DEDICATION

To my family, my best editors and kindest critics:
Howard, Kathy and Susie.

Frontis Blanket, 1860-70, 151 cm x 90 cm. 12 warps, 72 wefts.
Handspun wool with natural and vegetal colors. Three-ply
commercial red yarn and two- and three-ply ravelled red. Gift
of Mr. and Mrs. Gilbert Maxwell, 63.34.122.

Copyright © 1987 by Marian Rodee.
Library of Congress Catalog Number: 86-63764.

Printed in the United States of America.
Hard cover ISBN: 0-88740-095-7
Soft cover ISBN: 0-88740-091-4
Published by Schiffer Publishing Ltd.
1469 Morstein Road, West Chester, Pennsylvania 19380

This book may be purchased from the publisher.
Please include $2.00 postage.
Try your bookstore first.

Acknowledgments

My deepest gratitude to the National Endowment for the Arts which funded the time for the preparation of this manuscript as well as the photography.

My thanks also to students Julie Ahern Wild and Elizabeth Wooley, who prepared much of the technical information on sizes, materials and counts. I am especially grateful to Anthony Richardson who did most of the photography, no matter how large the textile. His technical ability has brought out the true beauty of the textiles.

I could not have done this book without the support of the Maxwell Museum's Directors J.J. Brody and Garth Bawden. Most important of all, my thanks to the late Gilbert Maxwell whose gift forms the nucleus of the Museum's collection and to Edwin L. Kennedy whose donations have made this one of the finest collections of ceremonial pattern textiles in a museum.

Preface

When I began, this project was to be a new edition of *Southwestern Weaving*, my catalogue of the holdings of the Maxwell Museum of Anthropology at the University of New Mexico in Albuquerque which was published in 1977 and 1981. I was intending to illustrate the pieces acquired in the past ten years. However, the project soon turned into something much more. I decided to add, in the form of essays, the results of my research of the past five years. In a very real sense, the museum's collection inspired this research. Since we had such a large and fine collection of ceremonial pattern weaving, I became curious as to when the style began, and why. More important, I decided to meet the women who were just names on catalogue entries and to find out something about them. This is only a small beginning, but an interesting one, and a search which I can see continuing for many years.

Although I have done less new research on the Pueblo and Hispanic Southwestern textile traditions than the Navajo, I include them in this volume because all three weaving traditions are tied historically and stylistically.

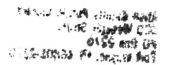

1 Serape, Saltillo, Northern Mexico, first half of the 19th century, 233.5 cm x 127.5 cm. 23 warps, 96 wefts. Woven in two pieces and sewn down the center. Handspun wool with natural and vegetal colors. Linen two-ply warp. Gift of Mr. and Mrs. Gilbert Maxwell, 63.34.87.

2 Blanket, Rio Grande, El Valle, 1890-1900, 192.5 cm x 109.5 cm. 9 warps, 30 wefts. This pattern, called "Vallero," was originated by Patricia Montoya (see Boyd 1974). Registered with the Laboratory of Anthropology, Santa Fe, no. 635. Woven in two pieces and sewn down the center. Four-ply aniline dyed commercial yarn. Cotton string warp. Gift of Mr. and Mrs. Gilbert Maxwell, 63.34.107.

3 Rug by Rose Lee. Photo courtesy of Cristof's Gallery, Santa Fe.

4 Half of woman's dress, 1860-75, 113 cm x 80.5 cm. 14 warps, 60 wefts. Handspun wool with natural and vegetal (indigo) colors. Two-ply ravelled red yarn. Gift of Dr. and Mrs. Lewis Binford, 73.56.1.

Glossary

The following definitions are used to describe each textile:

DATE Known dates of manufacture and of collection are specified as such. Most other dates are educated guesses based on style and materials.

SIZE Length always precedes width. Dimensions are expressed in centimeters and are taken to the nearest half-centimeter. The width is always measured across the warps regardless of the pattern. In anticipation of the entire country going to the metric system, the Museum has abandoned the English system. To convert from the metric divide each dimension by 2.54 cm. to obtain inches.

COUNT The fineness of textiles is expressed by the number of warps and wefts per inch. Where there is a significant difference in fineness from one yarn to another, this is noted. Fineness of over 80 wefts per inch (or 2.54 cm.) is considered "tapestry" quality. When thread counts are done the wefts are doubled, since for every weft visible on the surface there is one directly behind it.

WEAVE Unless otherwise stated, all textiles in the Navajo and Pueblo sections are in the tapestry technique.

BALANCED or 50/50 PLAIN WEAVE Warp and weft element are equally spaced and similar in size.

PLAIN, Weft threads pass alternately over and under successive warps.

TAPESTRY Weft-faced plain weave with the introduction of mosaic-like colored areas built up by weaving the weft back and forth within each individual area.

TWILL A single weft passed over and under two or more warps, with each row staggered.

WARP FLOAT Patterns are introduced by passing (or floating) warps over weft elements.

WRAPPED BROCADE Patterns are made by floating yarn across the surface of loosely woven plain weave fabric and wrapping it around one or two warps, producing thick ridges in the textile.

WARP-FACED, Plain weave with the warps concealing the wefts because they are more closely spaced and numerous than the wefts.

WEFT-FACED, Plain weave in which the wefts conceal the warps.

TYPE OF YARN

COMMERCIAL Factory made yarn processed by machine. Generally 3- or 4-ply. Weavers sometime separate 4-ply yarn into 2-ply elements. Terms such as "Saxony" and "Germantown" are avoided in the descriptions. What was once termed Saxony is described here as 3-ply vegetal dyed commercial yarn, and Germantown as 3-ply or 4-ply aniline dyed commercial yarn.

HANDSPUN Spun with a Navajo or Pueblo spindle.

RAVELLED Yarn made by separating the individual threads of a piece of commercially manufactured cloth and respinning.

STRING, Commercially manufactured cotton twine.

PLY, The twisting together of two or more strand of yarn.

TWIST The direction in which the yarn goes (S or Z) when it is plied. It is always the opposite direction from the spin.

DYES

ANILINE Commercially manufactured dyes obtained from coaltar derivatives. First manufactured in Europe in 1856, and still used today. Other chemical dyes are used today, but "aniline" is used as a generic synthetic dye.

CARDED Two colors blended or carded together to produce a third. For example, gray made by blending black and white wool, or pink by mixing red and white.

COCHINEAL A dye ranging in color from scarlet to rose/red, orange, or purple obtained from crushing a small parasitic beetle which lives on cactus.

INDIGO A vegetal dye grown commercially in Guatemala and the Carolinas during the 19th century. It is usually dark to pale blue in color but can be mixed with native yellow, usually from the rabbit brush, to produce a bright green.

NATURAL The color of the wool as it comes from the sheep (after cleaning).

VEGETAL The term used here is synonymous with the word "native" and refers to dyes made from plant and animal products even when imported. Although it is not completely accurate, since animal dyes are included, it is customary usage. When the specific organic material is known this is noted.

ACCESSION NUMBER The three part number each catalogue entry. Each item is identified within the Maxwell Museum by this number.

Contents

5 Chief's blanket rug, 1895-1910, 144 cm x 176 cm. 9 warps, 36 wefts. Rug in the pattern of a Phase III Chief's blanket. All handspun wool with natural, carded and aniline colors. Gift of the Maxwell Museum Association, 77.55.1.

6 Phase III chief's blanket, 1860-70, 159 cm x 182.5 cm. 12 warps, 52 wefts (handspun) and 12 warps, 60 wefts (ravelled). Collected by General O.B. Wilcox in 1870. See Maxwell 1963:12, fig. 4. Handspun wool with natural and vegetal colors (indigo). Two- and three-ply ravelled red yarn. Gift of Mr. and Mrs. Gilbert Maxwell, 63.34.112.

7 Bedroom of the Hubbell house, Hubbell Trading Post, 1985, showing use of weaving as bedspread. Photo by Susie Rodee.

8 Phase III chief's blanket, 1870-80, 140 cm x 199 cm. Textile has been chemically treated so the colors have a paler appearance. 8 warps, 50 wefts, handspun; 8 warps, 36 wefts ravelled, 8 warps, 50 wefts yarn. Handspun wool with natural and vegetal colors. Orange and pink are two-ply ravelled with Z-S spin and twist, while the rose is a three-ply commercial yarn. Gift of Edwin L. Kennedy, 85.52.2.

1. Pueblo Textiles

The ancestors of the modern Pueblo Indians began to use the large upright loom around A.D. 800 (Wheat: 1975) Pueblo weaving traditions are not only much older than those of the Navajo but are much more complicated. While a tapestry weave is the most common Navajo technique, twills, 50/50 plain weaves, and warp faced weaves are the usual Pueblo techniques. These weaves produce fabrics that make a suitable background for embroidery.

Pueblo men traditionally weave and embroider except at Zuni where the women do this work. Unlike the Navajo the Pueblos did not convert their blanket weaving tradition to a rug weaving one and their weaving has always been for Indian use. The introduction of white manufactured clothing has radically reduced the quantity of Pueblo weaving; traditional garments have been replaced by industrially made goods for everyday wear and only the need for ceremonial costumes has kept Pueblo weaving alive. Even so, almost no weaving is done at the Rio Grande Pueblos and most Pueblo textiles of the last sixty years have been made at Hopi for sale and trade to other villages.

In this section, the textiles are divided according to their function as men's or women's clothing. The basic woman's garment is the manta which does double duty as a shawl thrown over the shoulders or as a dress when sewn up the side. Frequently, the plain white wedding manta, presented by the groom for the wedding ceremony, was later embroidered along the top and bottom.

Traditional men's garments represented in the Maxwell Museum's collection are the kilt, sash, shoulder blanket, shirt, stockings, and leggings. Kilts are generally embroidered while sashes are executed in a wrapped brocade technique giving the appearance of embroidery. The main fabric of a sash is cotton with wool decoration floated over its face and wrapped around approximately every seventh warp. The design of the sash is always the same, a stylized head of the Broadfaced Kachina.

Small belts in the warp float technique are commonly woven today and are frequently worn as a belt on a modern European style dress.

9 Manta, Hopi, 1870-80, 99 cm x 127 cm. 30 warps, 18 wefts. Warp face weave with embroidery. Handspun natural white cotton. Embroidery done in handspun two-ply vegetal dyed wool and two-ply ravelled cochineal red wool. Gift of Mr. and Mrs. Bruce T. Ellis, 70.56.1.

10 Manta, Zuni, 1880-1900, 104 cm x 149.5 cm. Diagonal twill with wide bands of embroidery along top and bottom and narrow strips along sides. When the black first faded the entire dress was redyed, thus giving the embroidery a black cast. Handspun overdyed natural wool. Embroidery in one- and two-ply indigo dyed handspun. Gift of Mr. and Mrs. Gilbert Maxwell, 63.34.136.

11 Dress, Zuni, 1880-1900, 113.5 cm x 131.5 cm. Diagonal twill weave with embroidery along top and bottom edges and narrower bands of embroidery along the sides. The two parts of the dress are sewn together halfway down the edge with red yarn. When the black first faded the entire dress was redyed, thus giving the embroidery a black cast. Handspun overdyed natural wool. Embroidery done in one- and two-ply handspun indigo dyed wool. Gift of Mr. and Mrs. Gilbert Maxwell, 63.34.137.

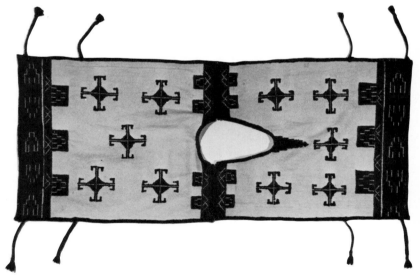

12 Skirt, Jemez, c. 1940, 75 cm in length. Juanita Lee, maker. Made for Mrs. Maxwell's initiation into the Jemez Tribe. It forms a costume with the following blouse. Embroidery done in four-ply aniline dyed wool yarn. Gift of Mr. and Mrs. Gilbert Maxwell, 75.322.4.

13 Blouse, Jemez, c. 1940, 56.5 cm x 48 cm. Made for Mrs. Maxwell's initiation into the Jemez Tribe. It forms a costume with the preceding skirt. The blouse is woven in two pieces and sewn together at the shoulders. Plain weave. All handspun natural white cotton. Embroidery done in four-ply aniline dyed wool yarn. Gift of Mr. and Mrs. Gilbert Maxwell, 75.322.5.

14 Manta, Acoma, 1870-80, 111 cm x 146 cm. Diagonal twill with red and green embroidery in strips at the top and bottom. Handspun wool with natural color overdyed with aniline. Embroidery done in two-ply ravelled aniline red and handspun aniline dyed green wool. Gift of Mr. Tom Bahti, 71.26.1.

15 Blanket, Rio Grande, 1850-70, 218 cm x 134.5 cm. 5 warps, 28 wefts. Woven in two pieces and sewn together. All handspun wool with natural and indigo colors. Two-ply warp. Gift of Mr. and Mrs. Gilbert Maxwell, 63.34.76. See page 39 for Spanish American weaving.

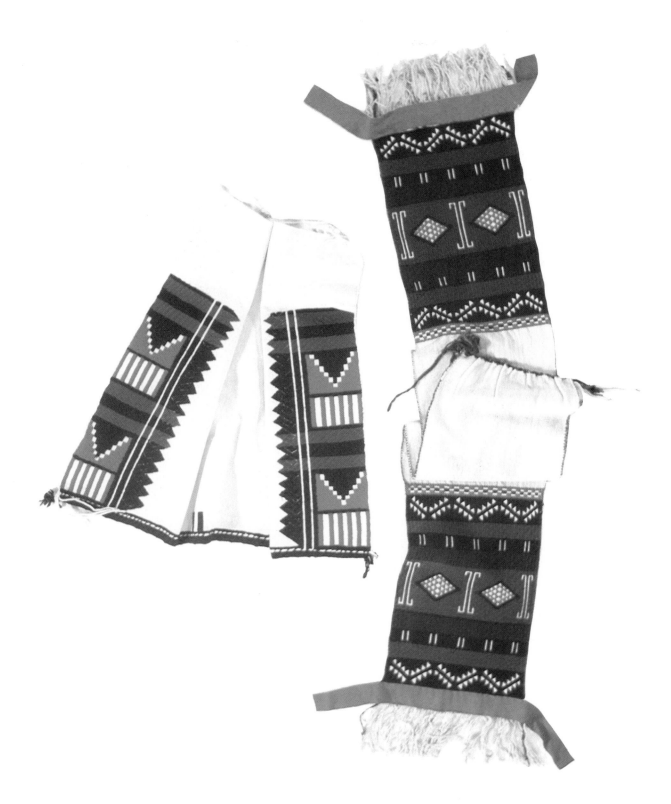

16 Left. Hopi kilt, ca. 1950, 117 cm x 69 cm. 32 warps, 12 wefts. Handspun natural white cotton with cotton string warp. Embroidery done in four-ply aniline dyed commercial yarn. Purchase, 67.33.6.

Right. Hopi Sash, ca. 1950, 212 cm x 29 cm. 14 warps, 10 wefts. Four-ply natural white commercial wool yarn and cotton string wefts and cotton string warp. Brocading done in four-ply aniline dyed commercial wool yarn. Gift of Mr. and Mrs. Gilbert Maxwell, 63.34.167.

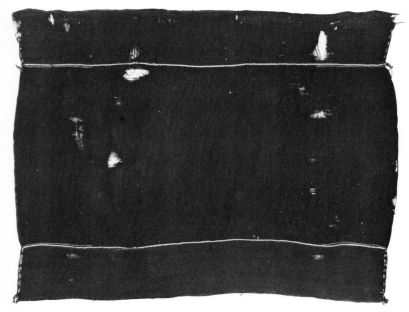

17 Manta, Zuni, 1880-1900, 103 cm x 130 cm. Diagonal twill with diamond twill in blue at top and bottom. Thick bands of plain embroidery added at inner edges of borders: blue, yellow extend all the way across and red one-fifth of the way in on either side. All handspun overdyed black wool and indigo wool. Embroidery done in two-ply vegetal dyed handspun and four-ply vegetal dyed commercial yarn. Gift of John Gilleland, 64.86.1.

18 Manta, Zuni, c. 1940-60, 103 cm x 64.7 cm. All handspun wool with aniline and indigo dyes. Gift of Edwin Kennedy, 85.52.8.

19 Manta, Hopi, c. 1950, 84.5 cm x 92 cm. Plain and diagonal twill weave. Handspun natural white cotton and commercial cotton string. Two-ply handspun aniline dyed wool. Gift of Morton Sachs, 70.74.1.

20 Manta, Hopi, 1950-60, 94 cm x 132.5 cm. Diagonal and plain twill weave. Handspun natural white cotton and cotton string. Three-ply aniline dyed commercial yarn. Gift of Mr. and Mrs. Gilbert Maxwell, 67.126.2.

21 Dress, Zuni, 1880-1900, 97 cm x 125.5 cm. Diagonal twill with diamond twill in blue at top and bottom. The dress still has the original stitching holding it together on the shoulder. All handspun overdyed natural black wool and indigo dyed wool. Gift of Mrs. Joseph Imhof, the Joseph Imhof Collection, 61.3.506.

22 Wedding Manta, Hopi, 1940-60, 105.5 cm x 157 cm. 32 warps, 11 wefts. "E. Chapalla" in ink on one edge. Warp-faced weave. Handspun natural white cotton weft and cotton string warp. Gift of Mr. and Mrs. Gilbert Maxwell, 67.126.1.

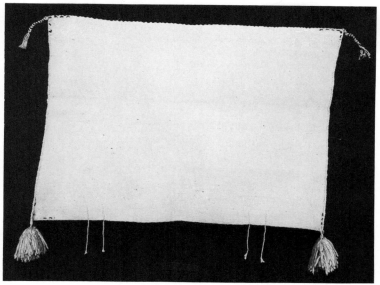

23 Child's Wedding Manta, Hopi, Kiakochomovi, 1971, 76 cm x 107.5 cm. 26 warps, 8 wefts. Frances Alpeche, weaver. Warp-faced weave with single line of embroidery in the four corners and two large tassels, one with a small feather tied in. Handspun natural white cotton wefts and cotton string warp. Touches of embroidery in handspun wool with orange/brown dye (ochre). Acquired from the Museum of Northern Arizona, 71.33.3.

15

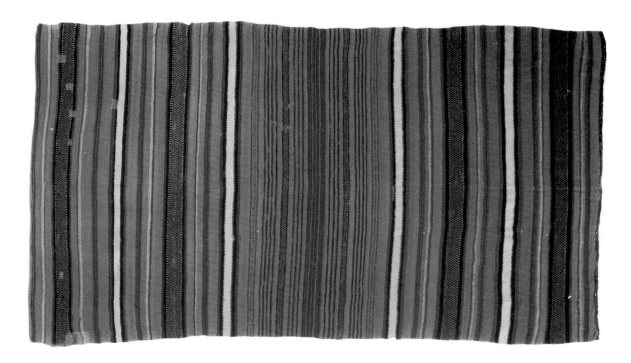

24 Blanket, Rio Grande, 1850-70, 243 cm x 134 cm. 5 warps, 30 wefts. Woven in one piece, six warps in the center are paired. All handspun wool with natural and vegetal colors. Two-ply warp. Transfer from Zimmerman Library, University of New Mexico, 65.42.154. See page 39 for Spanish American weaving.

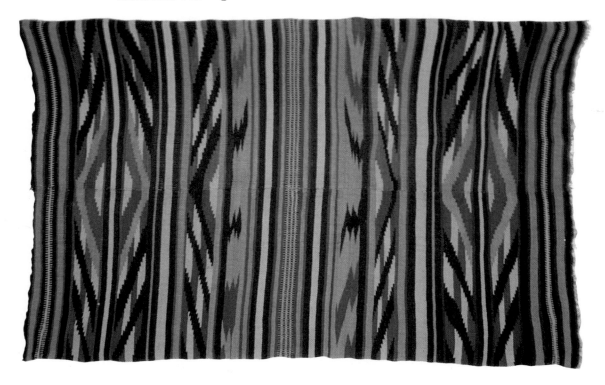

25 Blanket, Rio Grande, 1850-70, 224 cm x 142 cm. 6 warps, 28 wefts. Woven in two pieces and sewn down the center. All handspun wool with natural and vegetal colors. Two-ply warp. Gift of Mr. and Mrs. Gilbert Maxwell, 63.34.82. See page 39 for Spanish American weaving.

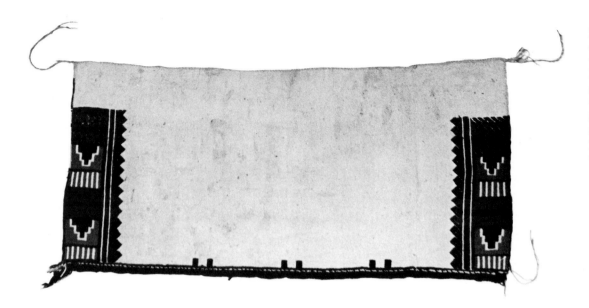

26 Kilt, c. 1910, 53 cm x 111 cm. 15 warps, 30 wefts. Plain weave with embroidery. Handspun natural white cotton with cotton string warp. Embroidery done in four-ply aniline dyed commercial wool yarn. Gift of Mr. and Mrs. Gilbert Maxwell, 63.34.171.

27 Kilt, 1900-20, 105.5 cm x 50 cm. 16 warps, 18 wefts. Identified as Cochiti by Mr. Imhof. Plain weave with embroidered ends and a black braided border sewn on. Handspun natural white cotton, embroidery done in four-ply aniline dyed commercial wool yarn. Gift of Mrs. Joseph Imhof, the Joseph Imhof Collection, 61.3.619.

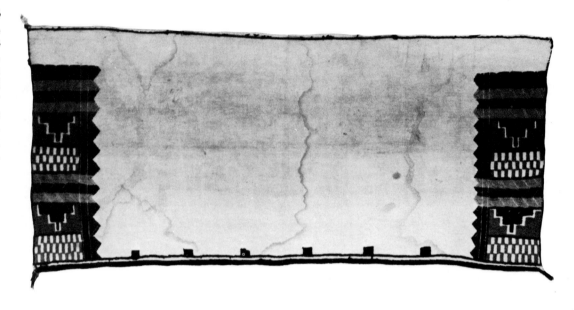

28 Kilt, 1900-20, 103.5 cm x 46 cm. 14 warps, 22 wefts. Identified as Cochiti by Mr. Imhof. Plain weave with embroidery and a green wool braided border sewn on. Handspun one- and two-ply cotton. Embroidery done in four-ply aniline dyed commercial yarn. Gift of Mrs. Joseph Imhof, the Joseph Imhof Collection, 61.3.618.

29 Kilt, Hopi, 1950-60, 107 cm x 63 cm. Jeanette Lamabuma, maker. Commercial cotton cloth, marked "Fulton Seamless" with embroidered ends and a black braided edging. Embroidery done in four-ply aniline dyed commercial wool yarn. Gift of Mr. and Mrs. Bruce T. Ellis, 66.89.1.

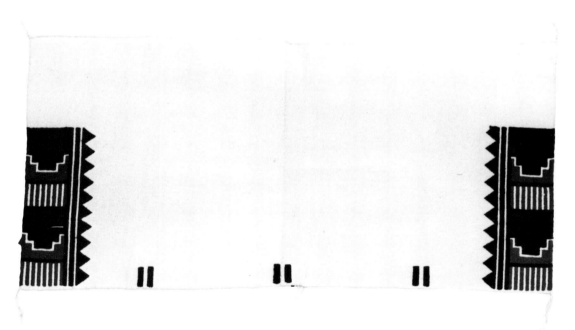

30 Kilt, Hopi, c. 1950, 125 cm x 63 cm. 24 warps, 10 wefts. Warp faced weave with embroidery. Four-ply natural white commercial wool with cotton string warp. Embroidery done in four-ply aniline dyed commercial wool yarn. Donor unknown, 76.1.37.

31 Kilt, Hopi, c. 1950, 117 cm x 69 cm. 32 warps, 12 wefts. Warp faced weave with embroidery and a braided edging. Handspun natural white cotton with cotton string warp. Embroidery done in four-ply aniline dyed commercial wool yarn. Purchase 67.33.6.

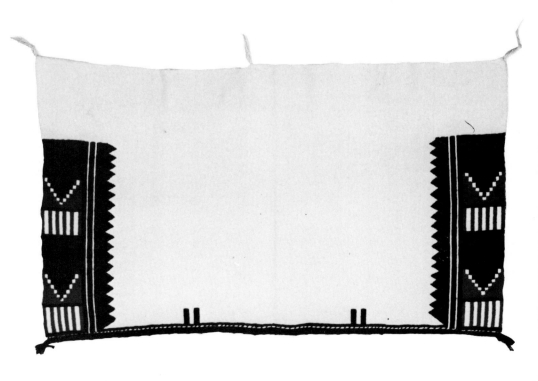

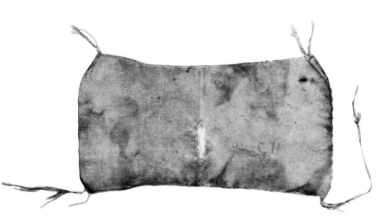

32 Boy's Kilt, Hopi, 1920-50, 53.5 cm x 30 cm. 26 warps, 12 wefts. Warp faced weave. Handspun natural white cotton with cotton string warp. Gift of Mrs. T.W. Ewing, 66.107.2.

33a (left) Half of a Sash, Hopi, c. 1900, 99 cm x 23 cm. 28 warps, 8 wefts. Forms a complete sash with 55.20.5b. Warp faced weave with wrapped brocading and long braided warp fringe. Natural white wool handspun and cotton string weft with cotton string warp. Brocading done in three- and four-ply aniline dyed commercial wool yarn. Gift of Mrs. Richard Wetherill, 55.20.5a.

33b (right) Half of a Sash, Hopi, c. 1900, 98 cm x 22 cm. Forms a completed sash with 55.20.5a. Gift of Mrs. Richard Wetherill, 55.20.5b.

34 Sash, 1900-20, 218 cm (both pieces) x 28.5 cm. 14 warps, 18 wefts. Identified as Cochiti by Mr. Imhof. Two separately woven pieces sewn together. Warp-faced weave with wrapped brocading, a knotted warp fring, and red silk ribbon sewn on. Handspun natural white cotton and cotton string wefts and a cotton string warp. Brocading done in four-ply aniline dyed commercial wool yarn. Gift of Mrs. Joseph Imhof, the Joseph Imhof Collection, 61.3.162.

35a (left) Half of a Sash, 1880-1900, 106 cm x 28.5 cm. 26 warps, 7 wefts. Identified as Cochiti by Mr. Imhof. Warp faced weave with wrapped brocading and warp fringe. This forms a complete sash with 61.3.165. All handspun natural white wool. Brocading done in handspun wool with natural and vegetal (indigo) colors and three-ply red commercial yarn. Gift of Mrs. Joseph Imhof, the Joseph Imhof Collection, 61.3.163.

35b (right) Half of a Sash, 1880-1900, 110 cm x 28.5 cm. 22 warps, 8 wefts. This forms a complete piece with 61.3.163. Gift of Mrs. Joseph Imhof, the Joseph Imhof Collection, 61.3.165.

36 Half of a Sash, Hopi, 1900-20, 102.5 cm x 28 cm. 18 warps, 9 wefts. Warp faced weave with wrapped brocading and warp fringe. Four-ply natural white commerical wool and cotton string weft and cotton string warp. Brocading done in four-ply aniline dyed commercial wool yarn. Gift of Mrs. Joseph Imhof, the Joseph Imhof Collection, 61.3.481.

37a (left) Half of a Sash, 1880-1900, 101 cm x 31 cm. 24 warps, 13 wefts. Identified as Cochiti by Mr. Imhof. Warp faced weave with wrapped brocading and warp fringe. Two pieces of red flannel sewn on—one on either side of brocading. Handspun natural white wool. Brocading done in handspun aniline dyed wool and three-ply aniline dyed commercial wool yarn. Gift of Mrs. Joseph Imhof, the Joseph Imhof Collection, 61.3.164.

37b (right) Half of a Sash, 1880-1900, 99 cm x 28 cm. 24 warps, 13 wefts. Forms a complete sash with preceding piece. Gift of Mrs. Joseph Imhof, the Joseph Imhof Collection, 61.3.166.

38 Sash, Hopi, c. 1950, 214 cm (both halves) x 22.5 cm. 18 warps, 12 wefts. Warp faced weave with wrapped brocading and a warp fringe. Two halves laced together. Four-ply natural white commercial wool yarn and cotton string wefts with cotton string warp. Brocading done in four-ply aniline dyed commercial wool yarn. Gift of Mr. and Mrs. Gilbert Maxwell, 67.126.3.

39 Sash, Hopi, c. 1950, 212 cm x 29 cm. 14 warps, 10 wefts. Warp faced weave with wrapped brocading and a warp fringe. Strip of red baize sewn on above fringe. Four-ply natural white commercial wool yarn and cotton string wefts and cotton string warp. Brocading done in four-ply aniline dyed commercial wool yarn. Gift of Mr. and Mrs. Gilbert Maxwell, 63.34.167.

42 Man's Wearing Blanket, Hopi, c. 1930, 107.5 cm x 137 cm. Diagonal twill weave. All handspun wool in natural colors. Gift of Mr. and Mrs. Gilbert Maxwell, 63.34.141.

40 (left) Half of a Sash, Hopi, c. 1950, 99 cm x 26.5 cm. 15 warps, 12 wefts. Warp faced weave with wrapped brocading and braided warp fringe. Four-ply aniline dyed yellow commercial wool yarn and cotton string warp. Brocading done in four-ply aniline dyed commercial wool yarn. Gift of Mr. Gilbert Maxwell, 68.46.46.

41 (right) Fragment of a Sash, Hopi, c. 1960, 42 cm x 18 cm. 14 warps, 9 wefts. Warp faced weave with wrapped brocading and warp fringe. Natural white cotton string in two sizes. Brocading done in four-ply aniline dyed commercial wool yarn. Donor unknown, 68.1.31.

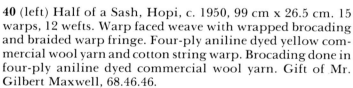

43 Shirt, San Juan, 1969, 52.5 cm x 40 cm (across shoulders). A copy of a Hopi type shirt. The design represents lightning, the fringes rain. Crocheted with commercial cotton yarn. Gift of Mr. and Mrs. Bruce T. Ellis, 69.55.1.

44 Vest, Hopi, 1900-20, 45 cm x 42 cm. Vest made from a cut-up sash. Knitted red wool panel under each arm and the back is faced with green velvet. All natural white cotton string. Brocading done in four-ply aniline dyed commercial wool yarn. Gift of Mr. Maurice Maisel, 64.18.22.

21

46 Stockings, Zuni, c. 1930, 36 cm x 14.5 cm. Knitted with dark blue aniline dyed four-ply commercial wool yarn. Gift of Mr. and Mrs. Gilbert Maxwell, 63.34.166.

45 Leggings, Hopi, c. 1950, 54.5 cm x 18.5 cm. Crocheted with three-ply natural white commercial cotton yarn. Gift of Mr. and Mrs. Gilbert Maxwell, 63.34.189a, b.

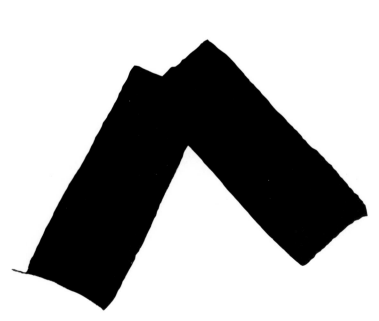

47 Stockings, Hopi, Hotevilla, 1971, 33.5 cm x 13 cm. Sidney Namingha, maker. Knitted with black aniline dyed four-ply commercial wool yarn. Acquired from the Museum of Northern Arizona, 71.33.2.

48 Stockings, Hopi, c. 1965, 35 cm x 14.5 cm. Knitted with black aniline dyed four-ply commercial wool yarn. Purchase, 67.33.4a, b.

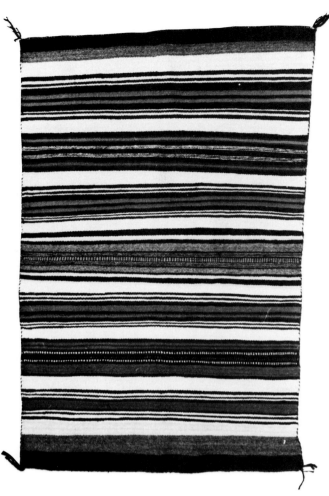

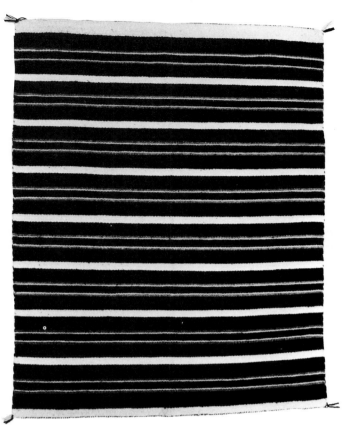

49 Saddle Blanket, Hopi, Moencopi, 1952, 150 cm x 97 cm. 6 warps, 30 wefts. Big Phillip, weaver. All handspun wool with natural, carded and aniline colors. Gift of Mr. and Mrs. Gilbert Maxwell, 63.34.156.

50 Rug/Blanket, Hopi, c. 1960, 183 cm x 141.5 cm. 5 warps, 16 wefts. Handspun wool with natural, carded and aniline colors with a cotton string warp. Gift of Mr. and Mrs. Edwin L. Kennedy, 69.67.21.

51 Blanket, probably Zuni, 1860-1900, 187 cm x 125 cm. 6 warps, 18 wefts. Collected by donor's father, Robert O. Brown of Santa Fe on a trip with Jesse Nusbaum, around 1915. All handspun wool with natural colors and indigo. Gift of Eloisa B. Jones, 82.30.1.

The following group of sashes are commonly known as "rain sashes," as the long fringe flowing from the cotton covered squash blossom-like cornhusk ring is considered to represent rain falling from the clouds. These sashes were generally made by a complicated braiding technique (Underhill 1944:70—75). One of the Museum's pieces (76.1.39) was woven on a loom as are most modern rain sashes.

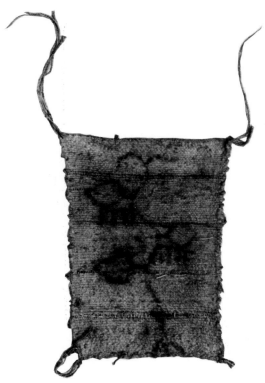

52 Pictorial Rug, Jemez, c. 1900-20, 37 cm x 26.5 cm. 12 warps, 8 wefts. This piece was given to Mrs. Wetherill's son by a Jemez man who said it represented the Jemez watershed. It is supposedly woven with fiber from the cottonwood tree and painted with brown stain from puffballs. Plain weave with painted design and remnants of feathers (duck according to Mrs. Wetherill) woven into four rows about 7 cm. apart. All handspun one- and two-ply natural white cotton. Gift of Mrs. Richard Wetherill, 55.20.51.

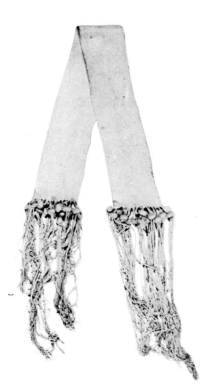

53 Sash, 1890-1920, 131 cm x 15.5 cm. Braided with two-ply natural white handspun cotton. Gift of Mrs. Richard Wetherill, 55.20.6.

54 Sash, 1900-20, 131 cm x 23.5 cm. Braided with two-ply natural white handspun cotton. Gift of Mrs. Joseph Imhof, the Joseph Imhof Collection, 61.3.620.

24

55 Sash, 1920-60, 119 cm x 10 cm. Braided with two-ply natural white handspun cotton. Gift of Mr. and Mrs. Bruce T. Ellis, 63.11.9.

56 Sash, 1900-50, 133 cm x 19 cm. Braided with five-ply natural white commercial cotton yarn. Donor unknown, 75.1.257.

57 Sash, 1900-50, 151 cm x 20.5 cm. 14 warps, 24 wefts. All handspun natural white cotton. Weft spun more tightly than warp. Donor unknown, 76.1.39.

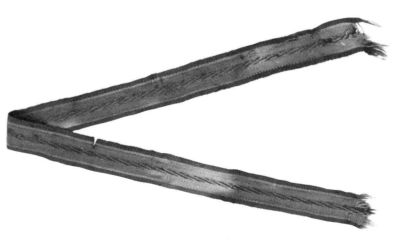

58 Child's Belt, Hopi, c. 1880, 125 cm x 6 cm. 40 warps, 10 wefts. Given to Mrs. Wetherill when she visited a kachina dance as a girl. Warp float weave. All four-ply aniline dyed commercial wool yarn. Gift of Mrs. Richard Wetherill, 55.20.7.

59 Belt, 1900-20, 167 cm x 8 cm. 36 warps, 12 wefts. Warp float weave. All four-ply aniline dyed commercial wool yarn. Gift of Mrs. Joseph Imhof, the Joseph Imhof Collection, 61.3.483.

60 Belt, 1900-20, 197 cm x 9 cm. 40 warps, 11 wefts. Warp float weave. Four-ply aniline dyed commercial wool yarn and cotton string warps. Cotton string weft. Gift of Mrs. Joseph Imhof, the Joseph Imhof Collection, 61.3.484.

61 Belt, Taos? 1900-20, 224.5 cm x 6 cm. 44 warps, 12 wefts. Warp float weave. All four-ply aniline dyed commercial wool yarn. Gift of Mrs. Joseph Imhof, the Joseph Imhof Collection, 61.3.482.

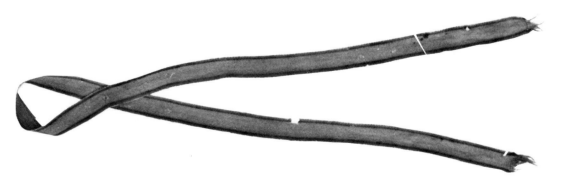

62 Belt, Taos? 1900-20, 63 cm x 3.5 cm. 40 warps, 13 wefts. Warp float weave. Four-ply aniline dyed commercial wool yarn with cotton string weft. Gift of Mrs. Joseph Imhof, the Joseph Imhof Collection, 61.3.485.

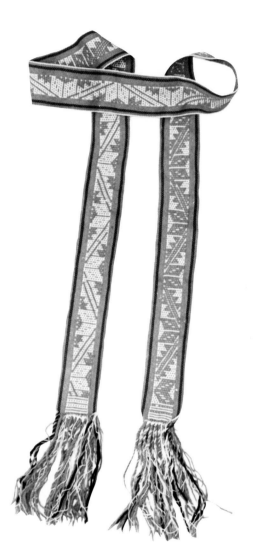

63 Belt, Taos? 1900-20, 236.5 cm x 9 cm. 44 warps, 8 wefts. Warp float weave. All four-ply aniline dyed commercial wool yarn. Gift of Mrs. Joseph Imhof, the Joseph Imhof Collection, 61.3.486.

64 Belt, Taos? 1900-20, 176 cm x 6 cm. 40 warps, 16 wefts. Warp float weave. Four-ply aniline dyed commercial wool yarn and cotton string warp. Cotton string weft. Gift of Mrs. Joseph Imhof, the Joseph Imhof Collection, 61.3.487.

65 Pair of Garters, Hopi? 1900-20, 51.5 cm x 3 cm. (a) and 40 cm x 3 cm (b). 36 warps, 15 wefts. Warp float weave. Four-ply aniline dyed commercial wool yarn with cotton string weft. Donor unknown, 74.28.22a, b.

66 Belt, Taos, 1925, 205 cm x 10 cm. 36 warps, 13 wefts. Warp float weave. Four-ply aniline dyed commercial wool yarn and cotton string warp and a cotton string weft. Gift of Mrs. Thomas Bush, 61.2.5.

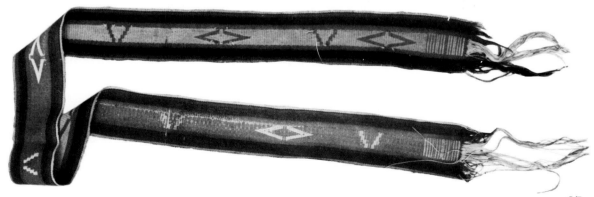

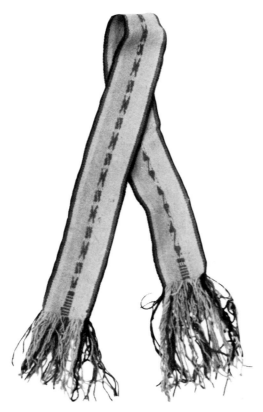

67 Belt, Taos? 1900-20, 97 cm x 7.5 cm. 30 warps, 13 wefts. Warp float weave. All four-ply aniline dyed commercial wool yarn. Gift of Mrs. Joseph Imhof, the Joseph Imhof Collection, 61.3.488.

68 Belt, Hopi, 1900-30, 90 cm x 5 cm. 56 warps, 16 wefts. Warp float weave. Four-ply aniline dyed commercial wool yarn and cotton string warp and cotton string weft. Transfer from Zimmerman Library, University of New Mexico, 73.30.24.

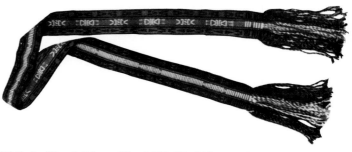

70 Belt, Hopi, Hotevilla, 1970-71, 212 cm x 9 cm. 40 warps, 10 wefts. Jack Pongyesvia, weaver. Warp float weave. All four-ply aniline dyed commercial wool yarn. Acquired from the Museum of Northern Arizona, 71.33.4.

69 Belt, Hopi, 1950-60, 66 cm x 5 cm. 68 warps, 20 wefts. Warp float weave. Two-ply handspun aniline dyed wool and cotton string warp. Cotton string weft. Gift of Mr. and Mrs. Gilbert Maxwell, 67.126.5.

71 Belt, c. 1950, 200 cm (without fringe) x 9.5 cm. 40 warps, 12 wefts. Warp float weave. Four-ply aniline dyed commercial wool yarn and cotton string warp. Cotton string weft. Gift of Mr. and Mrs. Gilbert Maxwell, 63.34.187.

2. Northern Mexico Textiles

The distinctive blanket patterns of the Saltillo region of nothern Mexico influenced both Navajo and Rio Grande weaving. Saltillo wearing blankets, or serapes, are long and narrow, made in two pieces and sewn together with a slit left in the center for the head. The patterns usually have an elaborate central figure, either circular or diamond shaped, on a ground filled with small vertically arranged parallelograms, the whole surrounded by a narrow border. When worn, the central figure forms a collar covering the shoulders and upper body. Saltillo region weavers may have come directly from Spain, bringing the design system with them in its fully developed form. The basic pattern may derive from a Persian rug style originating in the Sarouk area (Boyd 1973: personal communication).

The Maxwell Museum's series of Saltillo area serapes ranges from early cochineal—and indigo—dyed specimens of the early nineteenth century, through the aniline—dyed ones of the late nineteenth century, until about 1915 when the style was replaced by textiles with nationalistic motifs such as Aztec calendar stones.

The Maxwell Museum owns only a few pieces of Indian weaving from northern Mexico. Even less is known and written about the indigenous weaving than about the Saltillo tradition. The blankets tend to be coarse utilitarian items.

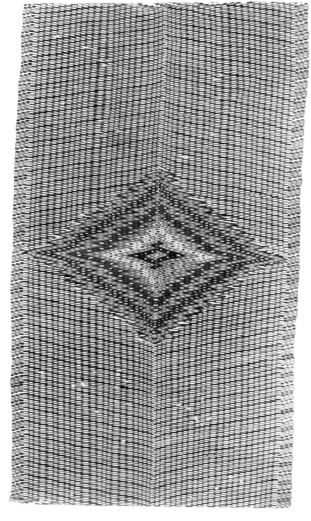

72 Serape, Saltillo, first half of the 19th century, 241 cm x 151 cm. 22 warps, 84 wefts. Woven in two pieces and sewn down the center. Handspun wool with natural and vegetal colors. Two-ply linen warp. Gift of Mr. and Mrs. Gilbert Maxwell, 63.34.89.

73 Serape, first half of 19th century, 241 cm x 123 cm. 12 warps, 60 wefts. Woven in two pieces and sewn together. Handspun wool with natural and vegetal colors. Two-ply linen warp. Gift of Dr. Scott Adler, 70.65.1.

74 Serape, Saltillo, first half of 19th century, 253.5 cm x 126 cm. 14 warps, 60 wefts. Woven in two pieces and sewn down the center. Handspun wool with natural and vegetal colors. Two-ply linen warp. Gift of Mr. and Mrs. Gilbert Maxwell, 63.34.157.

75 Serape, Saltillo, first half of the 19th century, 235 cm x 131 cm. 22 warps, 104 wefts. Woven in two pieces and sewn down the center. On either side of the central diamond are a pair of sheep with baskets in their mouths. Handspun wool with natural and vegetal colors. Two-ply linen warp. Gift of Mr. and Mrs. Gilbert Maxwell, 63.34.88.

76 Blanket, mid-19th century, 184 cm x 130 cm. 18 warps, 94 wefts. Saltillo Serape. Woven in two pieces and sewn together. All handspun wool with natural and vegetal dyes, linen warp. Gift of Edwin L. Kennedy through the Maxwell Museum Association, 79.45.85.

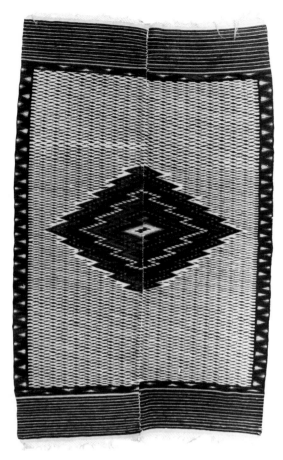

77 Serape, Saltillo, 1870-1900, 190 cm x 110 cm. 12 warps, 30 wefts. Woven in two pieces and sewn down the center. Handspun wool with natural and aniline colors. Cotton string warp. Gift of Mr. and Mrs. Gilbert Maxwell, 63.34.163.

78 Serape, Saltillo, 1880-1900, 216.5 cm x 116 cm. 14 warps, 56 wefts. Woven in two pieces and sewn down the center. Handspun wool with natural and aniline colors. Two-ply linen warp. Gift of Mr. and Mrs. Gilbert Maxwell, 63.34.161.

79 Serape, mid-19th century, 205.5 cm x 117 cm. 14 warps, 44 wefts. All handspun with natural and vegetal dyes and a linewarp. Gift of Edwin L. Kennedy, 85.52.12.

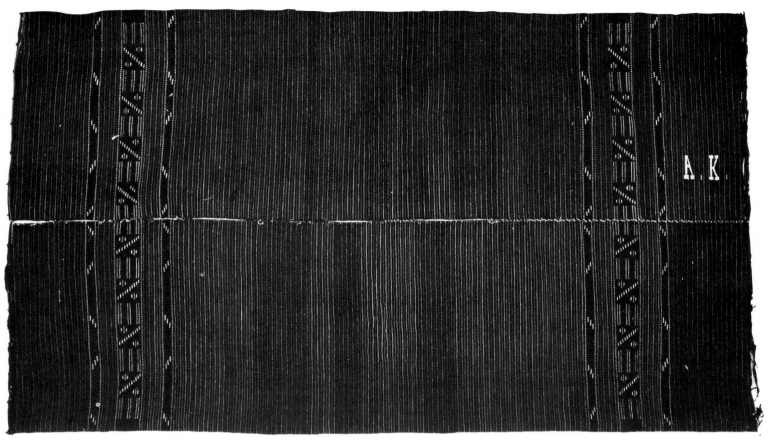

80 Blanket, 1880-1900, 209 cm x 122 cm. 10 warps, 56 wefts. Woven in two pieces and sewn down the center. Initials A.K. woven into one corner. Cotton string warp with all handspun natural white and two shades of indigo blue. Gift of Edwin L. Kennedy through the Maxwell Museum Association, 79.45.84.

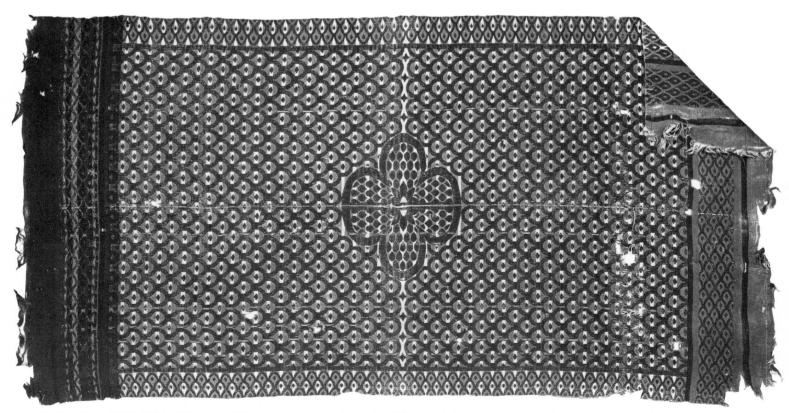

81 Blanket, 1880-1900, 228 cm x 116 cm. 12 warps, 90 wefts. Unusual double weave technique. All handspun wool with natural and aniline colors. Gift of Edwin L. Kennedy through the Maxwell Museum Association, 79.45.81.

82 Serape, Saltillo, c. 1915, 217.5 cm x 195 cm. 24 warps, 72 wefts. Woven in two pieces and sewn together. Handspun wool with natural and aniline colors. Two-ply handspun wool warp. Gift of Mr. and Mrs. Gilbert Maxwell, 63.34.164.

83 Rug, 214 cm x 135 cm. 7 warps, 26 wefts. All handspun wool in natural and aniline colors. This piece is unusual in that all the wool is "S" spun. Gift of Dr. Homer B. Martin, 76.51.1.

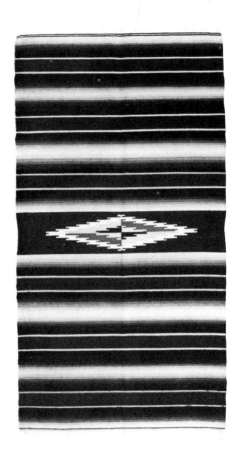

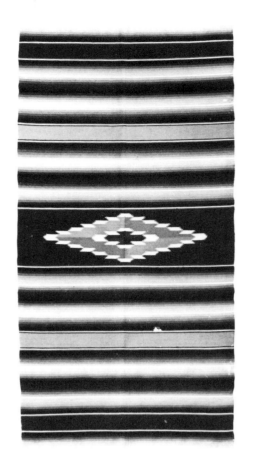

84 Rug or table throw, Northern Mexico, c. 1950, 118 cm x 58 cm. 20 warps, 50 wefts. Woven in one piece. Handspun wool in natural and aniline colors and cotton string. Cotton string warp. Gift of Mrs. Elaine Hudson, 68.101.8.

85 Rug or table throw, Northern Mexico, c. 1950, 119 cm x 57 cm. 20 warps, 64 wefts. Woven in one piece. Handspun wool in natural and aniline colors and cotton string and cotton string warp. Gift of Mrs. Elaine Hudson, 68.101.7.

86 Blanket, Tarahumara, c. 1935, 223 cm x 116 cm. 5 warps, 16 wefts. All handspun wool in natural colors. Warp is two-ply handspun. Gift of Mr. and Mrs. Gilbert Maxwell, 63.34.154.

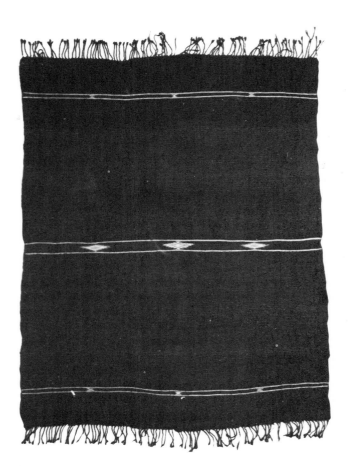

87 Blanket, Tarahumara, c. 1950, 208 cm x 96.5 cm. 5 warps, 14 wefts. All handspun natural wool. Anonymous gift in honor of Dr. W.W. Hill, 66.80.1.

88 Blanket, Tarahumara, c. 1938, 178 cm x 137 cm. 7 warps, 20 wefts. Purchased in 1938 in Cuschcuriachick. All handspun wool in natural and vegetal colors. Gift of Mr. and Mrs. Gilbert Maxwell, 63.34.155.

89 Skirt, 190 cm x 59 cm. 5 warps, 32 wefts. Purchased from Edmond Faubert. Precise place of origin unknown, from the Yoquivo-Urighique Ride area. Rare form, probably made for a seven to ten year old girl. Handspun wool, natural colors, three-ply red yarn. Gift of the Maxwell Museum Association, 78.54.26.

35

90 Sash, 1970's, 216 cm x 13.7 cm. Purchased from Edmond Faubert. Tarahumara Indian, Sariachique, Chihuahua. All handspun wool with natural and aniline colors. Gift of the Maxwell Museum Association, 78.54.27.

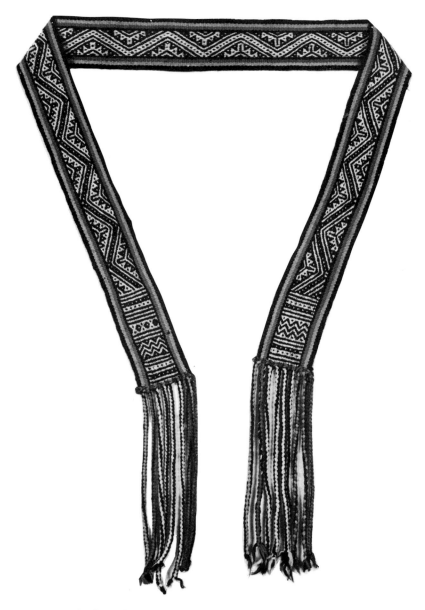

91 Sash, 1970's, 221 cm x 7.6 cm. Purchased from Edmond Faubert. Tarahumara Indian, Norogachi, Chihuahua. All handspun wool with natural and aniline colors. Gift of the Maxwell Museum Association, 78.54.11.

93 Sash, 1970's, 194 cm x 10.2 cm. Purchased from Edmond Faubert. Mayo Indian, Teachive, Sonora, Sash used in Pascola dance. All natural white handspun wool. Gift of the Maxwell Museum Association, 78.54.13.

92 Sash, 1970's, 254 cm x 7.5 cm. Purchased from Edmond Faubert. Tarahumara Indian, Choquita, Chihuahua. All handspun wool with natural and aniline colors. Gift of the Maxwell Museum Association, 78.54.12.

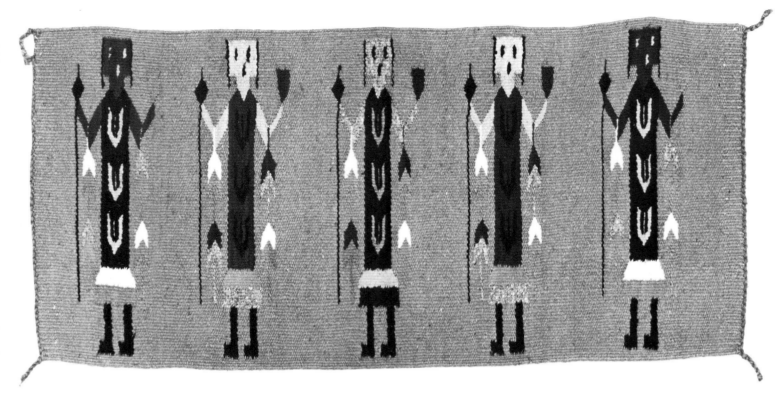

94 Rug, 1967-74, 101 cm x 49 cm. 6 warps, 22 wefts. Mexican copy of Navajo ye'ii rug. All handspun wool with natural and aniline colors. Gift of Tom and Goldie Neal, 82.56.4.

95 Rug, 1965-75, 206 cm x 128.5 cm. 6 warps, 14 wefts. Mexican copy of ye'ii bicheii rug from the Gilbert Maxwell Collections. Mr. Maxwell's book, *Navajo Weaving Past, Present and Future* was taken to Mexico where Native Americans wove copies on European looms. Notice the weaver has not understood the difference between Talking God who leads the line of dancers and Calling God who brings up the line. All handspun wool with natural and aniline colors. Gift of Andrew Nagen, 82.26.1.

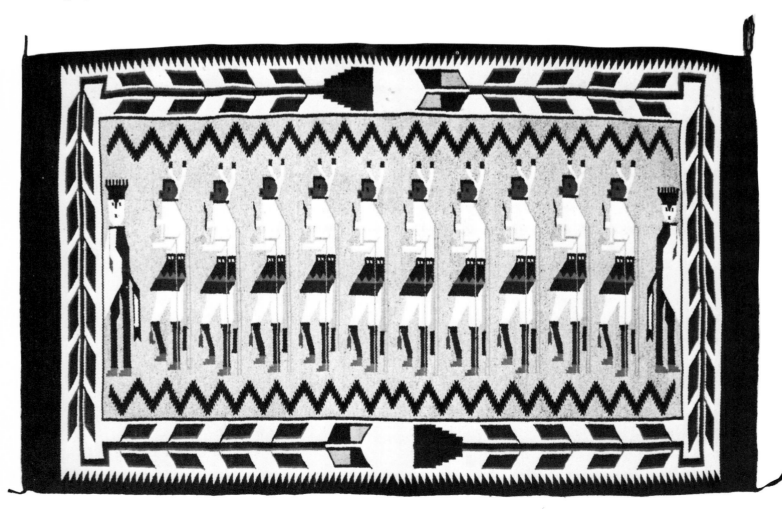

3. Rio Grande Textiles

Weaving done by the Spanish settlers of New Mexico and southern Colorado is commonly called "Rio Grande," because most was made at villages located along the drainage system of that river. The earliest Spanish settlers probably did not bring heavy looms with them, but rather the knowledge of how to build and use them. The combined production of both Indian and Spanish looms soon made textiles one of the province's chief exports.

The horizontal European loom used by the Spaniards is quite different from that used by Pueblo and Navajo weavers. The latter can be disassembled quite easily and carried anywhere and has simple stick heddles tied to the warps. The Spanish loom is a permanent installation with fixed heddles operated by a foot mechanism. Differences in manufacturing techniques based upon the construction of the loom can be used to distinguish Navajo or Pueblo from Rio Grande weaving. The Spanish loom can accommodate many yards of warp and as the weaving progresses the cloth is rolled on a beam. When all the warp on a loom is used the cloth is taken off, unrolled, and cut into individual pieces across the warps. The cutting leaves a fringe of warps that must be secured by being knotted together. The Navajo and Pueblo warps are continuous, being wound back and forth within the textile, producing a finished edge along the top and bottom as well as the sides. The texture of Rio Grande textiles is different also, due to the low proportion of thick 2-ply warp elements and high proportion of loosely spun wefts.

The Rio Grande loom was narrow, but textiles wider than the loom were produced in either of two ways. Two identical pieces could be sewn together longitudinally but the patterns then frequently did not exactly match. Alternatively, the loom could be double warped.

Weaving was then begun from left to right, and when the right edge was reached, the weft was passed around, under, and woven back to the left. This process always left at least one doubled warp in the center and the full width was not seen until the textile was taken off the loom. In the 1890's, a wider loom was introduced at the village of Chimayo by the Santa Fe trader J. S. Candelario, thus simplifying the weaving of wider textiles (Mrs. Richard Wetherill n.d.: unpublished journal).

Many of the dyes used by the Navajo and Pueblo weavers were also by the Rio Grande Spanish. Indigo was imported from the south, and rabbit brush and mountain mahogany (called logwood) were found locally. Rio Grande weavers also used aniline dyes and commercial yarns when they became available. A few examples of cochineal dye used on handspun wool are evidence that the Spanish-American weavers had access to this dye that seems not to have been available to Navajo or Pueblo weavers except by unraveling industrially made cloth or in the form of commercial yarn.

The history of Rio Grande weaving is not well documented. Most of the Maxwell Museum's Rio Grande textiles are dated, as are the Navajo ones, by the presence of certain yarns and dyes; however, further research may date them earlier than the nineteenth century.

The term "Chimayo" is often applied to Rio Grande textiles in much the same way as "Hopi" is used as a name for Pueblo textiles, and for the same reasons. Both communities kept old weaving traditions going long after they had been abandoned in other towns. Chimayo has an active weaving industry to this day, but textiles labeled Chimayo are not always made there.

96 Blanket, Yaqui-Mayo, 1930-60, 211 cm x 111 cm. 7 warps, 30 wefts. All handspun wool in natural, carded, vegetal and aniline colors. Gift of Dr. W.W. Hill, 69.2.1.

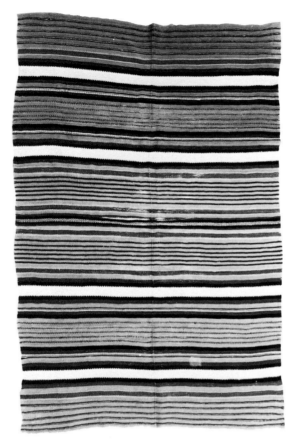

98 Blanket, Rio Grande, c. 1850-70, 213.5 cm x 130 cm. 6 warps, 36 wefts. Woven in one piece with a group of four warps in the center. All handspun wool with natural and vegetal colors. Two-ply warp. Transfer from Zimmerman Library, University of New Mexico, 65.42.152.

97 Blanket, Rio Grande, 1850-70, 237 cm x 130 cm. 7 warps, 32 wefts. Woven in one piece, two paired warps in the center. All handspun wool with natural and indigo colors. Two-ply warp. Gift of Mr. and Mrs. Gilbert Maxwell, 63.34.77.

99 Rug fragment, Rio Grande, 1860-80, 51 cm x 56 cm. 6 warps, 18 wefts. All handspun wool with natural and indigo colors. Two-ply warp. Donor unknown, 74.28.23.

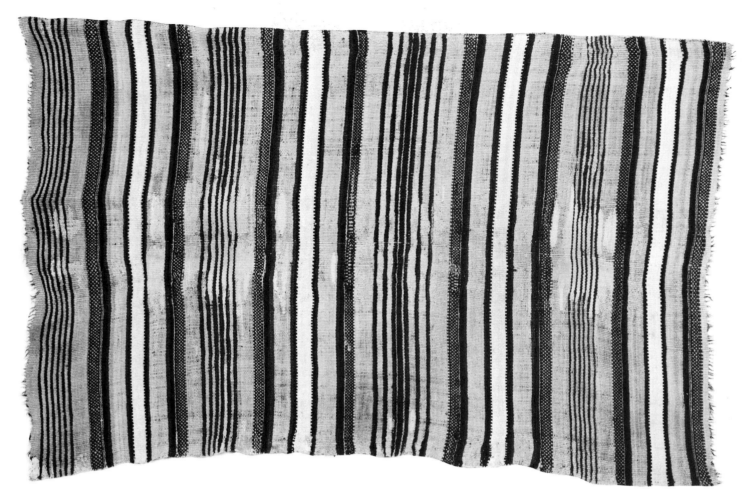

100 Blanket, 1850-70, 181 cm x 124.5 cm. 6 warps, 40 wefts.
All handspun wool and natural, vegetal and indigo colors.
Transfer from the Harwood Foundation, Taos, 80.51.99.

101 Blanket, Rio Grande, 1850-70, 235 cm x 124 cm. 6 warps, 34 wefts. Purchased from Fred Harvey Company in 1945. Formerly in J.F. Huckle Collection. Woven in one piece, two paired warps in center. All handspun with natural and vegetal dyes. Two-ply warp. Gift of Mr. and Mrs. Gilbert Maxwell, 63.34.81.

102 Blanket, Rio Grande, 1850-60, 233 cm x 117 cm. 5 warps, 36 wefts. Woven in one piece, four warps paired in the center. All handspun wool with natural and vegetal dyes. Two-ply warp. Transfer from Zimmerman Library, University of New Mexico, 65.42.153.

41

103 Blanket, 1880-1900, 203 cm x 145.4 cm. 9 warps, 32 wefts. Woven in two pieces and sewn together. All handspun wool with natural and aniline colors. Gift of Edwin L. Kennedy through the Maxwell Museum Association, 79.45.80. See Mexican Textiles on page 29.

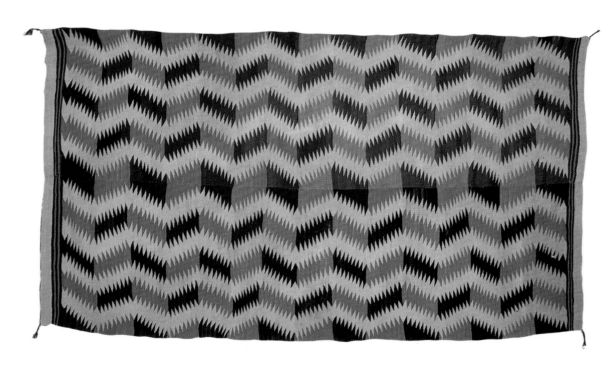

104 Blanket, 1860-80, 242 cm x 142.5 cm. 6 warps, 26 wefts. Woven in two strips and sewn together. Blanket was later repaired by a Navajo who added edge cords and tassels. All handspun wool with natural colors and indigo blue. Areas of reweaving are done in shades of brown three-ply commercial yarn. Gift of Edwin L. Kennedy through the Maxwell Museum Association, 79.45.78.

105 Blanket, 1850-70, 200 cm x 131.5 cm. 6 warps, 50 wefts. All handspun wool with natural and two shades of indigo colors. Transfer from the Harwood Foundation, Taos, 80.51.96.

106 Blanket, 1850-70, 208 cm x 128 cm. 6 warps, 38 wefts. Woven in two pieces and sewn together. All handspun wool with natural colors and indigo blue. Gift of Edwin L. Kennedy through the Maxwell Museum Association, 79.45.79.

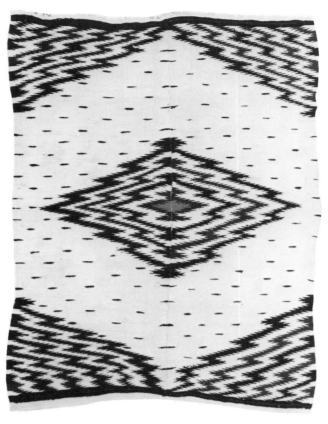

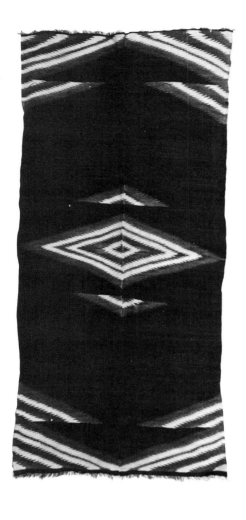

108 Blanket, Rio Grande, c. 1850, 213 cm x 95.5 cm. 8 warps, 36 wefts (handspun) and 8 warps, 46 wefts (commercial yarn). Woven in two pieces and sewn down the center. Handspun wool with natural and indigo colors. Three-ply red commercial yarn. Two-ply warp. Gift of Mr. and Mrs. Gilbert Maxwell, 63.34.79.

107 Blanket, Rio Grande, c. 1850, 189 cm x 134 cm. 5 warps, 40 wefts. Formerly in the Jim Seligman Collection. Woven in two pieces and sewn down the center. Handspun wool with natural and indigo colors. Three-ply red commercial yarn. Two-ply warp. Gift of Mr. and Mrs. Gilbert Maxwell, 63.34.84.

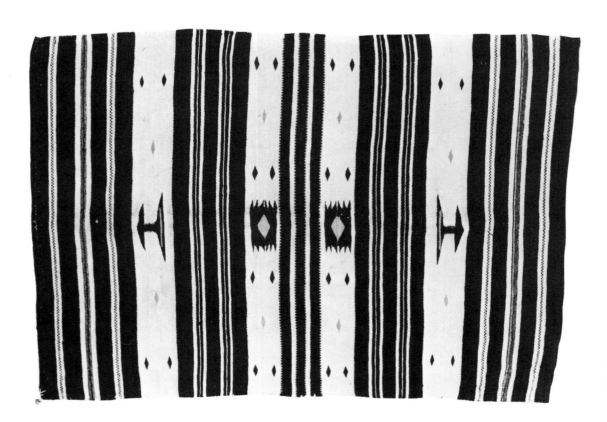

109 Blanket, Rio Grande, 1850-70, 167 cm x 117.5 cm. 6 warps, 36 wefts. Woven in one piece, warp paired in center. All handspun wool with natural, indigo and aniline colors. Two-ply warp. Both warp and weft cords added by a Navajo reweaver. The discontinuous warp is tucked back into the blanket. The unusual design motifs were also added by the reweaver. Previously called a ''slave blanket'' because of this combination of Mexican pattern with Navajo technique. Gift of Mr. and Mrs. Gilbert Maxwell, 63.34.85.

110 Blanket, Rio Grande, 1865-75, 212 cm x 122 cm. 7 warps, 30 wefts. Design is based on the Saltillo serape. Woven in two pieces and sewn down the center. Handspun wool with natural and indigo colors. Two- and three-ply aniline dyed commercial yarn. Two-ply warp. The commercial green, purple/blue, red/green, and gray yarns are all used in pairs. Warp repaired by a Navajo with a cord weft, last three warps are paired. Gift of Mr. and Mrs. Gilbert Maxwell, 63.34.83.

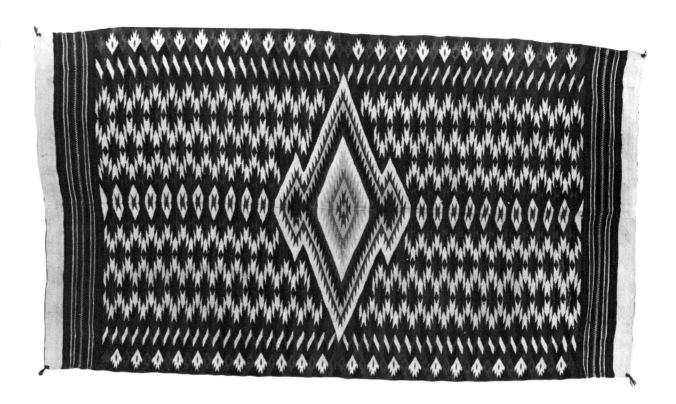

111 Blanket, Rio Grande, 1880-1900, 178 cm x 123 cm. 6 warps, 32 wefts. Woven in two pieces and sewn down the center. Handspun, two-ply natural and aniline color wool. Cotton string warp. A mottled effect is created by weaving two-ply strands of several colors together but without plying them. Gift of Mr. and Mrs. Gilbert Maxwell, 63.34.80.

112 Blanket, Rio Grande, 1880-1900, 210 cm x 121.5 cm. 6 warps, 24 wefts. Woven in one piece, warp paired in center. Handspun wool with aniline colors. Cotton string warp. Gift of Miss Lillian Colish, 71.35.1.

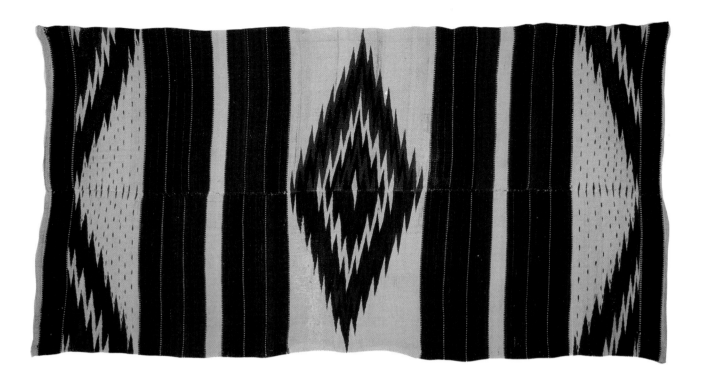

113 Blanket, 1850-70, 235.5 cm x 127 cm. 7 warps, 30 wefts. All handspun wool with natural and indigo colors. Transfer from the Harwood Foundation, Taos, 80.51.97.

114 Blanket, 1880-1900, 168 cm x 121.4 cm. 6 warps, 30 wefts. All handspun wool with natural and aniline dyes and a cotton string warp. Transfer from the Harwood Foundation, Taos, 80.51.93.

115 Blanket, 1870-85, 192 cm x 122.5 cm. 7 warps, 24 wefts, handspun, 7 warps, 28 wefts commercial yarn; 7 warps, 20 wefts ravelled. This textile is very unusual, incorporating technical features of both Navajo and Spanish American. Probably woven on a European loom and later repaired by a Navajo using both warp and weft edge cords. Handspun wool with natural and vegetal colors. The red is a three-ply commercial yarn used in pairs. Gift of Edwin L. Kennedy, 85.52.1.

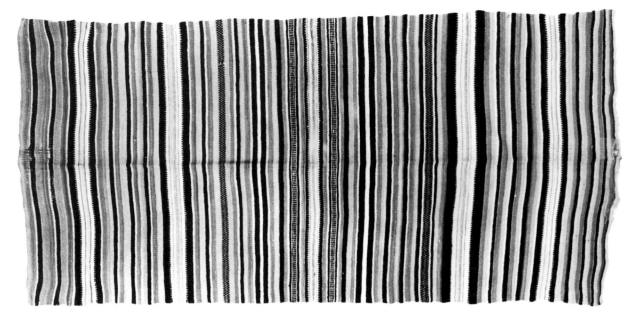

116 Blanket, Rio Grande, 1890-1900, 227.5 cm x 110 cm. 6 warps, 24 wefts. Woven in one piece. Handspun wool with natural, indigo and aniline colors. Two-ply warp. Gift of Mr. and Mrs. Gilbert Maxwell, 63.34.103.

117 Blanket, Rio Grande, 1880-90, 228 cm x 138 cm. 5 warps, 20 wefts. Woven in one piece. All handspun wool with natural and aniline colors. Two-ply warp. Gift of Mr. and Mrs. Gilbert Maxwell, 63.34.98.

118 Rug, Rio Grande, c. 1900, 330 cm x 200 cm. 5 warps, 36 wefts. Woven in one piece, one set of paired warps in center. All handspun wool with natural and aniline colors. Two-ply warp. Transfer from the Office of the Dean of the College of Arts and Sciences, University of New Mexico, 71.39.1.

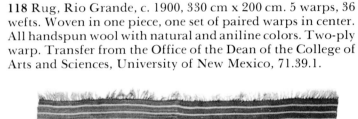
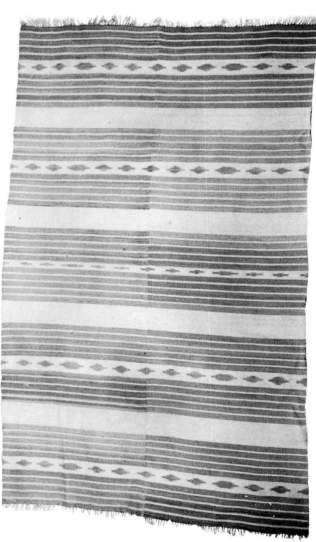

119 Blanket, 1880-1900, 208 cm x 114 cm. 7 warps, 44 wefts. Woven in two pieces and sewn together. Handspun wool with natural and aniline colors. Gift of Edwin L. Kennedy through the Maxwell Museum Association, 79.45.82.

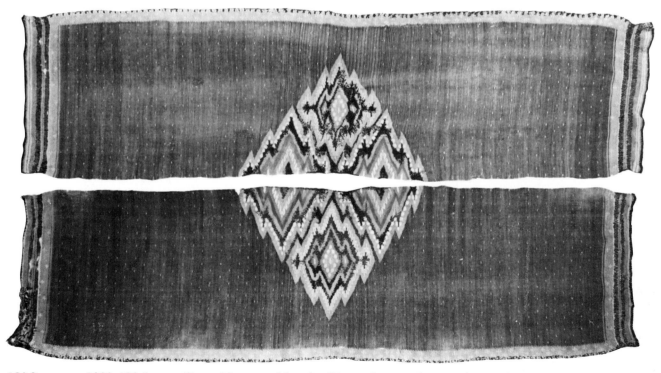

120 Serape, c. 1900, 180.5 cm x 47 cm. 18 warps, 30 wefts. Woven in two pieces and sewn down the center, but the pieces have been separated. Handspun wool with natural and aniline colors. Cotton string warp. Gift of Mrs. Richard Wetherill, 55.20.68a, b.

121 Rug, 1920-30, 79.5 cm x 42 cm. 8 warps, 30 wefts. All four-ply commercial yarn in natural and aniline colors. Transfer from the Harwood Foundation, Taos, 80.51.98.

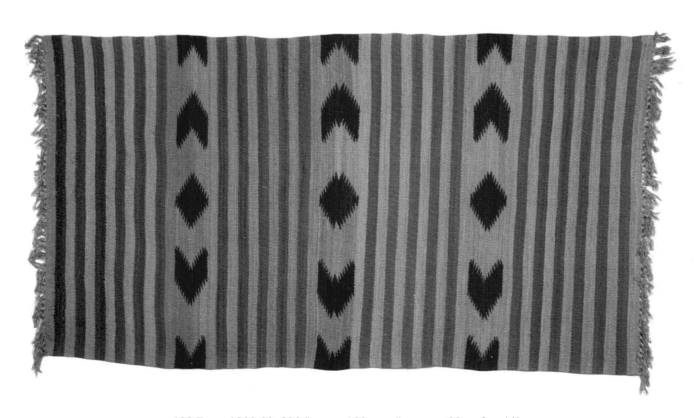

122 Rug, 1900-20, 206.5 cm x 120 cm. 5 warps, 22 wefts. All handspun wool with natural and aniline colors. Gift of John Durrie, 77.50.1.

Opposite page:
123 Rug, Chimayo, 1940-50, 426 cm x 264 cm. 9 warps, 22 wefts. The largest Spanish American rug known. Handspun wool with aniline colors. Gift of Andrew Nagen, 84.48.1.

124 & 125 Pair of Serapes, possibly Mexican, c. 1895, 205 cm x 101 cm. 14 warps, 64 wefts. Given to the Wetherills as a wedding present in 1896 by J.S. Candelario. Woven in one piece. Handspun wool with natural and aniline colors. A series of variegated four-ply aniline dyed yarns. Gift of Mrs. Richard Wetherill, 55.20.46 and 55.20.47.

126 Rug or chair throw, Rio Grande, Chimayo, c. 1890, 129 cm x 55.5 cm. 13 warps, 50 wefts. Owned by Richard Wetherill at time of his marriage in 1896. Woven in one piece. Handspun wool with natural and aniline colors. Two-ply warp. Gift of Mrs. Richard Wetherill, 55.20.45.

127 Serape, Rio Grande, Chimayo, c. 1896, 196 cm x 56 cm. 16 warps, 80 wefts. Woven in two pieces and originally sewn down the center, but separated for many years. Given as a wedding gift soon after 1896 by J.S. Candelario of Santa Fe. Handspun wool with natural and aniline colors. Gift of Mrs. Richard Wetherill, 55.20.48a, b.

128 Blanket, Rio Grande, Chimayo, c. 1900, 151 cm x 67 cm. 13 warps, 30 wefts. Woven in one piece. All handspun wool with natural and aniline dyes. Two-ply warp. Gift of Mrs. Richard Wetherill, 55.20.49.

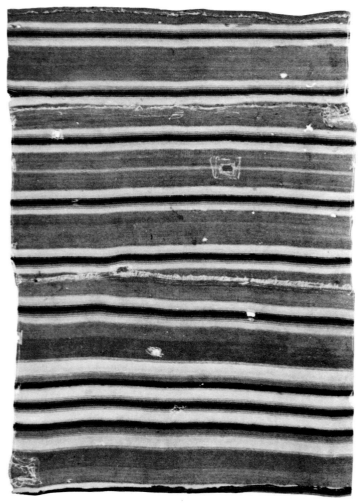

129 Fragment of a Serape, c. 1900, 99 cm x 69 cm. 12 warps, 60 wefts. Made up of fragments pieced together. All handspun wool with natural and aniline colors. Gift of Mrs. Richard Wetherill, 55.20.50.

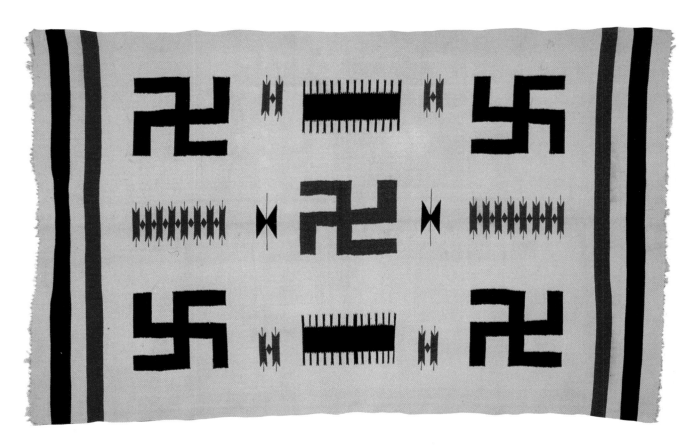

130 Rug, 1900-20, 195 cm x 126 cm. 11 warps, 35 wefts. A textile such as this clearly shows the movement of design motifs across the various cultures of the southwest. All commercial four-ply yarn with natural and aniline colors and a cotton string warp. Gift of Edwin L. Kennedy, 85.52.11.

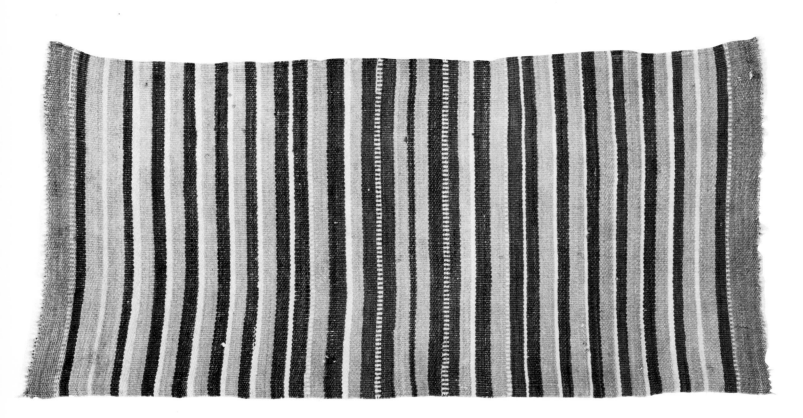

131 Blanket, 1910-30, 162 cm x 82.5 cm. 5 warps, 18 wefts. All handspun wool with natural and aniline colors. Transfer from the Harwood Foundation, Taos, 80.51.102.

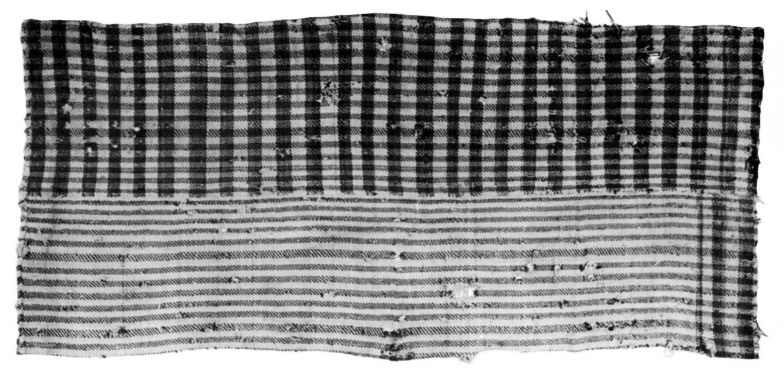

146 Jerga, 19th century, 230 cm x 116 cm. Woven in two pieces and sewn down the center. Twill weave. All natural brown and white handspun wool. Gift of Mr. and Mrs. Bruce T. Ellis, 69.70.4.

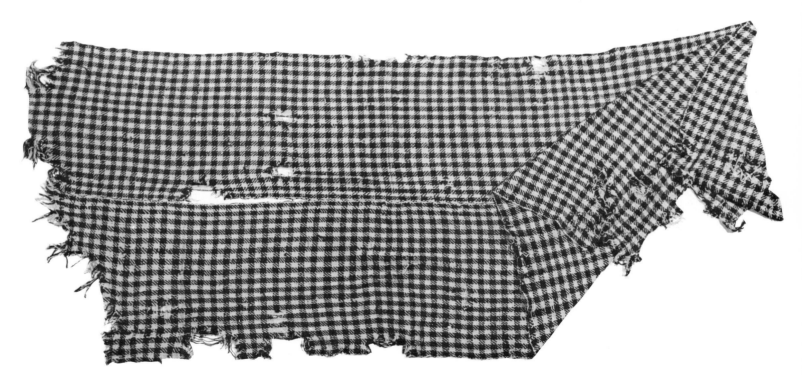

147 Jerga, Rio Grande, 19th century, 408 cm x 136 cm. Woven in two pieces and sewn down the center. Diagonal twill weave. All natural brown and white handspun wool. Gift of Mr. and Mrs. Bruce T. Ellis, 69.70.2.

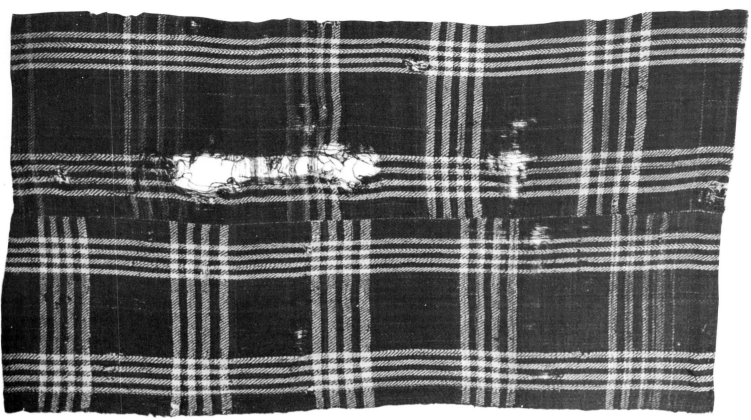

148 Jerga, Rio Grande, 19th century, 229.5 cm x 128.5 cm. Woven in two pieces and sewn down the center. Twill weave. All natural brown, white, and carded beige handspun. Gift of Mr. and Mrs. Bruce T. Ellis, 69.70.5.

149 Curtains in jerga cloth, 1930's, 219 cm x 89.5 cm (each piece). 7 warps, 10 wefts. Jerga curtains woven for the Harwood library during a federal work project in the 1930's. All handspun in natural and aniline colors. Transfer from the Harwood Foundation, Taos, 80.51.103 a-d.

4. Navajo Textiles

THE EARLY HISTORY AND THE BLANKET TRADE

It is generally stated that the Navajo learned the art of weaving from their Pueblo predecessors in the Southwest, although the date of this event is often debated. A date after the Pueblo Rebellion of 1680 and the reconquest of the province of New Mexico by the Spanish in 1692 is the most accepted one for, at this time, may Pueblos fled to live with the Navajo rather than face Spanish retribution. However, the Navajo Origin Myth states that Navajo women, when they arrived in their present homeland, wore dresses made of two hides or woven shredded cedar bark and covered the entrances of their houses with blankets woven of the same material (Matthews 1897, 141). The Navajo had migrated into the southwestern United States from somewhere in the northwest between 1000 A.D. and 1525 A.D. (Brugge 1983, 489). It is not known precisely from what area in the northwest the Navajo migrated, nor by what route, although today there are many Athabaskan—speaking groups in the interior of Canada. (Note: Navajo and Apache are both also Athabaskan languages.) Most ethnic groups living in the Northwest in the historic period, in particular the Salish of Puget Sound, wove garments and mats of

shredded cedar bark (Gustafson 1980, 15). Although no remnants of cedar bark garments have been found in early Navajo sites, their absence is not surprising since organic materials tend not to survive. It is quite possible that the Navajo entered the Southwest with the knowledge of weaving cedar bark garments on a simple frame, halfway between a true loom and basket weaving. It is logical to assume that when the Navajo first used cotton and then wool, they also adapted the Pueblo technology of the vertical loom.

In a report covering the years 1706 to 1743, Rabal, Governor of Northern Mexico, reports the Navajo wove wool blankets (Hill 1948, 397), thus indicating they were using the true loom in the early 18th century. In 1780, Teodor de Croix, the Commander General of the Interior Provinces of New Spain, wrote that the Navajo wove blankets and clothes of wool (Amsden (1934) 1971, 130). Just fifteen years later in 1795, Governor Fernando de Chacon reported that the Navajo "work their wool with more delicacy and taste than the Spaniards" (Amsden (1934) 1971, 132). In 1791, Fernando de la Concha, Governor of New Mexico, is reported to have "intiated trade by the Navajoes in the exporting of pelts and coarse blankets" (Bloom 1927, 232). Further, in 1812, Pedro Pino wrote of the Navajo:

150 Blanket, two fragments from Massacre Cave, Canyon de Chelly, before 1804, 119 cm x 134.5 cm. 4 warps, 12 wefts. See Maxwell 1963:10, fig. 1, and Kahlenberg and Berlant 1972:21. All handspun wool with natural colors. Gift of Mr. and Mrs. Gilbert Maxwell (large section) and Mr. R. Plummer (small section), 63.34.69.

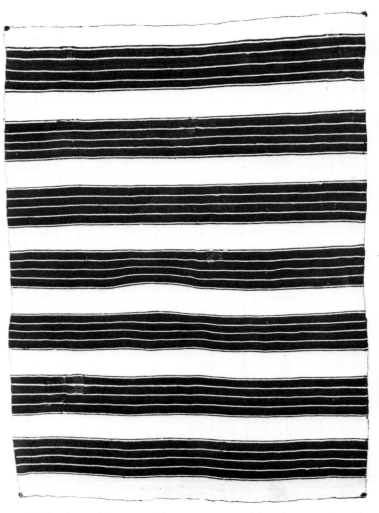

151 Blanket, bought in Chinle in 1934, c. 1850-1900, 176.5 cm x 130 cm. 7 warps, 16 wefts. All handspun wool with natural and carded colors. Gift of Dr. W.W. Hill, 65.47.2.

152 Blanket, 172 cm x 127 cm. 6 warps, 24 wefts. Purchased from Fred Harvey Co. 1955. All handspun wool with natural and vegetal colors (indigo). Gift of Mr. and Mrs. Gilbert Maxwell, 63.34.104.

"their woolen fabrics are the most valuable in our province (New Mexico) and Sonora and Chihuahua (as well)" (Amsden (1934) 1971, 133). These Spanish reports indicate not only that the Navajo were weaving in the 18th century, but also by the early 19th century were the finest weavers in the region, a position they have never relinquished. To balance this inequity, the Viceroy in Mexico, Joseph de Yturrigarcy, tried to improve the Spanish weaving in New Mexico by sending the master weavers Ignacio and Juan Bazan there to teach settlers the art (1805). The Viceroy had also initiated an annual trade fair in Chihuahua to stimulate the flow and production of goods (Bloom 1927, 234). No Navajo or Spanish weaving from the 17th or early 18th centuries in what is now New Mexico and Arizona is known to survive. Pieces found at Massacre Cave in Canyon de Chelly, Arizona constitute all the firmly dated extant early pieces of Navajo weaving. The Massacre Cave pieces were found with the remains of Navajo killed by a patrol of Spanish soldiers in the winter of 1804-05. See also page 71. By inference, these pieces date to the late 18th and very early 19th centuries. (Note: Part of a woman's dress found in a cave and now in the Durango Collection

may also date to the mid-or late-18th century (Shared Horizons 1980 cat. no. 1). These early textiles range from very fine to coarse, proving the technical ability of the weavers. The patterns are very simple, being stripes with a simple range of colors-black, white, brown, indigo blue, red and yellow.

The Spanish colonists valued the weaving skills of the Native Americans, both Navajo and Pueblo, and taxes were paid in the form of lengths of hand woven textiles (Fisher 1979, 11). Indeed, along with animal skins, weaving was the chief export of the province of New Mexico. Most of the textiles went to clothe the miners in Chihuahua, but none have apparently survived this hard usage. Josiah Gregg in *Commerce of the Prairies,* published in 1844, states:

They now also manufacture a singular species of blanket, known as the Serape Navajo, which is of so close and dense a texture that it will frequently hold water almost equal to gum-elastic cloth. It is therefore highly prized for protection against the rains. Some of the finer qualities are often sold among the Mexicans as high as fifty or sixty dollars each. (p. 199)

The Franciscan Fathers describe a blanket which they say was made especially for the Mexican trade as follows:

> The center was woven in a belt of blue flanked by narrow strips of white, black, the remainder of the blanket alternating in belts of white, black and blue, interspersed at optional intervals. (p. 247)

Early Navajo weaving was heavily influenced by Mexican styles and designs which were freely interchanged between the two traditions.

The opening of the Santa Fe Trail in 1822 brought more trade goods into the southwest, this time from the eastern United States rather than Mexico. However, with the acquisition of the territory by the United States in 1848, knowledge of Navajo weaving increases. The first official exploration party was that of Lt. James Simpson in 1849. Early military parties not only made maps of the new territories but recorded the lifestyles and costumes of the inhabitants. One of the earliest representations of the Navajo and their weaving is a lithograph based on a drawing by H.B. Mollhausen, the artist on the Colorado Exploring Expedition of 1857. (**166**). Military men, followed by anthropologists and settlers entered the southwest and bought textiles, a few pieces of which were given to eastern museums. It is difficult to say how the tastes of these early American visitors affected Navajo weaving. A photograph dated 1873 shows Governor Arny with a weaver and a textile on her loom in the pattern of an American flag. This type of pictorial, as well as others with names, military and fraternal insignia, and cattle brands, are obvious influences on Navajo patterns and probably are specifically commissioned works, as are other very large or unusual pieces (Rodee 1978). Early blankets were either finely woven and thin (famous for being waterproof), or soft and loosely woven. There was very little weaving of middle quality. Patterns ranged from the simple arrangements of bands of stripes to elaborate combinations of stepped diamonds. Fifty-four by seventy-two inches is about the size of the typical large Navajo serape or wearing blanket of the early period. Weaving format, with the exception of the so-called chief's pattern, is always longer than it is wide. Borders are unknown until around 1875, and uncommon until ten years later. Most patterns continue to the edge of the textile with ½ to ¼ motifs as though the blanket were cut out of a larger bolt of cloth. The colors of early weaving are suprisingly different from those of today- predominately red, white, blue and black with small quantities of green and yellow. These are the same colors as are found in the very early fragments, but the imported reds and blues are used in greater quantities.

153 Blanket/rug, 1870-80, 177 cm x 137 cm. 6 warps, 18 wefts. All handspun wool with natural, vegetal and carded colors. Purple is ravelled red and white carded together. Gift of Mrs. W.H. Loerpabel, 65.46.1.

154 Blanket, 1870-80, 184 cm x 114 cm. 8 warps, 34 wefts. Formerly in the Jim Seligman Collection. All handspun with natural and vegetal colors (indigo). Gift of Mr. and Mrs. Gilbert Maxwell, 63.34.139.

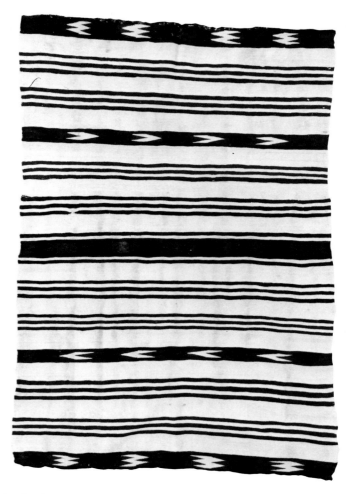

156 Blanket, 1860-75, 144 cm x 96 cm. 13 warps, 44 wefts. Handspun wool with natural and vegetal colors. Ravelled red in two- and three-ply. Gift of Miss Erna Fergusson, 64.60.24.

155 Blanket, c. 1860, 176 cm x 113.5 cm. 10 warps, 56 wefts (handspun) and 10 warps, 60 wefts (ravelled). Formerly in the Earl Morris Collection. Handspun with natural and vegetal colors (indigo). Ravelled red in two- and three-ply. Gift of Mr. and Mrs. Gilbert Maxwell, 63.34.123.

157 Half of a saddle blanket, 1860-70, 66.5 cm x 75.5 cm. 14 warps, 64 wefts. Handspun wool with natural and vegetal colors. Three-ply ravelled red. Gift of Miss Erna Fergusson, 64.60.23.

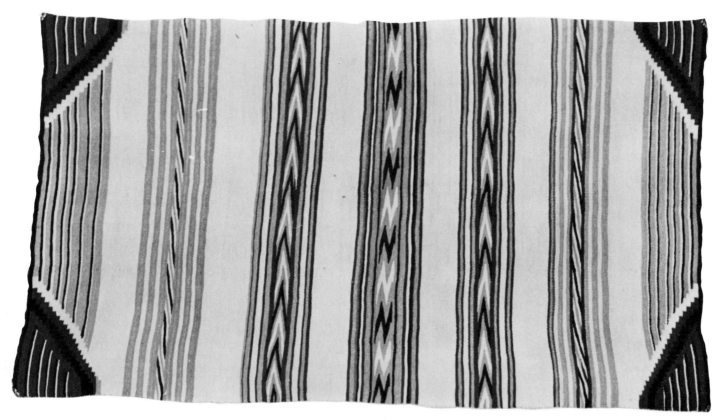

158 Double saddle blanket, 1860-70, 135 cm x 82.5 cm. 11 warps, 46 wefts. There is a break in the selvages 41 cm. from one end with small tassels as if for tying. Handspun wool with natural and vegetal colors. Three-ply commercial red and pink yarn. Gift of Mr. and Mrs. Gilbert Maxwell, 63.34.124.

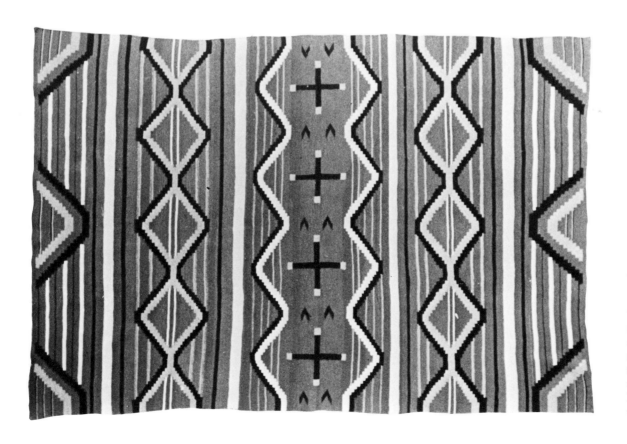

159 Blanket, 1870-80, 286.5 cm x 132 cm. 11 warps, 46 wefts. Collected by Stanley Stokes in 1880. Formerly in Frederick H. Douglas Collection. See Maxwell 1963:42, fig. 36. Handspun wool with natural, carded and vegetal colors. Three-ply commercial red and yellow yarn. Gift of Mr. and Mrs. Gilbert Maxwell, 63.34.142.

161 Blanket, 1875-80, 176 cm x 125 cm. 9 warps, 60 wefts. Handspun wool with natural and aniline colors. Ravelled two-ply yarn and commercial 3-ply yarn. Gift of Dr. Scott Adler, 70.65.2.

160 Blanket, 1860-70, 145.5 cm x 83 cm. 13 warps, 46 wefts (handspun), 13 warps, 50 wefts (ravelled). See Kahlenberg and Berlant 1972:73. Handspun wool with natural and vegetal colors (indigo). Ravelled two- and three-ply red yarn. Ravelled and carded pink. Gift of Mr. and Mrs. Gilbert Maxwell, 63.34.121.

Trade in Raw Materials

Among the raw materials for their weavngs, the Navajo had handspun wool from their own flocks. It was available in a wide range of natural colors from white through grays and browns to the relatively dark shades of yearling black sheep.

Many other colors were produced from native dyes which the Navajo had previously used on their basketry materials and leather. There was an especially fine black dye made in a lengthy process using pinyon-pitch, sumac and yellow ochre (Matthews, (1884), 3-4). The fine rich blue was obtained from indigo imported from Mexico and grown either there or in Guatemala. Indigo is usually sold in small pressed cakes and the knowledge of its preparation was probably traded along with the dyestuff as it requires urine mordant and preparation in a copper pot. Indigo is the only known foreign dye which was traded to the Navajo. Spanish American weavers were using other dyes, but these were evidently not available in trade to the Navajo. Exceedingly fast and long lasting, indigo produces an array of shades from pale blue to a deep, nearly black tone, the former from using a dye bath which has been almost exhausted of its color. Green is formed by mixing indigo with native yellow.

Red is one of the more difficult colors to obtain from southwestern plants, most of which produce tones of gold and brown. Washington Matthews reports two native red dyes being used in the 1800's the bark of *Alnus incana* and the bark or the root of *cercocarpus parvifolius* (Matthews (1884), 4). The best reds were supplied by a commercial trade cloth called baize or bayeta. Bolts of this factory made cloth colored with natural dyes such as cochineal or lac (both derived from crushed insects) were imported first from Mexico and later from the eastern United States after the opening of the Santa Fe Trail. The baize, which is a loosely woven, rather coarse fabric, is pulled apart or unravelled and the resulting yarn is reused as part of the wefts in the blanket. Pink is also obtained by taking small pieces of red, unravelled from the cloth, along with natural white and carding them together. These processes are very time consuming, but there is an interesting parallel practice in Navajo ceremonialism—a ritual unravelling of medicine bundles and the rubbing or pulling of the ties and bundle contents across the body of the patient (Reichard, (1920) 1974, 731-32). This is not to imply that the unravelling of trade cloth for reuse in weaving had a ritual connotation, but rather that there was a cultural precedent for this rather unusual practice of pulling apart an object.

Later, trade cloth colored with the synthetic dyes called "anilines" (invented in England in the mid-19th century) replaced the earlier natural-dyed red material. Often the aniline dyed trade cloth was called "American flannel" or "stroud cloth". Yarns of three and four-ply, spun on machines, were supplied to the Navajo as a result of the increasing trade as early as the 1860s (Amsden (1934) 1971, 182). The earlier natural-dyed yarns are traditionally called "Saxony" and the later aniline one "Germantown". The terms refer to a different center of manufacture, in Germany and Pennsylvania respectively. These yarns meant that weavers did not have to laboriously unravel blankets to get finely spun colorful yarns, but could buy or trade for materials in a ready-to-weave state.

162 Blanket, 1875-80, 226.5 cm x 106.5 cm. 14 warps, 46 wefts. A so-called slave blanket woven on a Navajo loom but with a Spanish-American pattern. Handspun wool with natural and indigo colors. Three-ply aniline commercial yarn. The commercial yarn may be an early Germantown. Gift of Mr. and Mrs. Gilbert Maxwell, 63.34.85.

Trade with other Native Americans

One important aspect of the 19th century history of Navajo weaving is the trade with other Native American groups. This history is difficult to document partially because there are few written comments on the trade and most of the actual pieces wore out with use. The Franciscan Fathers (1910) described a type of Navajo blanket especially made for trade with the Utes:

A similar blanket, and one much in demand by the Utes, was known as *alni na ljini,* or "the blanket with the black (streak) belt in the center". While the body of the blanket was laced with stripes of white and black, the center was mounted with a wide black belt, with additional red and blue stripes woven in between. Similar belts were woven in equidistant intervals between the center belt and the ends, though they were narrower than the center belt. The corners were narrower than the center belt. The corners were decorated with black tassels, making a very attractive blanket. (p. 24)

This verbal description translates into what is generally called a Phase I Chief's blanket (163). It is usually said that the Utes preferred a chief's blanket and some confusion has arisen because the final development of the chief's pattern, a so-called Phase III, has a large central diamond with half and quarter diamonds at the ends. Evidently the Utes continued to prefer the earliest form of this style. The actual trade value was five buckskins, a dressed buffalo robe, or a mare—although when trade increased, the value of the blanket dropped to one buckskin. The seemingly disproportionate value alloted here to one tanned buckskin may refer to ritually slain, often smothered, animals whose hide had not been pierced by any weapon. Blankets were the primary item brought to trade, and women began weaving six to nine months prior to a planned trip. Although the women usually did not accompany the men, they did receive a share of the profits. Some of the items the Navajo secured in exchange from the Utes were elk hides, storage bags, bandoliers, beaded bags and tweezers. Prized ceremonial items were also sought-beaverskins, buffalo tails for rattles, and pitch for rattles and baskets (Hill 1948, 392). In fact, a primary purpose of expeditions to the Utes was the procurement of ceremonial materials and the group was usually accompanied by a medicine man or singer. The journey to the Ute country was long and dangerous, partially because of the long-standing hostility between the two groups. The endeavour was undertaken with extensive rituals to insure the material success and personal safety of the party. It is interesting that when the Navajo reached a Ute settlement, they formed friendships and the trade was handled as a form of gift giving with the Navajo "giving" blankets to their friends and then making pointed comments as the types of items they wanted "given" in return. Such trading friendships were maintained over the years and apparently neither the Navajo nor the Utes had a class of professional traders. The exchange with the Pueblos was on a much more businesslike basis, a fact which the Navajo did not like.

163 Phase I chief's blanket, 1850-60, 128 cm x 161 cm. 10 warps, 56 wefts (handspun) and 10 warps, 64 wefts (ravelled). Acquired by Major General F. Funston in 1915. See Maxwell 1963:11, fig. 2; Kahlenberg and Berlant 1972:17. Handspun wool with natural colors. Two- and three-ply ravelled red yarn. Gift of Mr. and Mrs. Gilbert Maxwell, 63.34.114.

The Plains Indians were very fond of Navajo weaving, especially the chief's blanket in all three of its styles or phases. Early records frequently talk of "Spanish blankets", although when illustrated in Plains Indian pictorial histories or "winter counts", their design layout, i.e. wider than long, indicates Navajo rather than Spanish weaving. Winter counts were the painted chronicles of Plains bands with each winter indicated by a pictograph representing the outstanding event of that season. Thus, the winter of 1853-54 in the winter count of Lone Dog, a Yanktonai Sioux, is represented by a man dressed in white man's clothing (suit and hat) holding what can be identified as a Phase I Navajo chief's blanket (Hanson 1970, 4).

The early trade also was carried on by Mexicans travelling from Santa Fe and Taos to the Black Hills of South Dakota. In 1790, a French trader, Jacque D'Eglise, on a trip up the Missouri, found the Mandan supplied with Mexican goods and in 1806 Lt. Pike stated that the Spanish traded with the Pawnee once every three years. A group of trappers in 1811, "Spaniards of New Mexico", traded with the Arapahoes near the South Platte every year. Another early report (1826) by Peter Skene Ogden mentions that the Bannocks and Snakes regularly made trading trips down to Taos. The Mexicans did not have the limitless supplies of manufactured goods as did the French and American traders, but dealt in horses, foodstuffs and products of cottage industries—especially blankets, both their own and Navajo. Lists of goods brought by Mexican traders include flour, beans, pinole, strips of dried pumpkin, corn, salt, pepper, bread, onions and Taos lightning (whiskey).

The large, well-organized, and capitalized trading firms based in St. Louis (such as the American Fur Company) soon took business from the Spanish, although small independent traders tried to cut costs by bringing in goods from Santa Fe. One independent French trader on the Platte River, Geminien Beauvais, lost two wagon loads of goods in 1867 in a raid by the Cheyenne. Among the items stolen were "7 extra fine red Navajo blankets, 23 extra fine blue Navajo blankets", (Hanson and Walters 1976, 16-17). (Note the preference, or predominance at least, of blue over red by three to one.)

Although the foregoing account had made the picture of Navajo life seem one of peaceful trade with their neighbors, there is also another aspect, that of raiding, warfare and slave taking. The Navajo and Apache as semi-nomadic hunters and, in the case of the Navajo, shepherds and horticulturalists as well, frequently raided their Pueblo and Hispanic neighbors who lived in settled towns. This led to punitive expeditions and a round of intermittent hostilities. One such military party sent out by the Spanish government in 1805 caught a party of innocent Navajo unaware in Canyon de Chelly. The Navajo hid in a cave, but were discovered and killed by the soldiers. The site, called Massacre Cave, was left undisturbed by the Navajo for one hundred years as the Navajo have a deep fear of the deceased whose angry spirits they believe linger near the place of death. When, in the earlier part of this century, the remains were brought to the attention of a local trader, he realized the importance of the textile fragments that were found with the skeletons. He sold the textiles to anthropology museums all over the country (**150**). These so-called Massacre Cave textiles remain the largest body of early documented Navajo weaving.

Navajo raiding continued, and after the territories of present-day Arizona and New Mexico became part of the United States as a result of the Mexican War and the Treaty of Guadalupe Hidalgo in 1848, the Pueblo and Hispanic citizens petitioned the new government to control the Navajo depredations. In 1861, a campaign under Kit Carson was begun. Carson pursued a scorched-earth policy, burning Navajo crops and orchards and forcing the starving people to surrender. The captives were taken from Ft. Defiance on a march called the Long Walk to Bosque Redondo (Ft. Sumner) on the plains of New Mexico. At Bosque Redondo the government intended to turn the Navajo into farmers. However, drought combined with poor administration and provisioning by the government produced a series of failures. The Navajo were homesick for their cool mountain homelands and virtually dependent on the Army for food and clothing, so their leaders signed a peace treaty in 1868. This treaty provided for a federally recognized reservation in their former area of northern Arizona and New Mexico as well as allotments of food, clothing and livestock until they were re-established. The Navajo kept their promise and never waged war against their neighbors again and also very quickly became self-sufficient.

It is from this time, 1870, onward that examples of Navajo weaving become relatively common in museums and private collections. As part of the annuity goods, the Navajo were given looms (which they refused to use) as well as yarn, wool cards, dyes and baize blankets which they did use (Bailey and Bailey 1986, 51-52). In 1869, they were given "38 pairs of indigo blankets, 35 pairs of bayeta blankets to be unraveled and used in weaving, 2 boxes of indigo, 2,245 pounds of scarlet yarn, 700 pounds of assorted yarn and 148 pounds of red and white thread skeins. The scarlet yarn allotments were increased during the 1870's and in 1880 the price of "Mexican cloth" or baize went from $3 to $4 per yard and the government discontinued supplying baize and looked for a cheaper yarn substitute.

This cheaper substitute may have been Germantown yarn which is the generic name for three-or four-ply factory produced yarns dyed with the new bright aniline dyes invented by the Englishman William Perkin in 1857. These aniline dyes were commonly used in the American textile industry from the 1860's (Merrimac Valley Textile Museum 1977). They produced an incredible variety of colors which had not previously been available to weavers. In fact, the colors of textiles from about 1880 to 1900 were so bright that they were called "eyedazzlers" by early traders (**164-185, 189-192, 201-206**). It has only been recently that tastes have changed allowing us to appreciate, perhaps for the first time, the vibrant color combinations of eyedazzlers. Patterns also begin to change from rows or

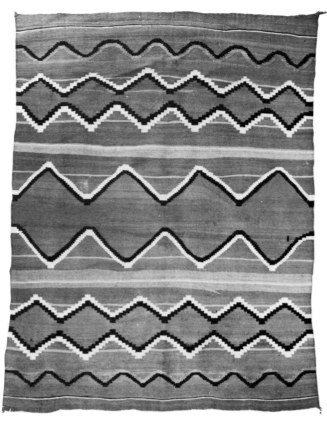

164 Blanket, 1880-85, 180 cm x 124 cm. 9 warps, 32 wefts. Formerly in the Earl Morris Collection. Purchased from F.M. Pierce who acquired it in Farmington in 1890. Handspun wool with natural, aniline, vegetal (indigo) and carded colors. Cotton string warp. Gift of Mr. and Mrs. Gilbert Maxwell, 63.34.73.

165 Woman's style blanket, 1875-80, 110.5 cm x 144.5 cm. 8 warps, 32 wefts. This type of blanket with narrow brown and beige stripes and three bands of pattern running horizontally is the equivalent to the chief's blanket for women. See Maxwell 1963:13, fig. 5. Handspun wool natural, aniline, vegetal (indigo) and carded colors. Gift of Mr. and Mrs. Gilbert Maxwell, 63.34.140.

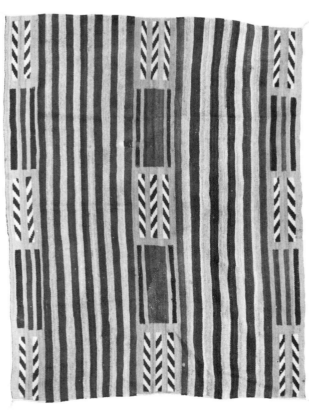

bands of horizontal motifs to vertical orientation or one all-over design. Instead of the early or classic period designs executed with small stepped or terraced edges, late 19th century textiles changed to diamonds with zigzag or serrated lines. Frequently, each design element is outlined with one or two contrasting color giving the entire design an electric effect.

Trade with Non-natives

As part of the treaty agreement, the government issued licenses to traders. The first was Lehman Spiegelberg in 1868 (Bailey and Bailey 1986, 58) and there were many traders operating without licenses just off the Reservation. The distribution of free Anglo-American goods by the government meant that the trader-for-profit was at a disavantage. However, after the Navajo had rebuilt their flocks and had surplus wool to trade (and annuity allotments ceased), trading posts began to flourish. In 1880-81 the Atchison-Topeka and Santa Fe railroad put through its southern line bringing in more and cheaper trade goods and also more visitors. This combination of more goods and people led to the development of the floor rug. Just as the Navajo had woven blankets for trade, so they began providing items to trade at the new posts, along with their wool. The new customers were Anglos who would use the textiles not as wearing blankets but as floor rugs.

During the late 19th and early 20th centuries, some of the most popular domestic rugs in the East came from the Caucasus area of Russia and Turkey where semi-nomadic people made rugs, tent hangings and horse and camel trappings in both pile and tapestry weaves. In the mid 1890's, there was a move to change Navajo weaving away from the eyedazzler to rugs with fewer colors and simpler designs based on these oriental rug patterns. This period is frequently called "transitional" (1880 to 1910), the transition being from blanket to rug. At first, in the 80's weavers made borderless blanket patterns as rugs which are frequently distiguished from wearing blankets only because they are larger and heavier. During the 1890's, many coarse rugs were woven out of handspun wool colored with pre-packaged aniline dyes. These rugs are called "pound blankets" because they were weighed and bought by the pound, much like wool top and supposedly canny weavers did not clean their wool but pounded sand and other impurities into the rug so they would weigh more (Maxwell 1963, 15). The 1890's were very bad for the Navajo. First, the national depression of 1893 lowered the price for wool if it could be sold at all. The depression was compounded by severe reservation-wide drought which forced the Navajo to sell much of their livestock to survive. As the drought continued through the decade, many Navajo were close to starvation (Bailey and Bailey 1986, 102-103). It is generally true that when wool prices are low, more women weave wool into rugs to get as much money as possible. The low price of wool and the generally bad conditions during the "90's" may help to explain the pound blanket phenomenon. It is certainly unlikely that many women could afford the greater expense of commercial yarns.

H.B. Mollhausen. Del.   Lith. of Sarony, Major & Knapp, 449 Broadway NY.

NAVAJOS.

166 The Navahoes. H.B. Mollhausen. Plate VII in *Report upon the Colorado River of the West*. 1861. Color lithograph.

167 Blanket, 1860-70, 119.5 cm x 87.5 cm. 13 warps, 50 wefts. Formerly in the Clay Lockett Collection. See Maxwell 1963:41, fig. 34. Handspun wool with natural and vegetal colors. Ravelled red and green two-ply yarn and three-ply commercial yarn. Gift of Mr. and Mrs. Gilbert Maxwell, 63.34.119.

168 Blanket, 1870-80, 190.5 cm x 34.5 cm. 12 warps, 48 wefts. Formerly in Alfred Barton Collection. See Maxwell 1963:42, fig. 35. Handspun wool with natural, vegetal and aniline colors. Two-ply ravelled red yarn and three-ply red commercial yarn. Cotton string warp. Gift of Mr. and Mrs. Gilbert Maxwell, 63.34.120.

169 Blanket, 1880-90, 192 cm x 131 cm. 7 warps, 26 wefts. All handspun wool with natural and aniline colors. Gift of Mr. Read Mullan, 64.26.2.

170 Rug/blanket, 1880-90, 189 cm x 128 cm. 9 warps, 32 wefts. All handspun wool with natural, vegetal (green) and aniline colors. Gift of Mr. Charles B. Popkin, 72.31.1.

171 Blanket, 1880-90, 177 cm x 127 cm. 8 warps, 24 wefts. Formerly in the Earl Morris Collection. All handspun wool with natural and aniline colors. Gift of Mr. and Mrs. Gilbert Maxwell, 63.34.176.

172 Rug, 1880-90, 138 cm x 83 cm. 6 warps, 30 wefts. All handspun wool with aniline colors. Gift of Mrs. C.W. Franklin, 74.27.1.

173 Blanket, 1875-80, 120 cm x 78.5 cm. 8 warps, 48 wefts. Formerly in Earl Morris Collection. Handspun wool with natural and vegetal (indigo) colors. Two- and three-ply ravelled aniline dyed yarns. Gift of Mr. and Mrs. Gilbert Maxwell, 63.34.118.

174 Blanket, c. 1890, 124 cm x 29.5 cm. 10 warps, 54 wefts. Formerly in the Earl Morris Collection. All four-ply aniline dyed commercial yarns. Warps are not continuous at one end, but are cut and doubled back into the fabric. Gift of Mr. and Mrs. Gilbert Maxwell, 63.34.160.

175 Blanket, 1880-95, 211 cm x 126 cm. 10 warps, 26 wefts (handspun) and 10 warps, 30 wefts (commercial). See Maxwell 1963:33, fig. 17. Purchased in 1895 by Earl Morris. Handspun wool with natural and aniline colors, four-ply aniline dyed yarn. The yellow commercial yarn appears in the center only. Gift of Mr. and Mrs. Gilbert Maxwell, 63.34.125.

176 Rug/blanket, 1885-95, 160 cm x 139 cm. 4 warps, 16 wefts. Handspun wool with natural and aniline colors. Gift of Mr. and Mrs. Gilbert Maxwell, 63.34.99.

177 Rug/blanket, 1880-1900, 187 cm x 141.5 cm. 5 warps, 16 wefts. All handspun wool with natural and aniline colors. Gift of Mrs. Gilbert Milne, 63.33.6.

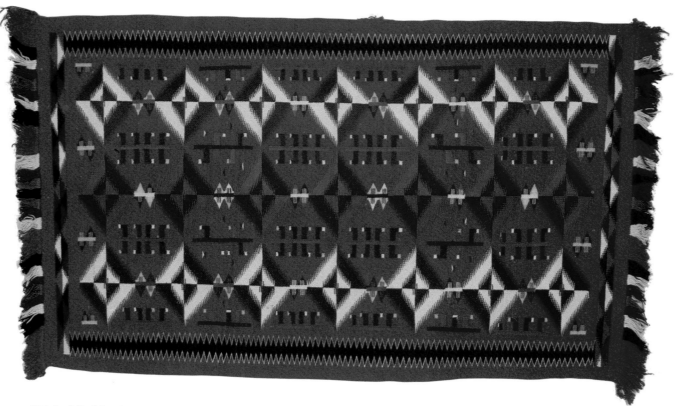

178 Saddle blanket, 1900-23, 143 cm x 87 cm. 11 warps, 42 wefts. Formerly in the Ethel Mae Bratton Collection. Exhibited at First National Intertribal Indian Ceremonial at Gallup, New Mexico in 1923 by C.N. Cotton. It won the first prize for weaving. Four-ply aniline dyed commercial yarn. Cotton string warp. Gift of Dr. Andrew C. Bratton, 73.26.2.

179 Blanket, 1890-1900, 122 cm x 91 cm. 8 warps, 40 wefts. All four-ply aniline dyed yarns. Salt and pepper yarn is tie-dyed. Cotton string warp. Gift of Mr. and Mrs. Gilbert Maxwell, 63.34.147.

180 Rug, 1890-1900, 200 cm x 123.5 cm. 5 warps, 16 wefts. All handspun wool with natural, carded and aniline colors. Gift of Mr. Irving D. Townsend, 53.10.1.

181 Blanket/rug, 1885-95, 178.5 cm x 121.5 cm. 6 warps, 24 wefts. All handspun wool with natural, carded and aniline colors. Gift of Mrs. Loretta Dohner, 65.43.1.

78

182 Blanket, 1880-90, 111 cm x 75.5 cm. 12 warps, 40 wefts. All four-ply aniline dyed commercial yarn. Gift of Mr. and Mrs. Gilbert Maxwell, 63.34.159.

183 Saddle blanket, 1880-1900, 74 cm x 67 cm. 12 warps, 48 wefts. Four-ply aniline dyed commercial yarn. Handspun white wool warp. Gift of Mrs. Maurine Grammer, 75.329.1.

184 Blanket, New Mexico, 1885-93, 160.5 cm x 119.5 cm. 7 warps, 32 wefts. Collected originally in New Mexico between 1888 and 1893. All handspun with natural and aniline colors. Gift of Mr. and Mrs. Gilbert Maxwell, 63.34.173.

185 Rug, 1880-90, 344 cm x 328.5 cm. 11 warps, 52 wefts. Four- and three-ply aniline dyed commercial yarn. Cotton string warp. Warps are cut at top and bottom and tucked back in for about one inch. Gift of Mr. and Mrs. Gilbert Maxwell, 63.34.149.

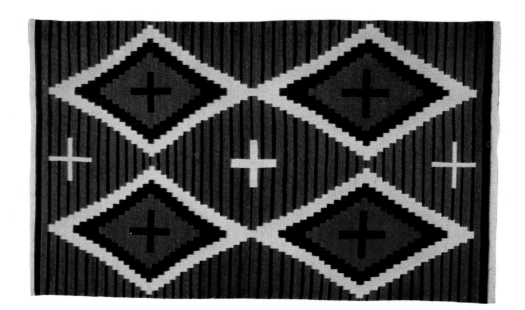

186 J.B. Moore, 1903 Catalog, Plate I.

187 J.B. Moore, 1911 Catalog, Plate XV.

188 J.B. Moore, 1911 Catalog, Plate XIX.

189 Rug/blanket, 1890-1900, 194.5 cm x 124.5 cm. 6 warps, 24 wefts. All handspun wool with natural, carded and aniline colors. Gift of Mr. Raymond Jonson, Vera Jonson Memorial Collection, 65.57.13.

190 Blanket, 1880-1900, 171.5 cm x 132 cm. 6 warps, 34 wefts. Formerly in the Earl Morris Collection. Pulled warp or wedge weave. See Maxwell 1963:41, fig. 41. All handspun wool with natural, carded and aniline colors. Gift of Mr. and Mrs. Gilbert Maxwell, 63.34.111.

191 Rug/blanket, 1890-1900, 264 cm x 150.5 cm. 7 warps, 14 wefts. Handspun wool with natural, vegetal, aniline and carded wool. Cotton string warp. Gift of Mrs. Leigh E. Smith in memory of Mary Augustus Brown, 67.123.2.

192 Rug/blanket, 1890-1900, 227 cm x 120 cm. 5 warps, 20 wefts. All handspun wool with natural and aniline colors. Gift of Mr. and Mrs. William K. McNaught, 71.29.1.

193 Blanket, 1885-95, 131.5 cm x 81.5 cm. 9 warps, 56 wefts. Four-ply aniline dyed commercial yarn with cotton string warp. Donor unknown, 74.28.2.

194 Blanket, 1885-90, 74 cm x 72.5 cm. 10 warps, 48 wefts. Four-ply aniline dyed commercial yarn with a cotton string warp. Gift of Mrs. Richard Wetherill, 55.20.29.

195 J.B. Moore, 1911 Catalog, Plate XX.

196 J.B. Moore, 1911 Catalog, Plate XXIII.

197 J.B. Moore, 1911 Catalog, Plate XXIV.

198 J.B. Moore, 1911 Catalog, Plate XXV.

199 J.B. Moore, 1911 Catalog, Plate XXIX.

200 J.B. Moore, 1911 Catalog, Plate XXX.

201 Rug, 1880-1900, 192.5 cm x 154 cm. 8 warps, 44 wefts. Four-ply aniline dyed commercial yarn. Two-ply aniline dyed red warp. Salt and pepper yarn is tie-dyed. Gift of Dr. Scott Alder, 70.65.3.

202 Saddle blanket, 1885-95, 118 cm x 80.5 cm. 10 warps, 46 wefts. Purchased in Carlsbad in 1945. Fringe of four-ply commercial yarn aniline dyed red, purple, and white. Four-ply aniline dyed yarn. Cotton string warp. Gift of Mr. and Mrs. Gilbert Maxwell, 63.34.158.

203 Rug, 1890-1900, 187.5 cm x 120 cm. 12 warps, 44 wefts. Handspun wool with natural and aniline colors. Cotton string warp. Purchase 67.14.2.

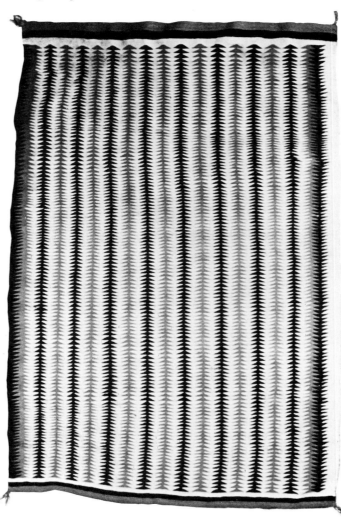

204 Saddle blanket, 1880-90, 95.5 cm x 75 cm. 8 warps, 40 wefts. Formerly in the Andrus Collection. Four-ply aniline dyed commercial year. Cotton string warp. Gift of Mr. and Mrs. Gilbert Maxwell, 63.34.144.

205 Rug, 1880-1900, 87.5 cm x 59 cm. 12 warps, 50 wefts. Four-ply aniline dyed yarn. Salt and pepper yarn is tie-dyed. Cotton string warp. Gift of A. Margaret Anson, 65.65.2.

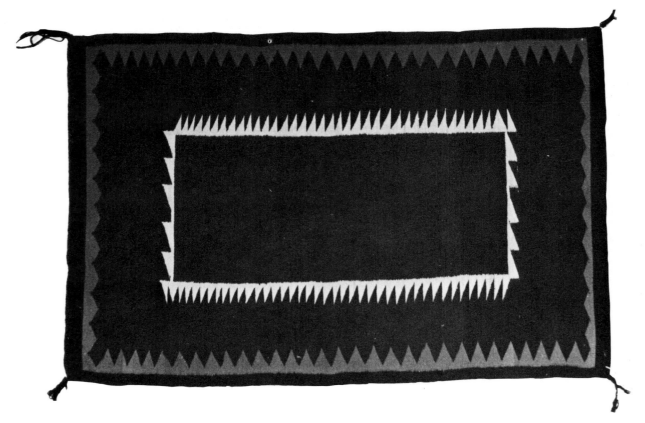

206 Rug, 1885-1900, 128 cm x 86 cm. 9 warps, 47 wefts. Purchased from Clay Lockett in 1948. Four-ply aniline dyed commercial yarn. White natural handspun. Cotton string warp. Gift of Mr. and Mrs. Gilbert Maxwell, 63.34.182.

207 J.B. Moore, 1911 Catalog, Plate XIV.

208 J.B. Moore, 1911 Catalog, Plate XXVII.

209 Rug, 1915, 216 cm x 132 cm. 7 warps, 24 wefts. Bought in 1915 at Crystal Trading Post by an unknown collector. All handspun wool with natural, carded and aniline colors. Gift of Mr. and Mrs. Gilbert Maxwell, 63.34.100.

Two early traders who worked to change rug styles around the turn of the century were John B. Moore of Crystal, N.M. and John Lorenzo Hubbell of Ganado, Arizona. Moore bought his trading post at Crystal in 1897 and began to market Navajo weaving with a newly popular Anglo merchandising technique, the mail order catalog. He issued one catalog in 1903 and another in 1911, along with single page flyers. These catalogs showed in black and white and color a series of rugs which the customer could order in several qualities and sizes (**186-188, 195-200, 207, 208**). Moore assured buyers that he and his wife had the wool commercially scoured at a mill and supervised the dyeing. Red and touches of blue were about the only bright colors used in these rugs. Most of the illustrations show a complete break with previous Navajo textile designs. In fact, they are quite strongly based on the Near Eastern rugs mentioned above. The textiles have borders and large central medallions with numerous "hooks" and filler elements in the background. Figures **209** and **210** illustrate two rugs purchased in 1915 at the Crystal post and figures **187** and **197** show the catalog illustrations on which they are based. Of course, no two Navajo rugs are ever exactly alike, and most Moore pieces are not absolutely identical to the catalog illustrations. Moore said his weavers created the designs and this is undoubtedly true, but the trader must have shown them some of the popular oriental patterns of the day. Moore left the post in 1912 and his partner carried on the business. The rug styles he began remained unchanged until about 1940 (**211**).

210 Rug, 1910-15, 203.5 cm x 137.5 cm. 7 warps, 18 wefts. Bought in 1915 at Crystal Trading Post by an unknown collector. See Moore 1911:Plate XIX; Maxwell 1962:36, fig. 24. All handspun wool with natural, carded and aniline colors. Gift of Mr. and Mrs. Gilbert Maxwell, 63.34.105.

211 Rug, Crystal, 1920-40, 181 cm x 107 cm. 10 warps, 30 wefts. All handspun wool with natural, carded and aniline colors. Gift of Edwin L. Kennedy through the Maxwell Museum Association, 79.45.83.

212 Navajo weaver at Visitors Center, Hubbell Trading Post copying a rug from a book. Photo by Marian Rodee.

213 Watercolor at Hubbell Trading Post. Photo by Kent Bush.

Lorenzo Hubbell was the second major trader who was working for changes in Navajo weaving in the 1890's. Hubbell, who had opened his trading post in 1876 at Ganado, Arizona, was a man who respected traditional Navajo culture and hence urged the weaving of Navajo blanket patterns. These textiles today are called "Hubbell Revival blankets". Many of them can be confused with original early pieces as was **291** until it was compared with a painting from the trading post, **213**. Revival pieces are almost always done in four-ply aniline-dyed yarns and indigo was replaced with a dark purple yarn which does not hold up well. Hubbell had small paintings made of older pieces he admired in collections throughout the U.S. The painter E.A. Burbank, who spent many summers in the Southwest, agreed to paint good blankets that he found in other parts of the country. These paintings were hung in the post for weavers to copy (**215-252**). They still hang in the rug room (**214**) at the post and weavers at Ganado employed today at the U.S. National Park Service Visitors' Center still make rugs to order from the paintings as well as from book illustrations (**212**).

214 Rug room at Hubbell Trading Post with early paintings of rugs on the wall. Photo by Marian Rodee.

215-252 Watercolor paintings at Hubbell Trading Post. Photos by Kent Bush.

215

216

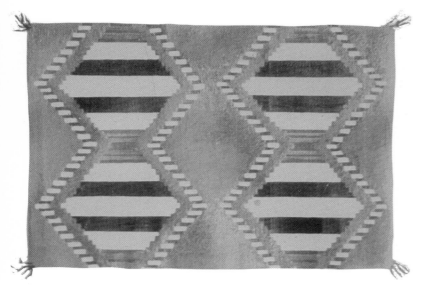

217

218

219

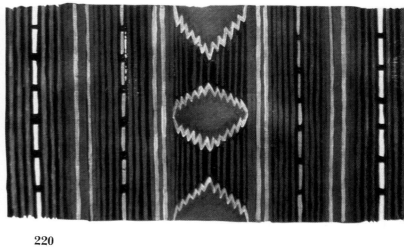

220

221

222

Watercolor paintings at Hubbell Trading Post. Photos by Kent Bush.

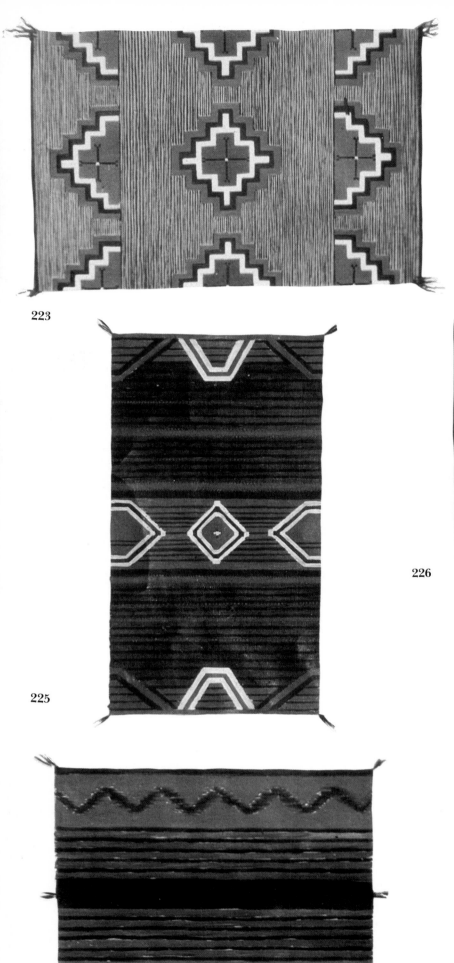

223

224

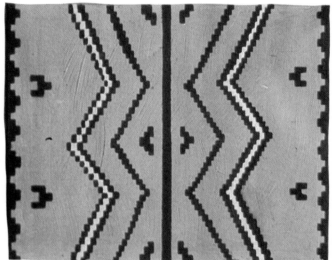

226

225

227

228

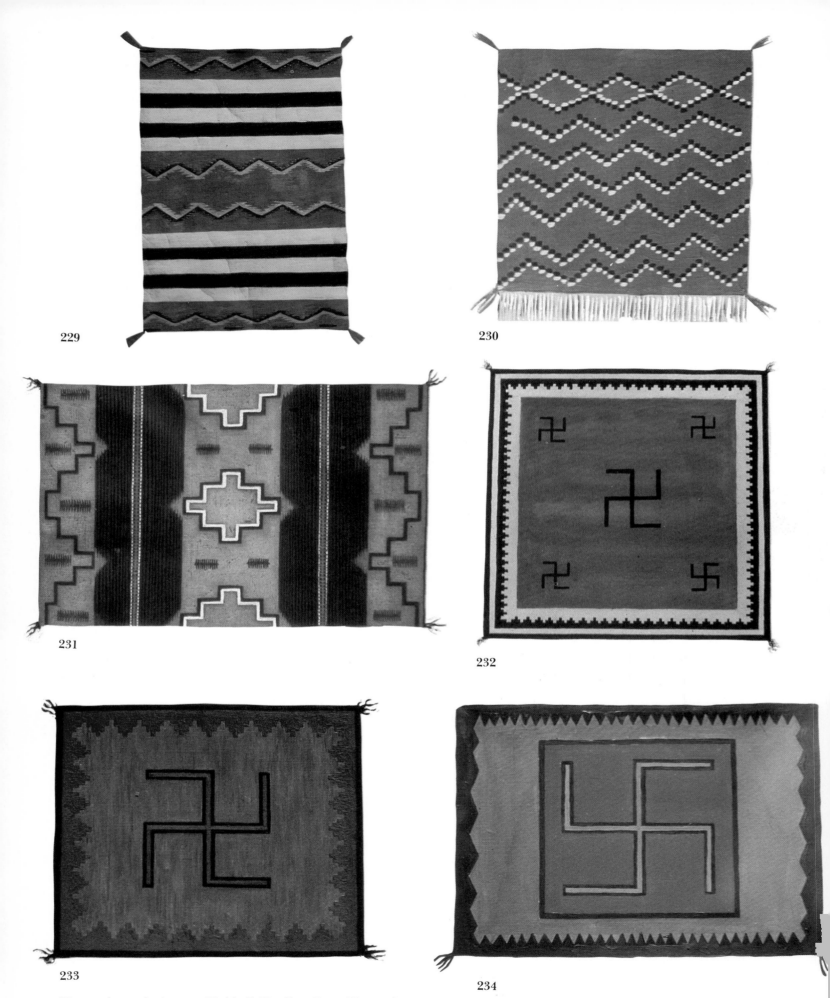

229

230

231

232

233

234

Watercolor paintings at Hubbell Trading Post. Photos by
Kent Bush.

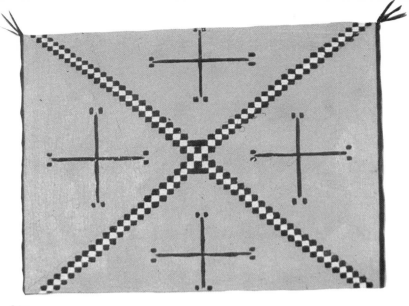

235

236

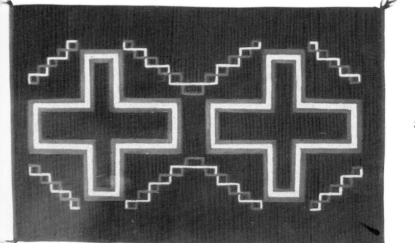

237

238

239

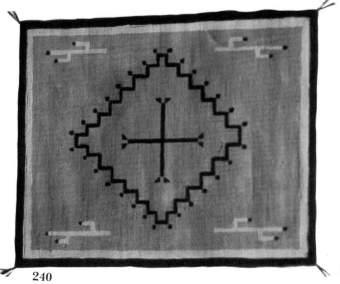

240

95

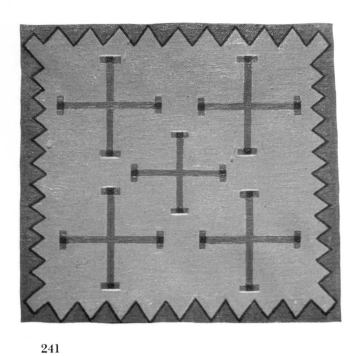

241

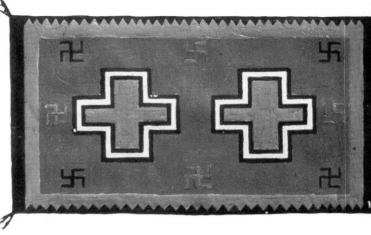

242

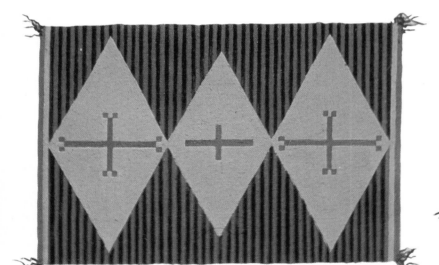

243

244

245

246

Watercolor paintings at Hubbell Trading Post. Photos by Kent Bush.

96

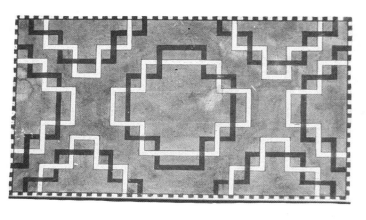

247

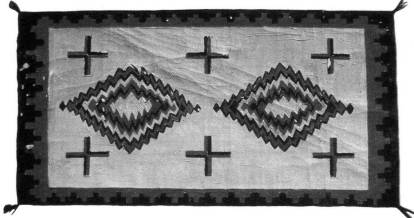

248

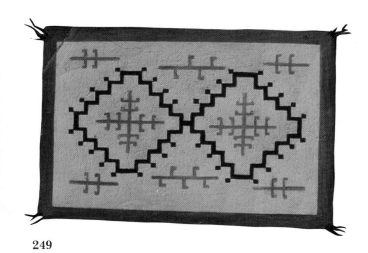

249

250

251

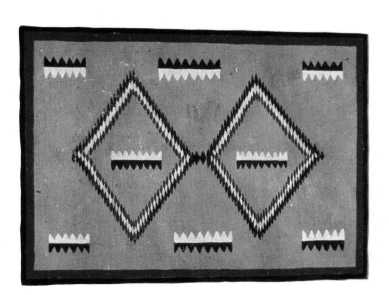

252

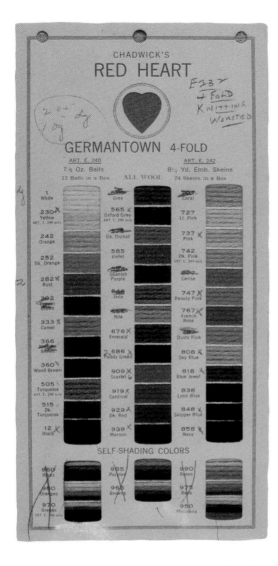

253 Red Heart yarn color chart in Hubbell Trading post with pencil notes indicating orders. Photo by Marian Rodee.

Although Hubbell's personal taste ran to the older blanket, he was running counter to contemporary taste. In a letter of 1905, Herman Schweizer, the buyer for Fred Harvey stores, said to Hubbell that his "shawl" (blanket) patterns did not sell at any price. Being essentially a business man, Hubbell gave up the blanket patterns in favor of those with borders, large central medallions or elements floating against the ground. The colors, as in Moore's, are simple red, black, white and gray. Hubbell still preferred traditional Navajo motifs such as the whirling logs or swastikas and crosses. Interestingly, both Moore and Hubbell borrowed, designs from one another. This sharing of certain popular rug patterns may be the result of C.N. Cotton, a Gallup wholesaler who was in partnership with Hubbell for a while. As a wholesaler, Cotton both supplied Reservation traders and purchased their rugs and wool crop. He undoubtedly had more influence than we know today, but his papers were lost in a fire.

Lorenzo Hubbell also helped with the materials for weavers in his area by supplying yarns (**253**) and dyes (**254**). At first, weavers had difficulty with the Diamond Dyes. A letter from the dye company's sales representative in 1912 states that the dyes should be fast if used according to their instructions. It could be that weavers with a limited amount of water were not able to rinse the wool as much as was necessary to remove excess dye. Although it is often said that the deep scarlet red so characteristic of Ganado rugs is a result of a double dye bath, the Diamond Dye chart indicated the color called "cardinal" will give this hue in one bath. Rugs based on the paintings were popular until the early 1930's when Lorenzo Hubbell died (1930) at which time the Ganado style became closer to that of Two Grey Hills. Some of the characteristics of the Ganado regional style at the earlier part of the century include: contrasting borders along a pair of sides, a row of three motifs—often crosses or crosses within diamonds, or an overall X-pattern. These rug types were very common during the first thirty years of this century, largely because Hubbell owned many posts, mostly in the central Reservation area, where these patterns were encouraged.

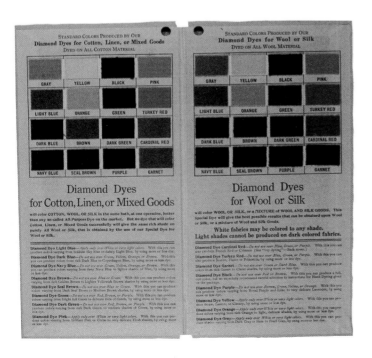

254 Diamond Dye color chart in Hubbell Trading Post. Photo by Marian Rodee.

On the eastern side of the Chuska Mountains, two traders living only a few miles apart worked together to develop a distinctive weaving style. Ed Davies at Two Grey Hills and George Bloomfield at Toadlena began as early as 1911 using the popular oriental rug-derived style of Moore at Crystal. The weavers supposedly had a natural dislike for red, and hence used only the natural sheep colors of wool. The style was fully developed by the early 1920's and has remained little-changed throughout the century (see pages 222-238).

Still another effort to change the course of Navajo weaving was undertaken by Mary Cabot Wheelwright, a Boston philanthropist and amateur anthropologist. Working with Cozy McSparron, the trader at Chinle, Arizona, Wheelwright supplied photos of old blankets to the weavers and the cash to buy their first efforts beginning in the early 1920's. Wheelwright preferred the 19th century classic pieces with their primarily horizontal borderless patterns rather than the bordered oriental-style rugs common elsewhere on the Reservation. She also encouraged softer colors derived from native dye plants (255). The first dye experiments produced shades of gold and green, but soon weavers experimented with more dyes to get an extraordinary range of colors not seen in older weaving. This vegetal revival style became very popular and was taken up by other traders, first at Wide Ruins in 1936, and then at Crystal around 1940 (Stoller 1976, 460).

A new style was developed in the 1970's by Bruce Burnham of Burntwater, Arizona. Called "Burntwater" after his post, this style combines vegetal dyed wools of the revival style with the elaborate Two Grey Hills patterns (256). Soon, this style had taken over the former position of Two Grey Hills as the most expensive of all Navajo weavings. The two pieces shown here are by a mother and daughter. Martha Duboise is an experienced weaver and her 14-year-old daugther Laura began weaving on her own. This is the first rug Laura brought into the post at Ganado for sale (257). She used her mother's wool, but the patterns are simpler. In a few years, she will be weaving the more intricate patterns of her mother's rugs.

255 Rug, probably Chinle or Crystal, 1920-40, 229 cm x 140 cm. 7 warps, 18 wefts. All handspun wool with natural and vegetal colors. Gift of Mr. Raymond Jonson, Vera Jonson Memorial Collection, 65.57.14.

256 Burntwater rug by Martha Duboise, 1985. Private Collection. Photo by Anthony Richardson.

257 First rug by Laura Duboise, age 14. Chinle style, 1985. The Duboises live in Oak Springs, Arizona. Private Collection. Photo by Anthony Richardson.

258 Rug or blanket, 1885-95, 195 cm x 138.5 cm. 11 warps, 28 wefts. All handspun wool with natural and aniline colors. Gift of Helen Chambers from the Jean Moore Estate, 76.54.1.

259 Saddle blanket, 1880-1900, 70.7 cm x 82.5 cm. 14 warps, 68 wefts. All four-ply yarn with natural and aniline colors and a brown cotton string warp. Gift of Muril E. Hagen through the Maxwell Museum Association, 83.39.6.

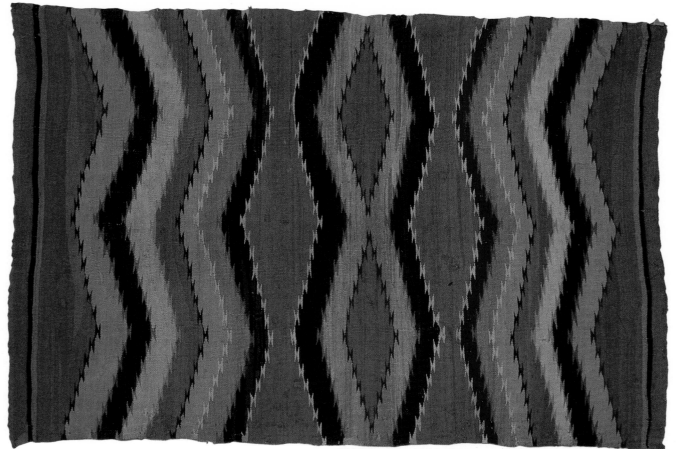

260 Blanket, 1880-1900, 187.5 cm x 128 cm. 7 warps, 26 wefts. All handspun wool with natural, aniline and indigo colors. Transfer from the Harwood Foundation, Taos, 80.51.89.

261 Rug, 1880-85, 171 cm x 115.5 cm. 10 warps, 52 wefts. Rug is illustrated in *Old Navajo Rugs*, Plate 2. All four-ply commercial yarns with aniline dyes and a cotton string warp. Gift of Mr. Edwin L. Kennedy, 85.52.4.

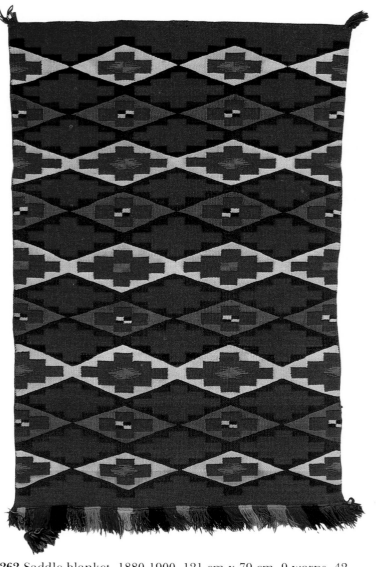

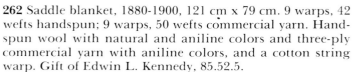

262 Saddle blanket, 1880-1900, 121 cm x 79 cm. 9 warps, 42 wefts handspun; 9 warps, 50 wefts commercial yarn. Hand-spun wool with natural and aniline colors and three-ply commercial yarn with aniline colors, and a cotton string warp. Gift of Edwin L. Kennedy, 85.52.5.

264 Saddle blanket, 1880-1900, 99 cm x 71 cm. 9 warps, 38 wefts. All four-ply yarns with natural and aniline colors. Gift of Dr. David Gale, 82.60.2.

263 Rug, 1880-1900, 254 cm x 146 cm. 10 warps, 60 wefts. All commercial four-ply yarn with natural and aniline colors and a cotton string warp. Gift of Edwin L. Kennedy, 85.52.7.

265 Rug, 1880-1900, 184 cm x 131 cm. 14 warps, 50 wefts. All three-ply commercial wool with natural and aniline colors and a cotton string warp. Gift of Edwin L. Kennedy, 85.52.6.

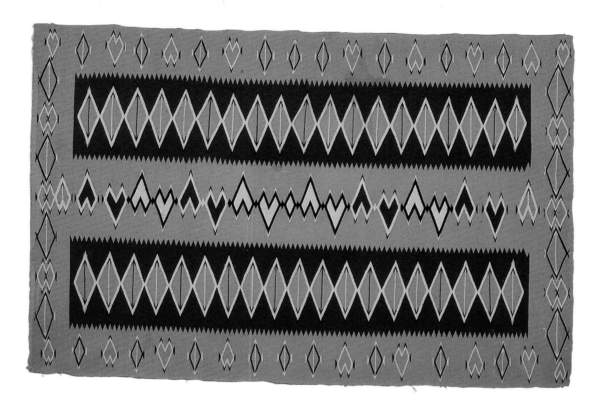

266 Rug, 1880-1900, 211 cm x 141 cm. 10 warps, 50 wefts. All four-ply commercial yarn with aniline dyes and a cotton string warp. Gift of R. Greiner, 77.59.1.

267 Rug/blanket, 1880-1900, 218 cm x 144 cm. 6 warps, 26 wefts. All handspun wool with natural and aniline colors. Gift of Edwin L. Kennedy through the Maxwell Museum Association, 79.45.72.

269 Rug, 1900-20, 245 cm x 147 cm. 6 warps, 16 wefts. All handspun wool with natural and aniline colors. Gift of Dorothy Latimer Teare, 83.28.2.

268 Rug, c. 1919, 204 cm x 128 cm. 7 warps, 34 wefts. All handspun wool with carded and natural colors. Purchased in Shiprock, N.M. in 1919. Gift of Mrs. Alice Howell, 76.83.1.

270 Rug, c. 1900, 208 cm x 170 cm. 8 warps, 40 wefts. The material may be the experimental carpet yarn introduced by **Lorenzo Hubbell. Note the similarity to no. 297. All three-ply** aniline dyed commercial yarn. In most of the border and in scattered areas in the center the weaver has used the yarn in pairs giving a coarser effect. Gift of Mr. and Mrs. Gilbert Maxwell, 63.34.110.

271 Pillow cover, 1890-1900, 52.5 cm x 55.5 cm. 10 warps, 48 wefts. Four-ply aniline dyed commercial yarn. Cotton string warp. Gift of A. Margaret Anson, 65.65.1.

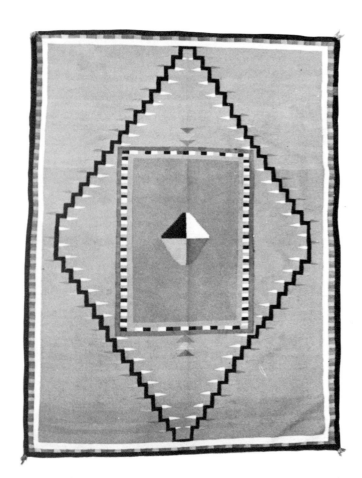

272 Rug/blanket, 1885-95, 198 cm x 126 cm. 9 warps, 26 wefts. All handspun wool with natural, vegetal (indigo) and aniline colors. Gift of Mr. Read Mullan, 64.26.1.

273 Rug, 1885-95, 196 cm x 144 cm. 9 warps, 44 wefts. See Maxwell 1963:33, fig. 18. All four- and two-ply aniline dyed yarn. Gift of Mr. and Mrs. Gilbert Maxwell, 63.34.109.

274 Rug, 1890-1900, 149 cm x 99 cm. 7 warps, 14 wefts. Handspun wool with natural and aniline colors and a cotton string warp. Gift of Hazel Beebe, 81.46.78.

275 Rug, 1890-1900, 182 cm x 116 cm. 7 warps, 26 wefts. All handspun wool with natural and carded colors. Gift of Mr. and Mrs. Julian Shapero, 78.36.2.

276 Rug, 1880-1900, 272 cm x 128 cm. 11 warps, 48 wefts. All four-ply commerical yarn with natural and aniline colors. Gift of Edwin L. Kennedy, 85.52.3.

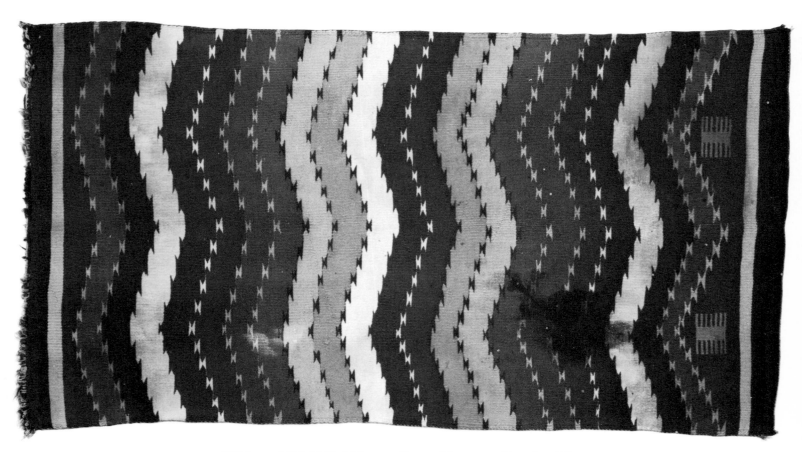

277 Rug, 1880-1900, 130 cm x 71 cm. 10 warps, 40 wefts. All four-ply aniline dyed commercial yarn. Gift of Hazel Beebe, 81.46.76.

278 Rug, 1880-1900, 117 cm x 80 cm. 11 warps, 40 wefts. All commercial four-ply yarn with aniline dyes. Gift of Hazel Beebe, 81.46.75.

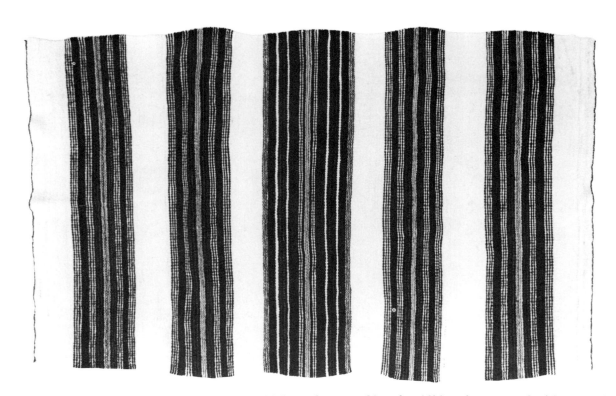

279 Rug/blanket, 1890-1910, 186.5 cm x 111.5 cm. 8 warps, 20 wefts. All handspun wool with natural vegetal and aniline colors. Gift of Mrs. W.H. Loerpabel, 65.46.2.

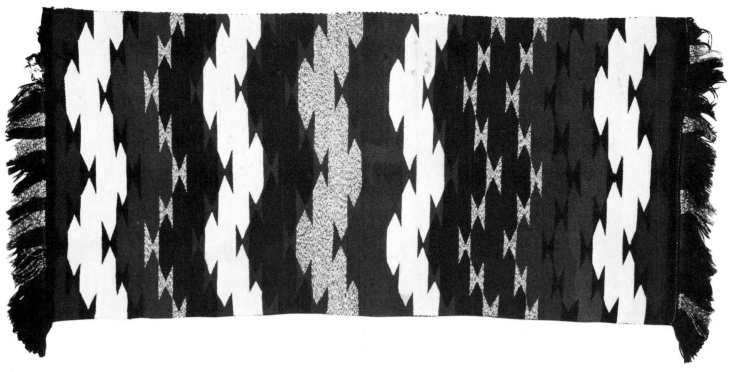

280 Saddle blanket, 1880-1900, 132 cm x 65.5 cm. 9 warps, 56 wefts. All commercial four-ply wool with natural and aniline colors and a cotton string warp. Gift of Edwin L. Kennedy, 85.52.10.

281 Saddle blanket, 1875-85, 89 cm x 76 cm. 12 warps, 44 wefts. All four-ply commercial yarn in natural and aniline colors. Gift of Hazel Beebe, 81.46.73.

282 Rug/blanket, 1880-1890, 186 cm x 144.5 cm. 9 warps, 30 wefts. All handspun wool with natural and aniline colors. Gift of Edwin L. Kennedy through the Maxwell Museum Association, 79.45.73.

283 Rug, 1880-1900, 181 cm x 135.5 cm. 9 warps, 32 wefts. All handspun wool with natural, carded and aniline colors. Gift of Mrs. H.A. Batten, 79.43.6.

284 Rug, 1890-1900, 256 cm x 151 cm. 5 warps, 18 wefts. All handspun wool with natural, carded and aniline colors. Gift of Mr. and Mrs. Julian Shapero, 78.36.1.

285 Rug, 1880-1900, 155.5 cm x 107.5 cm. 6 warps, 22 wefts. All handspun wool with aniline colors and a cotton string warp. Gift of Edwin L. Kennedy, 85.52.9.

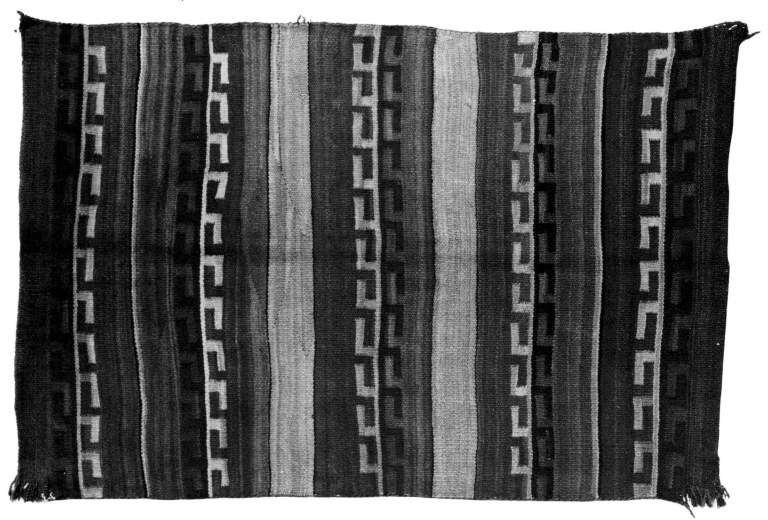

286 Rug, 1890-1900, 234 cm x 137 cm. 6 warps, 20 wefts. All handspun wool with natural and aniline colors and a cotton string warp. Gift of Dorothy Latimer Teare, 83.28.3.

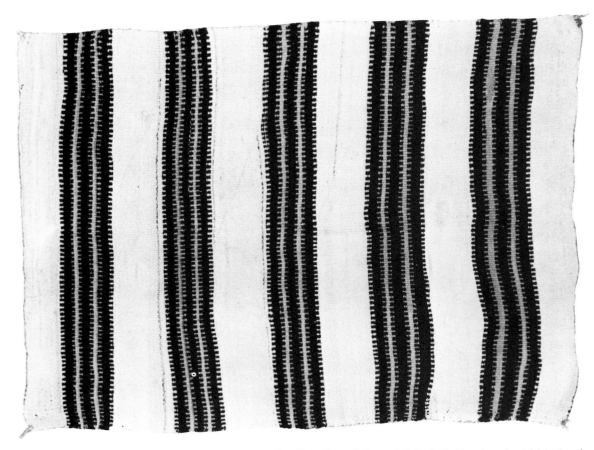

287 Blanket, 1880-1900, 166 cm x 121 cm. 4 warps, 16 wefts. Purchased from Maisel Collection in 1944. Registered with Laboratory of Anthropology, Santa Fe, no. 647. All handspun wool with natural and aniline colors. Gift of Mr. and Mrs. Gilbert Maxwell, 63.34.117.

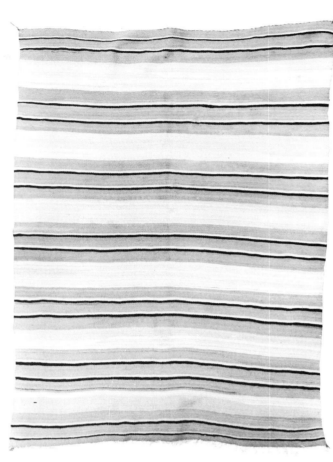

288 Blanket, 1890-1900, 155 cm x 120 cm. 6 warps, 16 wefts. All handspun wool with natural carded and aniline colors. Gift of Mrs. Prudence E. Oakes, 66.113.2.

290 Rug, 1890-1900, 153 cm x 82 cm. 8 warps, 24 wefts. All handspun wool with natural and aniline colors. Gift of Mrs. Prudence E. Oakes, 66.113.2.

289 Blanket, 1885-95, 176 cm x 126 cm. 7 warps, 30 wefts. Purchased from Carlsbad Caverns Supply Co. in 1946. Registered with Laboratory of Anthropology, Santa Fe, no. 644. All handspun wool with natural, carded and aniline colors. Gift of Mr. and Mrs. Gilbert Maxwell, 63.34.174.

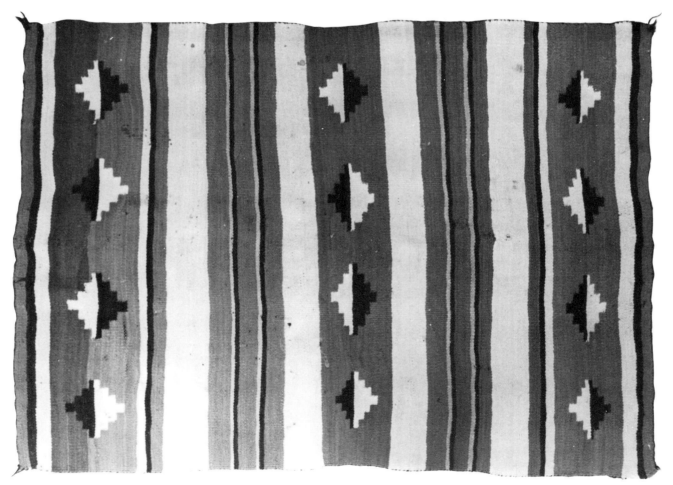

291 Blanket, 1885-1900, 202 cm x 153 cm. 15 warps, 64 wefts. Purchased from Fred Harvey Co. See Maxwell 1963:34, fig. 19. All commercial two- and three-ply aniline yarn. Gift of Mr. and Mrs. Gilbert Maxwell, 63.34.151.

292 Rug, 1910-15, 222 cm x 132.5 cm. 6 warps, 36 wefts. Crystal, see Moore 1911:Plate XXVII. All handspun wool with natural, carded and aniline colors. Gift of Mr. and Mrs. Gilbert Maxwell, 63.34.102.

293 Blanket, Ganado, Arizona, c. 1900, 254 cm x 144 cm. 10 warps, 54 wefts. Lorenzo Hubbell revival pattern from Ganado, Arizona. Purchased by Clark Field in 1931 from the Irving S. Cobb Collection. All four-ply aniline dyed commercial yarns. Gift of Mr. and Mrs. Gilbert Maxwell, 63.34.116.

294 Rug, 1900-20, 192.5 cm x 139 cm. 6 warps, 18 wefts. All handspun wool with natural, carded and aniline colors. Gift of Mike Robertson, 83.33.1.

295 Rug, 1900-15, 192 cm x 150 cm. 7 warps, 18 wefts. Crystal, J.B. Moore influence. The border is a type illustrated in Moore's catalog; the central design is similar to one shown in Moore 1902:Plate V. All handspun wool with natural, aniline and carded colors. Gift of Mr. George Meyers, 67.67.1.

296 Rug, 1900-15, 176 cm x 112.5 cm. 5 warps, 26 wefts. All handspun wool with natural, carded and aniline colors. Gift of Mrs. Willis S. Clayton, Jr., 57.6.3.

297 Rug, 1900-10, 277 cm x 219 cm. 5 warps, 20 wefts. Note the similarity of design to no. 270. All handspun wool with natural, carded and aniline colors. Gift of Mrs. Lewis Kohlhaas, 74.37.1.

299 Saddle blanket, Tucson, 1900-20, 129 cm x 67 cm. 13 warps, 28 wefts. Bought in Tucson in 1948. Handspun natural and carded colors. Cotton string warp. Gift of Mr. and Mrs. Gilbert Maxwell, 74.67.1.

298 Hall rug, 1900-10, 447 cm x 92 cm. 9 warps, 22 wefts. Handspun wool with natural, carded and aniline colors. Cotton string warp. Gift of Mrs. Willis S. Clayton, Jr., 57.6.5.

300 Saddle blanket, 1900-20, 69 cm x 90 cm. 4 warps, 18 wefts. A knotted fringe tied to warps at one end. All handspun wool with natural and aniline colors. Red appears only in one small line extending in from the selvage for about 3½ inches. Gift of Miss Elizabeth Elder, 68.16.4.

301 Rug, 1910-20, 183 cm x 87.5 cm. 7 warps, 18 wefts. All handspun wool with natural, vegetal and carded colors. Transferred from Zimmerman Library, University of New Mexico, 65.42.162.

302 Rug, 1900-20, 196 cm x 142.5 cm. 8 warps, 18 wefts. Handspun wool with natural and aniline colors. Cotton string warp. Red has run uniformly making white background pink. Transferred from Zimmerman Library, University of New Mexico, 65.42.160.

303 Rug, 1900-20, 192 cm x 127 cm. 5 warps, 14 wefts. All handspun wool with natural and aniline colors. Given to donor's husband in 1924. Gift of Mrs. Albert Stern, 84.58.1.

304 Rug, 1900-20, 105 cm x 74.5 cm. 6 warps, 24 wefts. All handspun wool with natural and aniline colors and a cotton string warp. Transfer from the Harwood Foundation, Taos, 80.51.88.

305 Rug, 1890-1910, 155.5 cm x 112.5 cm. 4 warps, 12 wefts. All handspun wool with natural and aniline colors. Transfer from the Harwood Foundation, Taos, 80.51.90.

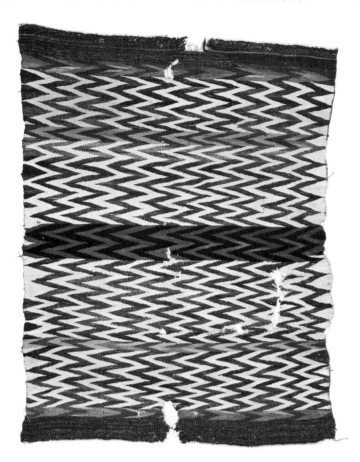

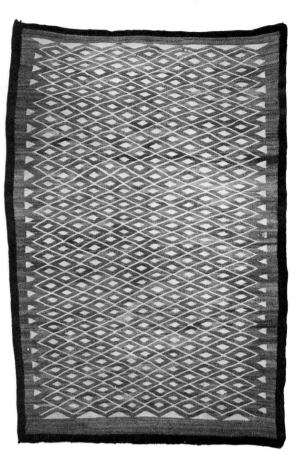

306 Rug, 1910-20, 186.5 cm x 135 cm. 6 warps, 10 wefts. All handspun wool with natural and aniline colors. Gift of Shirley Earickson, 76.76.1.

307 Rug, 1900-1920, 238 cm x 154 cm. 5 warps, 18 wefts. All handspun wool in natural and carded colors. Gift of Mr. and Mrs. W.H. Roberts, 79.57.1.

308 Rug, 1900-1915, 243 cm x 152 cm. 6 warps, 26 wefts. All handspun wool with natural and aniline colors. Possibly Ganado. Gift of Dorothy Latimer Teare, 83.28.1.

119

309 Rug, 1900-10, 188 cm x 131.5 cm. 6 warps, 16 wefts. Family history states it was made in the Zuni area about 1907. All handspun wool with natural, carded and aniline colors. Gift of Mr. and Mrs. Fred Goldworthy, 67.24.1.

310 Saddle blanket, South Kayenta—Shonto Area, 1900-25, 80 cm x 91.5 cm. 8 warps, 16 wefts. All handspun wool with natural and carded colors. Gift of Mrs. Lawrence Milne, 63.33.4.

311 Rug, c. 1908, 176 cm x 127 cm. 8 warps, 16 wefts. All handspun wool with natural colors. Purchased in Red Lake Arizona in 1908. A photograph of this rug appeared in *Old Navajo Rugs* (UNM Press: 1981) and a dealer identified it at a Tucson sale and offered it to the Museum. Gift of the Maxwell Museum Association in memory of Dr. Warren Brown, 82.22.1.

312 Blanket, 1875-85, 79 cm x 106 cm. This blanket has unusual Pueblo format and pattern. 9 warps, 40 wefts. Handspun wool, natural white, vegetal brown ravelled and recarded pink. Gift of Edwin L. Kennedy through the Maxwell Museum Association, 79.45.75.

Woman's dress

Early weaving was meant to be worn; most pieces dating before about 1880 were garments for men and women and occasionally children.

Before the adoption of white style clothing in the late nineteenth century, the usual dress for a Navajo woman was a two-piece woven garment sewn down the sides and at the shoulders. Each half had the same pattern with a black central portion and red and blue borders at the top and bottom.

A one-piece dress style formerly identified as Pueblo has now been attributed to the Navajo by Dr. Joe Ben Wheat of the University of Colorado. The Museum has four examples of this type of garment (313-316).

There are three types of Navajo women's dress, one of them being similar to that woven and worn by Pueblo women. It is folded along one edge and sewn on the other and worn over the left shoulder leaving the right shoulder bare. This dress (*manta*) is usually woven with a black center and red and indigo blue ends, and is secured by a belt, either woven or of silver. This one-piece manta could also be used as a shawl draped over the shoulders, and was reported by the Franciscan Fathers as woven in all-over red and white stripes (Franciscian Fathers 1910, 246). At the trading post at Ramah, older people remember *mantas* with black and white horizontal stripes as well as the red and white dresses (Kluckhohn *et. al.* 1971, 239). No such documented striped pieces are now known to have survived. **312** appears to be a Navajo woven interpretation of the embroidered Hopi *manta*. The usual type, which is well represented in museum collections, has a black wool center with indigo and red twill borders (313-316).

313 Woman's dress, Shiprock, 1900-10, 129 cm x 163 cm. Bought in Shiprock in 1910 by Earl Morris. Twill weave. Handspun wool with natural and aniline colors. Cotton string warp. Gift of Mr. and Mrs. Gilbert Maxwell, 63.34.133.

314 Woman's dress, c. 1880, 107 cm x 140 cm. Twill weave. Handspun wool with natural and vegetal (indigo) colors. Two-ply ravelled vegetal red. Gift of Mr. and Mrs. Gilbert Maxwell, 63.34.138.

315 Woman's dress, 1880-90, 110.5 cm x 152 cm. Plain twill weave with areas of diamond and herringbone. Handspun wool with natural, aniline and vegetal (indigo) colors. Ravelled three-ply vegetal red. Gift of Mr. and Mrs. Gilbert Maxwell, 63.34.130.

316 Woman's dress, 1875-80, 103 cm x 140 cm. Plain twill weave with areas of herringbone twill. Handspun with natural, aniline and vegetal (indigo) colors. 63.15.5.

317 Complete woman's dress, Arizona, 1850-60, 123 cm x 89.5 cm and 119.5 cm x 87 cm. 13 warps, 60 wefts. Formerly in the Earl Morris Collection. Mr. Morris acquired it in Holbrook, Arizona, in 1928. Handspun wool with natural and indigo colors. Ravelled two-ply vegetal red. Gift of Mr. and Mrs. Gilbert Maxwell, 63.34.145a, b.

318 Complete woman's dress, 1880-90, 126.5 cm x 81.5 cm and 128 cm x 87 cm. 13 warps, 44 wefts (handspun) and 11 warps, 52 wefts (ravelled). Registered with the Laboratory of Anthropology, Santa Fe, no. 628. Formerly in the Maisel and the Earl Morris Collections. Two halves sewn together at shoulders and down one side. Handspun wool with natural and vegetal (indigo) colors. Ravelled three-ply red yarn. Gift of Mr. and Mrs. Gilbert Maxwell, 63.34.126.

319a & b Complete woman's dress, 1860-65, 86 cm x 123 cm and 90 cm x 140 cm. 13 warps, 44 wefts. Formerly in the Clay Lockett Collection. Handspun wool with natural and vegetal colors. Two-ply ravelled red aniline. Gift of Mr. and Mrs. Gilbert Maxwell, 63.34.132a, b.

320a & b Rugs, 1920-40, 161 cm x 77.5 cm. 8 warps, 28 wefts. Weight of pieces indicates they were woven as rugs, but the pattern is that of the traditional Navajo woman's dress. All handspun wool with natural and aniline colors. Gift of Mrs. O.D. Johnson, 79.59.1a, b.

The two-piece dress which is far more common consists of a pair of identical woven rectangles, usually in black wool with indigo blue and red designs in the top and bottom borders (**317-319**). The two pieces were sewn together at the shoulders and down the sides and belted at the waist. This style was based on the two-piece buckskin dress of the Plains Indians and their own distant past. Since the wool was rather rough next to the skin, the Navajo, after their return from Bosque Redondo, lined the dresses with cotton (Kluckhohn *et. al.* 1971, 241). Both the two-piece dress and the man's blanket style, called a chief's blanket, are woven occasionally today. The dress is still worn by members of the Navajo Tribal band, although today examples are narrower to be form-fitting and may have notched collars woven in as well (**320-321**). While the old dresses could reach either to just below the knees or eight inches above the ankle (Kluckhohn *et. al.*, 241), modern girls prefer them to be knee-length. Most of the old two-piece dresses have been cut apart so that they can be sold separately to collectors. They are usually very finely woven but conservative in style with few changes in color or design evident in the last century and a half. Dresses have not been popular with collectors, perhaps because of their conservatism as well as the broad expanse of somber black in the center. Handwoven dresses must have been fairly expensive in their day, however. Son of Old Man Hat in the late 1870's says his mother was wearing dresses of plain white muslin, and a gift of calico and ready-made calico dresses was special (Dyk [1938] 1967, 248).

321 Two-piece woman's dress, 1970's, 82.5 cm x 51 cm. 9 warps, 44 wefts. Purchased from Natalie Pattison who in turn bought the dress at Pinyon in the 1970's. All handspun wool with natural and aniline colors. Gift of the Maxwell Museum Association, 80.34.1.

126

Wearing Blankets

The high point of Navajo weaving was the "serape Navajo" or man's wearing blanket (159). This was the largest of all early forms, about 55" by 72", and of elaborate design and very fine weave. The style of blanket called "chief's" in three progressive variations or phases was much in demand by the Plains Indians (163, 322-327, 329). Their width is always greater than their length, as in Pueblo textiles, and they are characterized by broad horizontal black and white stripes and three patterned bands. In the earliest chief's blankets, the Phase One style, the patterns consists of stripes of red and blue. Phase Two style is recognized by an elaboration of the three bands, generally with bars or ribbonlike designs. Phase Three chief's blankets are the most elaborate with each band containing three serrated or terraced diamonds or triangles.

322 Phase II chief's blanket, 1850-60, 142 cm x 183 cm. 11 warps, 58 wefts. See Maxwell 1963:12, fig. 3. Handspun wool with natural and indigo color. Ravelled three-ply red yarn. The blue wool is shorter and curlier than that used for other colors. Gift of Mr. and Mrs. Gilbert Maxwell, 63.34.113.

323 Phase III chief's blanket, c. 1900, 148 cm x 233 cm. 10 warps, 36 wefts (handspun) and 10 warps, 44 wefts (ravelled). Purchased by Gilbert Maxwell in 1947 from Annie Wahneka, Chee Dodge's daughter. Handspun wool with natural and aniline colors. Ravelled two-ply red yarn and commercial four-ply red yarn. The red commercial yarn appears only for one inch at one end of the blanket. Gift of Mr. and Mrs. Gilbert Maxwell, 63.34.128.

324 Phase III chief's rug, Lukachukai, c. 1934, 125 cm x 181 cm. 7 warps, 30 wefts. All handspun wool with natural carded and aniline colors. Gift of Dr. W.W. Hill, 65.47.1.

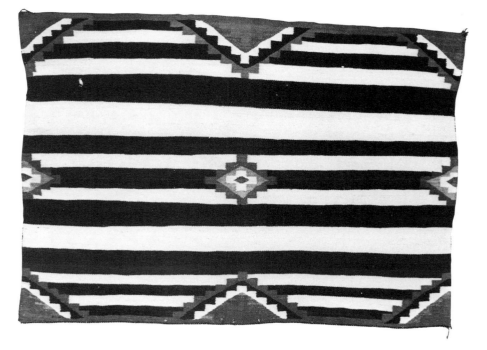

325 Phase III chief's rug, 1900-20, 147 cm x 182 cm. 7 warps, 32 wefts. All hand-spun wool with natural, carded and aniline colors. Donor unknown, 76.1.31.

326 Phase III chief's rug fragment, 1920-40, 148 cm x 114.5 cm. 6 warps, 22 wefts. All handspun wool with natural and aniline colors. Gift of Mr. George Johnson, 63.40.2.

327 Chief's saddle blanket, 1940-60, 69.5 cm x 87 cm. 11 warps, 26 wefts. All handspun wool with natural, carded and aniline colors. Gift of Mr. Michael Marshall, 71.9.1.

128

328 Chief's blanket rug, 1900-15, 134 cm x 139 cm. 7 warps, 30 wefts. Unusual rug in a Phase I pattern. Handspun wool with natural and aniline colors. Gift of Hazel Beebe, 81.46.74.

329 Phase II chief's rug/blanket, New Mexico, 1890-1910, 129 cm x 103 cm. 7 warps, 20 wefts. Purchased circa 1910 in New Mexico by D. Brown of Schenectady, New York. All handspun wool with natural and aniline colors. Some goat hair carded in. Gift of Mrs. Virginia Brockman, 62.5.1.

330 Saddle blanket, c. 1930, 124 cm x 74 cm. Twill weave. All handspun wool with natural, carded and aniline colors. Gift of Betty Karlson Lane, Muriel Karlson Memorial Collection, 60.27.124.

129

In spite of all the attention given in this century to the development of men's fine quality serapes during the 19th century, the most common blanket of that time was the simple handspun, white-background type, very loosely woven and generally with bands of stripes. This blanket, often called a *dyugie*, is seen in many photos of southwestern Indians in the late 19th and early 20th centuries, at least in those that were not posed in a photographer's studio (**279** and **287**). All three weaving traditions of the southwest, Navajo, Pueblo and Spanish American, produced wearing blankets of this type and it is often difficult to determine from an old photograph the exact origin of a textile. Such blankets are plain, unprepossessive, and little-collected; hence, much rarer in museum collections than their actual importance at the time would indicate.

Saddle Blankets

The saddle blanket, with the possible exception of the women's dress and the sash, is the only type of Navajo weaving still used by the Navajo themselves. These blankets are conservative in pattern still maintaining the striped design with quarter and half diamonds at the edges so characteristic of classic period weaving (**330**). In the early 19th century, only single saddle blankets were made, but later double size blankets were also woven. Amsden speculates that the change in size (30'' by 30'' for a single saddle and 30'' x 60'' for a double saddle) occurred at the time the Navajo began using the heavier American saddle (Amsden [1934] 1971, 104). The larger blanket was used folded double under the saddle to provide twice the padding. However, both size blankets continue to be produced. Today, saddle blankets are simple, coarse and of two main types. The first is primarily white, gray or brown with horizontal stripes, and the second is the twill with an over-two, under-two weave which makes for a thicker, fluffier blanket. These common quality modern blankets are passed over by collectors; but, especially in double size, are bought by tourists because they make bright, durable and affordable area rugs. Saddle blankets provide a trade product for the lower end of the market

331 Saddle blanket, Gallup, c. 1960, 141.5 cm x 85.5 cm. Diamond twill weave. All handspun wool with natural, carded and aniline colors. Gift of Mr. and Mrs. Gilbert Maxwell, 63.34.95.

332 Saddle blanket, Wide Ruins, c. 1948, 152.5 cm x 86 cm. See Maxwell 1963:49, fig. 38. Plain and diamond twill weave. All handspun wool with natural, carded and vegetal colors. Gift of Mr. and Mrs. Gilbert Maxwell, 63.34.96.

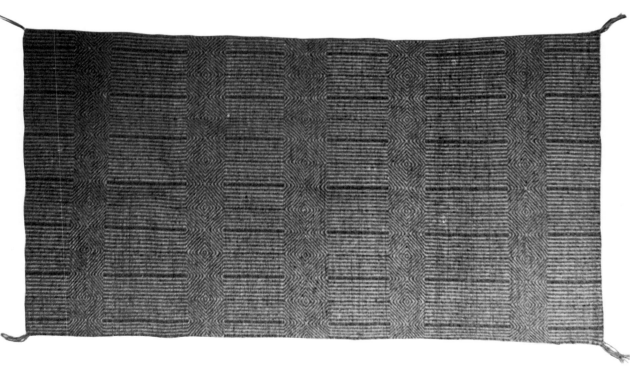

333 Saddle blanket, Gallup, c. 1960, 139.5 cm x 86.5 cm. Diamond twill weave. All handspun wool with natural and aniline colors. Gift of Mr. and Mrs. Gilbert Maxwell, 63.34.92.

335 Saddle blanket, Gallup, c. 1952, 147 cm x 82 cm. See Maxwell 1963:46, fig. 37. Twill weave. All handspun wool with natural, carded and aniline colors. Gift of Mr. and Mrs. Gilbert Maxwell, 63.34.94.

334 Saddle blanket, Gallup, c. 1960, 138 cm x 87.5 cm. Plain twill weave. Handspun wool with natural and aniline colors. Cotton string warp. Gift of Mr. and Mrs. Gilbert Maxwell, 63.34.93.

336 Saddle blanket, Gallup, c. 1960, 137 cm x 94.5 cm. Diamond twill weave. All handspun wool with natural and aniline colors. Gift of Mr. and Mrs. Gilbert Maxwell, 63.34.90.

and are still considered an ideal protection between horse and saddle (**331-336**).

Many collectors and dealers call small, 19th-century blankets of high quality, especially double saddle size, "children's wearing blankets". As such, they are more appealing than "horse blankets", but it is doubtful that such fine pieces of weaving would have been given to children. However, the Navajo do have a tradition of elaborately outfitting their horses with silver mounted bridles, expensive saddles and fine blankets. Many blankets of the late 19th century in the expensive Germantown 4-ply yarns have elaborate fringes and tassels which would show off well projecting from under the back and sides of the saddle (**183**).

Man's Shirt

The only piece of hand-woven clothing unique to men was the wool shirt. The Franciscan Fathers record two kinds—plain blue wool and red striped. They report the sleeves were woven separately and laced into tubes and then sewn to the rectangular body of the shirt. However, in the Ramah area there was said to be a type of shirt in black with sleeves woven in one piece with the shirt body, sewn down the sides but with the sleeves left open (Kluckhohn *et. al.* 1971, 254). If the report is correct, this is a very early example of shaped weaving which is generally thought to be a 20th century development.

Such shirts were probably adapted from the embroidered Pueblo type, the wearing of which seemed to disappear with the removal of the Navajo to Bosque Redondo.

337 Belt, c. 1880, 108.5 cm x 7.5 cm. 15 warps, 68 wefts. Worn by Mrs. Wetherill at a Corn Dance in 1885-86. Warp float weave. Four-ply aniline dyed commercial yarn. Cotton string in warp and weft. Gift of Mrs. Richard Wetherill, 55.20.41.

Sashes, Garters and Hair Ties

The costume accessories, sashes, garters and hair ties were woven on the narrow belt loom in the warp float technique and differed only in size (**337-342**). The predominant colors of these accesories are red with green, white and dark blue. All the colors are wool except the white, which is cotton. It is virtually impossible to distinguish Navajo from Pueblo belts, as there was a great deal of trade back and forth with each group making sashes in the styles perferred by the other. Most extant examples are made of commercial yarns often called "Germantown" which came to the Reservation during the 1880's and, with some variations, are still being used.

The principal use of the sash was to cinch-in the woman's dress. Nowadays, sashes are used with the long, flounced cotton or velveteen skirt, often with a silver concho belt over it. A secondary use as a brace to support a woman during childbirth has been also reported (Kluckhohn *et. al.* 1971, 244).

Patterns on garters and hair ties are most frequently plain stripes, while this pattern is never found on sashes. Sashes are generally four inches wide and four to six feet long; garters two inches wide by two feet long; hair ties one inch wide and eighteen inches long. Hair ties had the most intimate connection with the wearer (and the least commercial value) and were buried with the deceased. The same importance was not attached to sashes or garters and this might relate to the spiritual importance associated with human hair, a concept common all over native North America.

338 Belt, 1880-1900, 67 cm x 7 cm. 17 warps, 60 wefts. Warp float weave. Four-ply aniline dyed commercial yarn. Cotton string in warp and weft. Gift of Mrs. Richard Wetherill, 55.20.40.

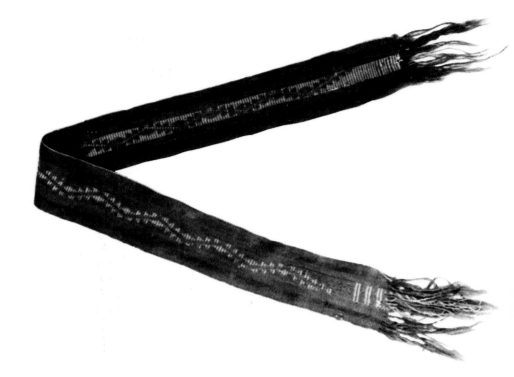

339 Belt, 1880-1900, 73 cm x 6 cm. 14 warps, 36 wefts. Warp float weave. Four-ply aniline dyed commercial yarn. Cotton string in warp and weft. Gift of Mrs. Richard Wetherill, 55.20.39.

340 Belt, 1880-1900, 80 cm x 6.5 cm. 20 warps, 64 wefts. Warp float weave. Two-ply aniline dyed handspun wool. Cotton string in warp and weft. Gift of Mrs. Richard Wetherill, 55.20.38.

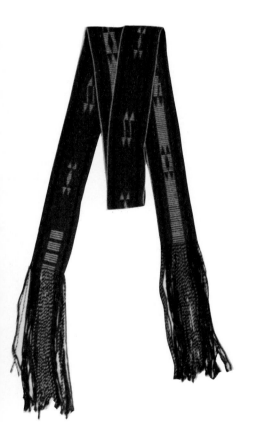

341 Belt, 1880-1900, 221.5 cm x 10 cm. 12 warps, 40 wefts. Warp float weave. Four-ply aniline dyed commercial yarn. Cotton string in warp and weft. Gift of Mrs. Richard Wetherill, 55.20.42.

342 Belt, 1880-1900, 200 cm x 12 cm. 12 warps, 48 wefts. Four-ply aniline dyed red commercial yarn. Two-ply handspun indigo dyed wool. Cotton string in warp and weft. Indefinite loan from Mr. and Mrs. Gilbert Maxwell, 68.46.48.

Miscellaneous Uses

One interesting and seldom mentioned use by the Navajo of their own weaving is as saddle bags. Blankets used for this purpose were of the larger sort "about the size of a Pendleton blanket" (Kluckhohn *et. al.* 1971, 89). The items to be carried were placed in either end of the blanket and the long ends then folded over and tied or sewn. The blanket was then thrown over the saddle so the "pouches" hung on either side. Blanket bags used on a long-term basis were destroyed when their owner died. There is evidence that smaller pieces, especially saddle blankets, were also used extemporaneusly as saddle bags. For example, when Son of Old Man Hat and his father filled their double saddle blankets with peaches and laced up the edges with soapweed stalks (Dyk [1938] 1967, 336). **343** shows a street at Zuni where donkeys are loaded with striped blankets filled with goods and a man wears a similar blanket.

Whether a special style of blanket was woven for this purpose is not certain, although the mid-20th century Navajo term "Mexican" for the woven saddle bag is the same as that recorded in 1910 by the Franciscan Fathers. Whether the "Mexican" pattern was the preferred one (though evidently not the exclusive one) for use as saddle bags is unclear.

343 Street in Zuni Pueblo, showing people and animals with saddle and carrying bags made out of native weaving. 1879. Photo by John K. Hilliers. Smithsonian Institution.

Hogan doorway covers were used to prevent drafts and rain from entering the dwelling and were originally twined and plaited of various materials such as yucca, juniper bark and cliff rose bark (Kluckhohn *et. al.* 1971, 157). The Navajo Origin Myth states that mats of shredded cedar bark were used over the doorway by The People when they first emerged (Matthews 1897, 141). The Franciscan Fathers in their *Ethnographic Dictionary* note only old wool blankets covering doorways (1910, 332). **344** shows a hogan photographed in 1892 by James Moody with just such an old tattered blanket over the doorway. A photo dated c. 1910 (**345**) shows a ceremonial sweat lodge with not one, but several blankets around the doorway, in this case to help keep steam from the hot rocks inside. Other old photos show Navajo women working outside in a shade or ramada as in **347** and using native woven blankets as screens, sun shades, cushions and even as area or work space dividers.

344 Nadespa in front of hogan. She wears a traditional two-piece dress and the hogan entrance is covered with a Navajo blanket. 1892. Photo by James Moody. Smithsonian Institution.

345 Sweat Lodge, covered with numerous Navajo blankets. 1905. Photo by Simeon Schemberger, St. Michaels, Arizona. Smithsonian Institution.

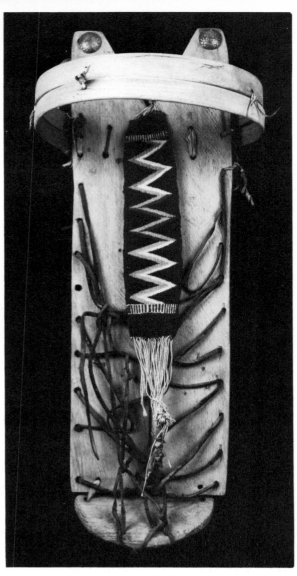

Another incidental use is for litters made of blankets and poles to carry injured people. While the poles were carefully disposed of after use so that their presence might not cause another sickness or injury, there is no report that the blankets were destroyed (Kluckhohn *et. al.* 1971, 102).

Saddle girths and carrying straps for cradleboards were woven right onto the iron rings used for attachment to the saddle or board (**346**). The pattern of zigzags shown in the Maxwell Museum's cradleboard strap is fairly typical, and its lightning-like character may be symbolic or protective in nature.

346 Navajo cradleboard with carrying strap. Maxwell Museum. Photo by Anthony Richardson.

347 Women in a shade, showing use of blankets as space dividers and seating. 1882-1887. Christian Barthelmess, Ft. Wingate, Arizona. Smithsonian Institution.

Non-Navajo Uses

The change from weaving blankets to producing floor rugs for the homes of Anglo-Americans has been documented (see page 72).

Although use as a floor rug was the primary function in homes at the end of the 19th and the beginning of the 20th centuries, there are other uses which are frequently overlooked. Victorian homes were a sea of cloth-covered surfaces: slip covers, chair backs, table runners, antimaccasars and mantle decorations. It was almost as though it were indecent to display an uncovered table or chair. The so-called "Gallup throw", small and with simple, bold patterns in medium grade weaves, was popular then and now. The sizes were 18" x 18" and 18" x 36", usually with a cotton string warp and often with a fringe at one or both ends. Gallup throws and earlier small pieces in Germantown yarn were ideal for chair and sofa backs, were sewn up as pillows, or

thrown over tables in the taste of a previous generation. A special type of table cover which is currently enjoying a revival was apparently invented in the Ganado area. With an equal barred or Greek cross shape, this weaving was made in this curious form so that each flap hangs over one of the four sides of a table. There are two such weavings in the collection of the Hubbell Trading Post National Monument which were commissioned by the Hubbell family in the 1930's to be used on tables in their homes. They were not woven for use in churches, as has been suggested by dealers. A less exotic shape is represented by the pair of table or bedroom bureau runners which were made for Mrs. Richard Wetherill in the 1890's and are now in the Maxwell Museum collection (348 and 349). They are small, rather long and narrow, and, being woven from some remnants of the red trade cloth called baize or bayeta, were too fine to walk on.

348 Table runner, 1895-1900, 168 cm x 36.5 cm. 12 warps, 34 wefts. From Mrs. Wetherill's notes: "The bayetta in this blanket was some that was manufactured in Boston. It was an experiment and while a good copy, it faded. We never handled it at our trading post, but Horbin at Thoreau has some. One of our Navaho women bought two yards for a dress, but her husband made her weave this blanket." Handspun wool with natural and aniline colors. Three-ply ravelled red yarn. Gift of Mrs. Richard Wetherill, 55.20.26.

349 Table runner, 1895-1902, 131 cm x 29 cm. 12 warps, 60 wefts. Purchased in 1902 in El Paso, Texas. Four-ply aniline dyed commercial yarn. Black is aniline dyed handspun. Cotton string warp. Gift of Mrs. Richard Wetherill, 55.20.28.

Another use for Navajo weaving that was once in fashion but is no longer popular is the *portiere* or door cover. This hanging served as a room divider or drape over an entryway between a main hall and the parlor or between two rooms, and hence was probably also a good draft retardant. A turn-of-the-century photograph of the Washington, D.C. parlor of anthropologist Matilda Coxe Stevenson shows such a *portiere,* in this case two very fine Navajo blankets, one of them a Phase III chief's pattern (**350**). In the Hubbell home next to the trading post at Ganado, Lorenzo Hubbell had a pair of *portieres* woven in Germantown yarn to cover the front of a large open closet. Such textiles are generally stitched to rings so they can be pushed back and forth on a rod above the openings.

Although the Navajo preferred vegetable fiber mats and sheepskins as bedding materials, many 19th century soldiers and cowboys preferred Navajo weaving for their own bedrolls because it was tightly woven and nearly waterproof. An Anglo extension of this use is that of a bedspread in more domestic surroundings, as seen in a Germantown yarn example with American flags in the corners commissioned by Governor O.B. Wilcox and now in the Denver Art Museum. Many bed-size textiles which have come down in excellent condition in Anglo families may have served this function in the past (**7**).

350 Portiere in the parlor of Matilda C. Stevenson's Washington, D.C. House, late 19th century. Smithsonian Institution.

351 Jacket, c. 1960, 57 cm x 49 cm. 9 warps, 32 wefts. Sleeves and collar woven separately and sewn on. All handspun wool with natural, carded and aniline colors. Gift of Mr. and Mrs. Gilbert Maxwell, 63.34.177.

352 Handbag, c. 1960, 31.5 cm x 29 cm. 8 warps, 20 wefts. Handbag with inner pocket, buttonholed flap and handle all woven in one piece and sewn down the sides. Handspun wool with natural and aniline colors. Cotton string warp. Gift of Mr. and Mrs. Gilbert Maxwell, 63.34.188.

Occasionally an Anglo garment is made as a novelty or perhaps on commission, such as vests and jackets (**351**). In the last generation, a flood of small purses, book bags, and glasses cases have been made. Many of these items are enthusiastically used by young Navajos especially when they go away to school—something to remind them of their families and ethnic identity.

The most important non-Navajo use of Navajo weaving today is that of art objects. Many textiles are still bought to be used as floor rugs, but as the prices climb, more buyers are hanging them on the walls of their homes. Weaving is still made in quantity, but rugs of medium to coarse weaves are produced less often than the fine to very fine grades. The best weavers are rewarded more for their time than are average ones. Frequently, an average rug will not sell at all, while the best rug attracts many collectors. Rugs with a count of over eighty wefts per inch are often called "tapestries", even though the majority of Navajo textiles are technically tapestries. (Tapestry in the strictest sense defines a technique.) Dealers today use the term tapestry to mean a textile so incredibly fine and thin that it should only be used as a wall hanging (a tapestry in the medieval sense).

The Navajo, like the Pueblo, have a four-directional and color symbolism; but, like the Tewa, they limit their geographical world by physically identifiable mountains (Pinxten 1983, 12). In the south is Mt. Taylor near Grants, N.M. (turquoise) and in the east is Blanca Peak in the Sangre de Cristo range near Alamosa (white shell). In the west are the San Francisco peaks near Flagstaff (yellow abalone), and in the north is the Hesperus Peak in La Plata Range or the San Juan Mountains (black jet). The navel of the world from whence the Navajo emerged into this world out of the last of four underworlds is represented by two geologic formations in northwest New Mexico: Gobernador and Huerfano, although individual Navajo informants claim that *their* particular region is the navel of the world. So similar are these cosmological ideas to those of the Pueblo, that they may have been adopted by the Navajo after they reached the Southwest. Like the Zuni, the Navajo believe the world is bounded by oceans.

Overall, the Navajo universe is conceived of as two slightly concave discs—Mother Earth below and Father Sky above (Pinxten 1983, 11). They are separated by air or winds, and if they should ever meet, the world would end. There are pillars of precious stones at the four directions holding them apart, and from Father Sky are hung the stars. In the east is an opening which is also essential for the well-being of the Navajo world.

The Navajo dwelling or hogan itself reflects this view of the world. It is always circular and the doorway, like the opening of the universe, faces east. The supports of the roof are clustered in the region of four directions. The hearth is, as the sun, in the center and the smoke hole, directly above, is the zenith. The division of, and use of, space within a hogan follows the cosmic order. Traditionally, men stay in the southern and women in the northern portions of the hogan. During a ritual held in a hogan, this sexual division is strictly adhered to and all movement is clockwise, or sunwise. This division of space in traditional households is carried over into everyday life, although only in a hogan (not a modern rectangular house). When a family occupies another type of house or a brush-roofed, outdoor space called a ramada, this division of male and female does not occur. It is only within the sacred circle of the hogan that such restrictions are imposed (Kent 1982, 128-131). The campus of the Navajo Community College at Tsaile, Arizona is organized in the same manner as the interior space of a hogan with the library occupying a position analagous to that of the man's sacred medicine bundles (Harry Walters, personal communication, 1979).

Just as the hogan is a model of the universe, so, too, is the Navajo coiled basket (Pinxten 1983, 9). Many baskets are made by Utes and Paiutes, today, to be sold to the Navajo who require baskets in their traditional wedding ceremony. When one travels through the Reservation today, trading posts with stocks of baskets in the salesroom will usually have a sign indicating the baskets are for sale to Navajos only. Coiled basket construction spirals out from the center in a clockwise direction, just as the universe moved from the center at creation. These baskets have a design break in one side which is emphasized by the edge of the basket that is finished with the end of the last coil over the design break. Thus, when the surface of the basket is covered with corn meal or pollen for the ritual offerings, the direction of the opening can be directed to the east, that is, to the great opening in the universe and the point where the sun rises.

Just as the hogan and basket are models of the Navajo universe, so, too, is the woman's woven dress. Similarities in pattern between baskets and textile weavings frequently have been noted (Rodee 1981, Fig. 32) (317-319). The dress consists of two identical woven rectangles. The center is a solid expanse of black, and the wide top and bottom panels are red with pattern elements in black and indigo blue. Only occasionally is another small amount of color introduced. The patterns of the upper and lower dress panels are usually limited to plain stripes, opposed stepped triangles, and the equal barred cross, and all these elements also are found on their baskets. The cross is a directional symbol (Reichard 1950, 162), and one might speculate that the stepped triangles are directional mountains and/or the pillars supporting the sky. Although the materials and dyes have changed over the years, unlike all other forms of Navajo weaving, the patterns and colors of women's dresses have scarcely changed during the nearly two centuries that their existence has been recorded. The dress has long-since passed out of fashion, and even one hundred years ago when it was more common, it was an expensive article of apparel which only a wealthy woman could afford. Now they are made in very small numbers by mothers or grandmothers for young girls. For instance, all the female members of the Navajo Tribal Band wear this type of dress. Perhaps in a symbolic sense, a woman wearing such a traditional garment becomes mother earth or Changing Woman, the mythic representation of the diurnal changes of the earth. In this way, the three dimensional broken circle encompasses her with her own navel replacing that of the earth.

The broken circle permeates Navajo religious thought. In the arts, the break in both the design and edge finish of baskets has been noted. Another form of the broken circle is the so-called "spirit trail" or "weaver's pathway". To understand this technical phenomenon, it is necessary to consider the history of Navajo weaving.

Fragments of early weaving are known from the mid-18th and early 19th centuries, but they are few. There are no significant numbers of firmly datable textiles until the 1840's (Amsden [1934] 1971, 205-209). These early pieces were primarily blankets woven first of indigenous cotton and later of wool from the sheep the Spanish introduced into the Southwest. As garments, they were produced by the women for their families' own use and for trade to other ethnic groups. They included the two-piece woman's dress, saddle blankets and outer wearing blankets which functioned like overcoats. Later, they were sold as bedding to soldiers, ranchers and the occasional anthropologist. It is largely the textiles sold to the soldiers and anthropologists that have made their way into museum collections and come into the notice of textile historians. These earliest blankets had all-over patterns and frequently were arranged in bands of design often with the four corners and center strongly emphasized, but never did a continuous border appear around the blanket. Around 1875, borders started to appear on four sides as multicolored stripes or a fret pattern. By 1900, unbordered textiles had nearly disappeared. This change was a result of the gradual shift in the market from garments made for local use to rugs for the tourists who were, after 1880, beginning to come through the southwest on the new railroads. Borders, along with other pattern changes, are then found on a heavier, coarser fabric more suited to the floor than the human body.

After enclosing the design with a border, the "weaver's pathway" was created as a woven break in the edge design of a rug. This break is most commonly accomplished by a weft thread from the background of the central pattern being woven through to the edge of the rug (Bennett 1974, 8) (**532**). Although most weft threads alternate back and forth, the pathway thread extends to the edge and is broken off and left to a physical as well as a visual break. Again, although there are exceptions, the pathway is usually woven near the end of the rug, and always to the weaver's right. (The right represents the east, while the left represents the north from whence evil comes.) The meanings of the pathway are diverse, although the term commonly used by Anglos for the break, "spirit trail", is not correct. This pathway is not a trail to let evil spirits or a devil out. This erroneous explanation may have resulted from a confusion in the pronunciation of two similar-sounding Navajo words: that for "spirit"—especially that of the dead—and "mind". Most Navajo weavers interviewed by Bennett described the break as a pathway for their own minds or creative energy that was put in as a protection from physical exhaustion or even insanity (Bennett 1974, 34). It is dangerous for a weaver, or any other Navajo, to over-do and put too much energy into a project. The weavers may inadvertently enclose, or trap, their own spirit into a rug, and the path is protection against this happening. So, the pathway is more of an escape route for the weaver's own spirit and not for evil.

It is highly dangerous to be enclosed or encircled, the Navajo believe. Bennett related a cautionary story, told by a Navajo weaver, of a mother who warned her daughter always to weave four stripes into her dress so

353 Rug, Two Grey Hills, c. 1970, 233 cm x 154 cm. 10 warps, 42 wefts. All handspun wool with natural colors. Gift of Edwin L. Kennedy through the Maxwell Museum Association, 80.5.6.

that if she were ever in trouble she would be able to escape in any of the four directions. The daughter did not take her mother's advice and was murdered (Bennett 1974, 59-60). Over the generations, the use of this weaver's pathway has declined and is seldom found in rugs today. Needless to say, it never appears in pieces with old style, borderless, striped patterns such as those produced at Crystal or Wide Ruins.

In looking at Navajo weaving of the nineteenth century, some modern Anglo authors have suggested that the stepped triangles and stripes represent rock-striated mesas, and the streaked colors of the desert sunset (Berlant and Kahlenberg 1977, 148). This is probably an overly romantic view. Navajo artists, like their Pueblo neighbors, may be unconsciously effected by their striking environment, but there is no evidence that they intended their geometric patterns to illustrate the sky or landscape. There may be a personal symbolism involved, as when a weaver includes a bow and arrow in a rug because she had been thinking about her brothers going hunting—although of course they were using modern weapons (Pearl Sunrise 1978, personal communication). Most patterns result from far more prosaic concerns. Streaky wool results from faulty dyeing when there is a scarcity of water in washing and dyeing the weft yarns. The stepped motifs results from the nature of the loom. Wherever this type of simple vertical loom is used in the world, strikingly similar patterns can be seen. Technique often determines style more than does environment.

An exception to the technique-determines-style idea is a group of 20th-century textiles that are really miniature landscape paintings. In Navajo weaving, pieces that show actual, everyday objects such as soup can labels, sheep, cartoon characters and mountains are called, quite appropriately, "pictorials". Today, common pictorial style shows the impressive natural landmark called Shiprock located in the northwestern corner of New Mexico south of Farmington. Naturally, the term "shiprock" is an Anglo one, the formation reminding early settlers of a huge sailing ship riding on the ocean of the flat desert. To the Navajo, however, it is a creature called "Cliff Monster" who once roamed over Navajo land (Reichard 1950, 22). Traditionally, the Divine Twins, Monster Slayer and Born for Water, killed fierce and terribly large creatures and made the world safe for people. The unburied bodies of these creatures litter the landscape, forever reminding the Navajo of the history of their homeland. The depiction of Shiprock in Navajo weaving is as a souvenir item for Anglo tourists more than anything else. Sometimes Monument Valley also appears on rugs, but this is a fairly recent development.

A new type of landscape pictorial developed in the 1970's and is called by traders and dealers "reservation roads" (**354**). In these, the more complex segments of the Navajo landscape are shown with clouds and mesas and, remarkably, the highways, houses and vehicles found on the Reservation, too. In these pieces, more emphasis is placed on non-natural elements. Often the scene is quite compressed including every style of house and outbuilding imaginable and a wide range of cars, pick-up trucks, trains, horses and wagons. A large

number of these pictorials come from the post of Donnehotso in the Monument Valley. In fact, the style may have originated there. Because of the spectacular rock formations in the Valley, one or two are usually included in the backgrounds of these scenes. Some weavers depict small domestic scenes such as a woman weaving or cooking mutton or even large, complex views of the entire community gathered for a Squaw Dance. Perspective is not much in evidence, although objects in the distance are shown as elevated and smaller than those in the foreground. The aim of these pieces apparently is to illustrate all the objects a tourist would see driving through the Navajo Reservation; but none of the scenes appears to be in any specific geographic location. The houses and vehicles are a bit blocky, but the technique is a *tour-de-force* of weaving. Because so much effort is put into the actual weaving process, the weaver usually uses a commercial yarn bought at the local trading post for them rather than her own homespun wool. The majority of these pieces are small (about two feet by three feet is the average) although there are larger ones. The "reservation roads" rugs are expensive curio or souvenir items, but ones which are admired by collectors as a type of folk art.

The representation of true Navajo symbolism is done in drypainting, a sacred art form which is primarily executed by men. (See also the Sacred Symbols section, pages 145-149.) Drypaintings accompany curing ceremonies which consist of numerous prayers or chants performed on behalf of the patient. The ceremonies, because of the predominance of prayers, are called "chants" or "sings". Each chant is based on the adventures of a hero who brings power from the world of the supernaturals back to earth for the benefit of mankind. The paintings, executed on the floor of the hogan in colored sands and crushed plant parts, represent actual events in mythic adventures (Wyman 1983). The holy people are believed to be flattered to see their portraits and are therefore attracted to the ceremony. In return for this honor done to them, they restore the health of the patient. The paintings are laid out in a directional manner with the east facing the door of the hogan. Most paintings are encircled with a protective guardian figure, most frequently the rainbow goddess. She extends only around three sides of the painting, for an opening is always left in the east. This eastern opening enables the evil and disharmony-causing illness to leave, and goodness and health to enter. The patient is seated on the paintings, and spiritually-charged sand is touched to his or her body. All who attend the sing are blessed as well. This is, in essence, an ephemeral art form; the power involved is so great that the painting must be destroyed the same day to avoid dangerous consequences. When the dry-paintings were first studied by anthropologists, the Navajo were fearful of the consequence, but the desire to preserve their culture for the future outweighed their concerns. Today, a few women weave exact copies of the holy designs, and both men and women make the paintings on glue-covered boards. Again, these are made to be sold to Anglos, and in this form are not sacred, although in the minds of some Navajo not, perhaps, without some dangerous power.

Because so much has been written about Navajo religious symbolism, it was interesting to see whether any symbolic motifs have passed into their weavings, even on a sub-conscious level. The symbols are certainly too potent for most weavers to use casually. Color, of course, has its directional symbolism as it moves within all religious actions in a sunwise motion—that is from east to south to west to north. White, the color of the east, separates the sacred from the profane; blue is the color of happiness and fertility of the earth; black gives invisibility and, thus, protection; yellow is the color of corn and pollen and represents the fertility of the earth. Red is a strong color not only visually, but as a symbol of war, danger and witchcraft. It is also thought to protect one from danger (Wyman 1983, 77). Of interest is the fact that red, white, blue, black and yellow are the major colors of early Navajo weaving. When the Navajo were settled on a Reservation in 1869 and were subject to more Anglo influences, a wider range of colors was used. Even after the railroad had brought brightly colored yarns and new commercial dyes to the Navajo, the most popular color remained red with its variations.

The outlining (175) of a figure in a drypainting with a line of contrasting color had ritual meaning (Wyman 1983, 77). Likewise, weavers outlined a motif in one or even three or four colors popularly from 1880 to 1900 and still today in small numbers around the post of Red Mesa. Clouds and columns of clouds are shown in drypaintings as keystone and terrace shapes (Wyman 1983, 114), that is, the same form clouds have taken in Pueblo pottery.

The Navajo, like the Pueblo, have gone from a farming society to one in which the arts of weaving, ceramics and jewelry are of utmost importance to their survival. It is a tribute to their ability to survive that they have been able to adapt to the demand of the dominant society and still kept alive the concepts that are most important to them. Navajos and Pueblos do not have the luxury of viewing the southwestern landscape with the romantic eyes of Anglo artists who were attracted and inspired by the picturesque scenery. The land is beautiful, and the sacred place of their origin is delimited by mountains and rivers, but the land must be entreated for basic survival and must be placated by their rituals.

354 Rug, 1960's, 124 cm x 69 cm. 8 warps, 30 wefts. Pictorial called "Reservation Roads" which shows typical houses and vehicles found on the reservation. All handspun with natural, carded, vegetal and aniline colors and some three-ply green yarn. Gift of Edwin L. Kennedy, 80.5.4.

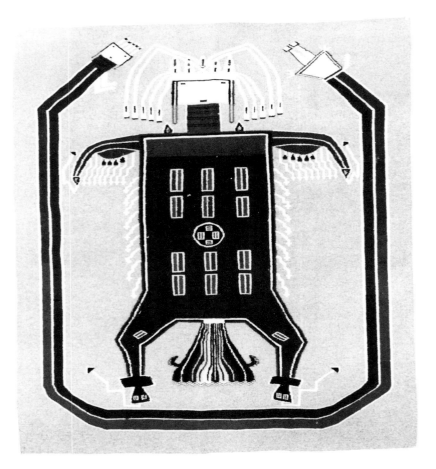

355 Rug, sandpainting, Red Rock, 1960's, 135 cm x 122 cm. 10 warps, 60 wefts. Beautyway: Big Thunder. Mrs. King Tutt, weaver. Two-ply aniline dyed commercial yarn. Handspun natural white warp. Gift of Mr. and Mrs. Edwin L. Kennedy, 69.67.15.

356 Rug, sandpainting, 1960's, 166.5 cm x 111.5 cm. 15 warps, 40 wefts. Beautyway: People with Weasel Skins (variation). Mrs. Tom Peshlakai, weaver. Four-ply and some two-ply aniline dyed commercial yarn. Handspun natural white warp. Gift of Mr. and Mrs. Edwin L. Kennedy, 69.67.31.

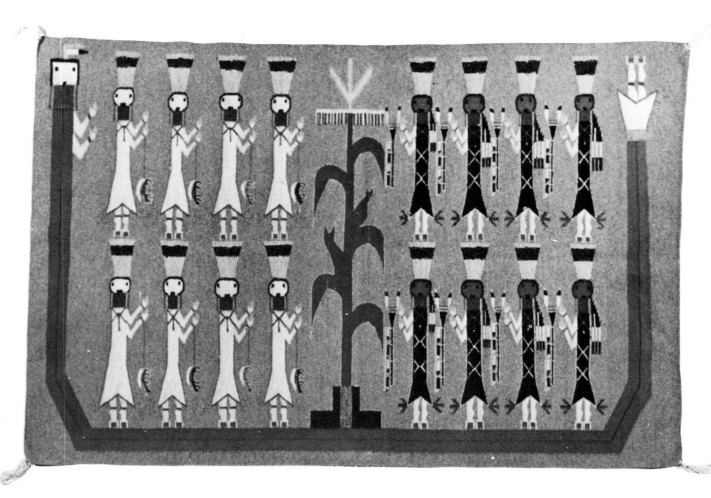

The sacred symbols which weavers use in their rugs are taken from drypainting—an integral part of traditional Navajo healing ceremonies called "sings" (because the prayers are chanted or sung). (See also pages 142-143.) Prayers, fasting, sweat baths, herbal medicines and songs are all part of the total ceremony. The chants are organized into eleven complexes; at one time there were many others, but they are no longer or seldom used. The eleven common complexes are: Shootingway, Flintway, Mountainway, Nightway, Navajo Windway, Chiricahua (Apache) Windway, Handtremblingway, Red Antway, Big Starway, Beautyway and Plumeway. Each chant, or "way", is based on a myth in which human or supernatural heroes have adventures to conquer evil and bring wondrous gifts to humankind. Because of the power of the images, a traditional woman making sandpainting rugs must have the chant sung over her before and/or after the rug is made. Most chants can be performed as Holyway—to attract good and to cure a patient—or Evilway—to exorcise witches or ghosts. Rugs are always based on the Holyway type of painting.

Drypaintings have several types of visual organization. There can be a single large central figure such as Big Thunder (355) or two such as Mother Earth and Father Sky (359). Linear compositions may be one or two rows of four or eight (important ritual numbers) (356) or as many as fifty-six, as in the First Dancers of Nightway. The repetition of the figures increases the power of the painting. Because the Navajo believe that the world is an equal balance of male and female, frequently half of the supernaturals are shown as one sex and half as the other. In circular paintings, the scene rotates in a sunwise or clockwise motion around a central circle representing either the place where the Navajo people emerged from the last of three underworlds, or one of the sacred lakes (357). Often incorporated into these circular paintings are the four sacred plants—corn, beans, squash and tobacco—which are the essence of Navajo subsistence.

357 Rug, sandpainting, Red Rock, 1960's, 133 cm x 135.5 cm. 12 warps, 60 wefts. Beautyway: Frogs. Anna Mae Lamson, weaver. Two-ply aniline dyed commercial yarn. Handspun natural beige warp. Gift of Mr. and Mrs. Edwin L. Kennedy, 69.67.14.

Each painting is encircled by a rainbow guardian to protect the sacred space. The paintings are executed on the floor of the hogan and have a break or opening in the rainbow to the east to let evil and sickness out and goodness and health in. This opening is aligned with the door of the hogan which always faces east. This eastern opening is also frequently guarded by a pair of creatures such as Big Fly, bats or corn beetles. Therefore, there is a real directional layout in the drypaintings as well as the rugs based on them. If the side with the opening in rainbow guardian is the east, then the left is the north, right is the south, and the fourth side is west. Usually, colors are associated with the four directions as follows: east, white; blue, south, yellow, west; and black, north. This color association is not absolute in Navajo religion, however.

There are twelve *ye'ii* (holy persons) but only eight are shown in paintings and rugs. Most *ye'ii* do not have the power of speech; they communicate by animal cries. Talking God, the only *ye'ii* with the gift of speech, is also called *ye'ii bicheii* (maternal grandfather of the *ye'ii*). He leads them in a dance during the Nightway. The dance is one of the most popular subjects for weaving, and the rugs actually show the masked dancers in profile led by Talking God (**358**). In rugs, the dancers are shown in natural proportions as human figures wearing masks. Newer rugs have added the figure of a woman holding a ceremonial basket at the head of the line of dancers (**361**).

The origins of Navajo ceremonial pattern weaving are rather obscure. George Wharton James, writing in 1914, indicated that they were a relatively new phenomenon (1914, 139). James attributes the rugs with *ye'ii* figures to an un-named weaver who specialized in pictorials with human and animal forms. Her first *ye'ii* rug, when hung in the trader's office, caused a furor among the local Navajo. In spite of strong protests and threats, the trader, un-named also, kept the controversial rug hanging until it was purchased by a collector for several hundred dollars. Thus encouraged, the weaver went on to do a total of six or seven *ye'ii* rugs. Recent research has shown some of James' information inaccurate and, at times, an outright fabrication (Kathy Bennett 1979, conference paper). The fact that James names neither the weaver nor the trader might seem peculiar, however, one must remember that James was writing of contemporaries in an emotionally charged situation and was probably trying to protect them. A number of these single figure *ye'ii* rugs still exist and technically they have the characteristics of 1900 to 1915 period textiles. James states that two of these *ye'ii* rugs were in the possession of Richard T.F. Simpson, the trader at Canyon Gallegos near Farmington, New Mexico (1914, 140). Simpson's Navajo wife, Yana pah, was a weaver who made *ye'ii* rugs (Willow Powers, 1986 personal communicator). It is tempting to speculate that Simpson is the un-named trader and the *ye'ii* style started under his sponsorship. The illustration in Amsden's book (p. 53) and (**360**) in the Maxwell collection are identical in style and most certainly by the same weaver. There is a naturalistic, almost humorous appearance to the large single *ye'ii* with western style

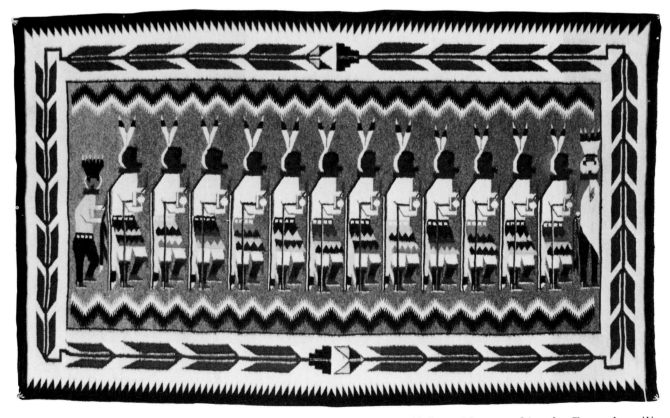

358 Rug, *Ye'ii Bicheii* Dance from Nightway, Shiprock, 1960, 172 cm x 107.5 cm. 12 warps, 34 wefts. Four-ply aniline dyed commercial yarn. Handspun white warp. Gift of Mr. and Mrs. Gilbert Maxwell, 63.34.150.

146

359 Rug, sandpainting, Two Grey Hills (Tohatchi), 1959, 156 cm x 184.5 cm. 14 warps, 30 wefts. Mother Earth and Father Sky, see Maxwell 1963:40, fig. 31. All handspun wool with natural, carded and aniline colors. Gift of Mr. and Mrs. Gilbert Maxwell, 63.34.74.

360 Rug, Ye'ii, Gallegos Canyon, 1910, 167 cm x 97.5 cm. 9 warps, 30 wefts. Handspun wool with natural, carded and aniline colors. Four-ply aniline dyed turquoise yarn. Cotton string warp. Gift of Mr. and Mrs. Gilbert Maxwell, 63.34.101.

361 Rug, 1978, 125.5 cm x 70 cm. 10 warps, 48 wefts. Anna Peshlakai, weaver. All two-ply aniline dyed commercial yarn. Gift of Edwin D. Kennedy, Jr. through the Maxwell Museum Association, 85.49.7.

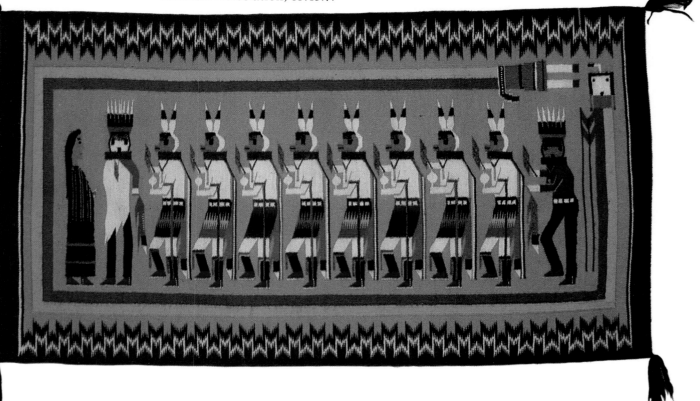

362 *Ye'ii* rug, c. 1900-1910. Stark Museum, Orange, Texas.

trousers and concho belt. The Farmington area has certainly always been one of the main centers of ye'ii and other ceremonial weaving. A fine example, and one almost identical to the illustrations in James' book, is in the Start Museum, Orange, Texas (**362**). Gilbert Maxwell, a trader in the Farmington area, also identified the weaver of this example as Mrs. Richard Simpson (Yanapah). A second type is more abstract in style, closer to the representation of ye'ii in drypaintings and are executed in commercial yarns and apparently are the work of a weaver other than Yanapah Simpson.

The origins of drypainting (called sandpainting in older terminology) pattern weaving are even older than those of the single "Holy Person", although actual examples are extremely rare. This fact is surprising as it would seem logical that weavers would first try a single figure and, barring disaster, go on to the more elaborate and religously dangerous complete drypainting. The earliest documented drypainting rug in the Museum of Indian Heritage, Indianapolis (**363**) is of saddle-blanket size with a black handspun wool background and the design elements in 4-ply aniline dyed yarns. It was woven in 1883 by Eston Naltha Chu near Farmington, New Mexico. This rug may depict an eagle ceremonial, although an exact identification is impossible. There are other Germantown wool, ceremonial pattern blankets that, on the basis of materials, but not on external evidence, date to the last quarter of the 19th century. Perhaps these blankets are a result of the same interest of anthropologists that was noted in the development of Hopi kachinas in the 19th century by Frederick Dockstader [1954] 1985, 86]. Dockstader suggested that kachina production was stimulated by the anthropologists who were working with the Hopis and collecting their material culture. The carved "dolls" would graphically illustrate Hopi religion for the patrons of their eastern museums. The natural place to look for such a connection was the archive of Washington Matthews in the Wheelwright Museum. Matthews documented both weaving of his period (1884) and religion (1902). However, there is no evidence in his papers that he commissioned a blanket based on religious symbolism. It is still a possibility that he or someone like him was influential to these early weavers.

Another documented example of drypainting weaving is noted by Wheat (1976, 48) as woven in 1896 in Chaco Canyon on order for a man on the Wetherill Expedition. Richard Wetherill had another blanket made for his own use (Parezo 1983, 46) and his brother John said that he had the first ye'ii made to be sent to the 1904 World's Fair in St. Louis (Tanner 1968, 80). There are scattered references to drypainting rugs discovered by Wheat in trading post records at Two Grey Hills and Newcomb between 1903 and 1911 (Parezo, p. 46). However, there is no visual evidence about the style or appearance of these rugs. The style did not gain momentum until Hosteen Klah and his nieces wove them, as will be explained ahead.

Why was there such an early and seemingly peaceful history for drypainting rugs and such an uproar over ye'ii figure rugs? Perhaps the intent of the weaver or the purpose for which the rug was intended has something to do with these reactions. Singers have been generally cooperative with ethnographers who wished to record their religious knowledge, realizing that the benefits outweighed the danger of sacrilege. Although the purpose of the 19th century ceremonial rugs is unknown, it may be that they served the same function as did the drawings. On the other hand, the single ye'ii rug appeared on the wall or floor of a trading post with a price, and its only purpose was to decorate a collector's home or be walked on. Thus, it had no "redeeming social value" and represented a real misuse of power. Navajo will bend the rules for a fitting purpose. If an Anglo museum were to display a medicine bundle or actual drypainting, most Navajo religious leaders would disapprove. However, the Navajo Community College Museum at Tsaile, Arizona, has the approval of the traditional religious leadership to display this very material because it was reasoned that the museum is the proper place to show drypaintings in order to instruct Navajo children in knowledge and respect for their heritage (Harry Walters 1981, personal communication).

Drypainting rugs were not made very frequently during the late 19th and early 20th centuries. Ye'ii rugs on the other hand, after the initial furor, became an established style in the Farmington area. Hosteen Klah in the Two Grey Hills area did much to break down the religious fear surrounding ceremonial weaving. Klah began his first drypainting rug in 1919 in spite of the objections of fellow singers (Newcomb 1964, 157). He felt that his power and control over the chants would protect himself and the Navajo community from any evil side effects, although he did express concern to Frances Newcomb (the trader's wife who worked with him in recording on paper his religious knowledge) that the textiles might be walked on. Only after he was assured that the rugs would be hung in museums did he begin to weave. Klah evidently regarded these woven replicas with the same respect as the drawings he assisted Newcomb in compiling. Only twenty-five rugs were produced by him and they all went to wealthy collectors who were seriously interested in the preservation of Navajo religious tradition (**364**). The majority were eventually deposited in the Wheelwright Museum, formerly the Museum of Navajo Ceremonial Art, by Mary Cabot Wheelwright (Newcomb 1964, 164). Klah was already an accomplished weaver in the geometric style before he undertook ceremonial weaving. (Lynette Newcomb Wilson 1981, personal communication). Interestingly, he collected and prepared his materials for weaving as carefully as he would have chosen the sand the pigments for an actual drypainting. He sorted the special brown wool from his family's flocks and prepared vegetal dyes and even cochineal, although later rugs contained commercial package dyes. Klah's protection extended to his nieces who also began weaving ceremonial pattern rugs under his direction. **366**, donated by Lynette Newcomb Wilson, daughter of Frances Newcomb, is the first ceremonial design piece done by Klah's niece Gladys (Mrs. Sam) Manuelito (1927). Klah's other niece Irene (Mrs. Jim) Manuelito also wove ceremonial pattern pieces and both women helped their uncle to finish his generally very large rugs.

149

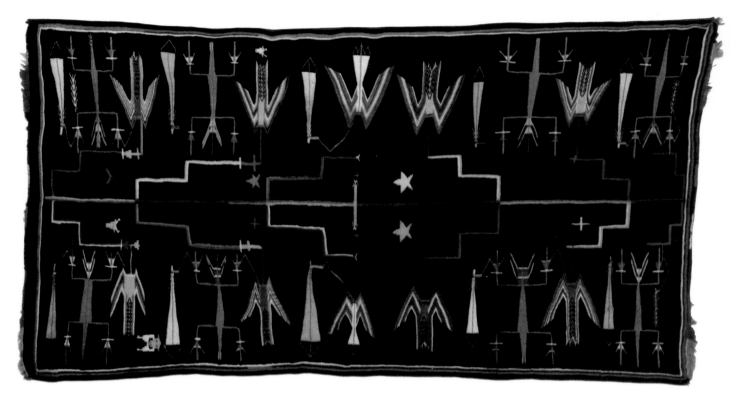

363 Ceremonial pattern blanket. Woven in 1883 by Eston Nalathe Chu, near Farmington, New Mexico. Museum of Indian Heritage, Indianapolis, Indiana.

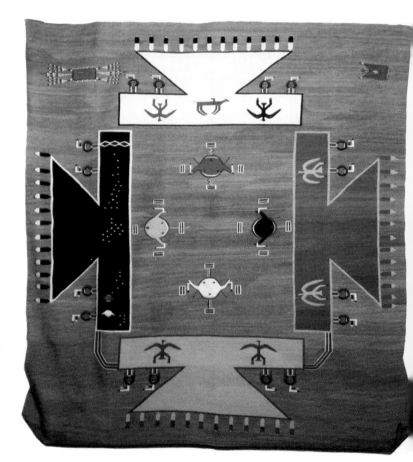

364 Hosteen Klah's last rug. Woven in 1937 and finished by his nieces, Gladys and Irene Manuelito. The Skies', Mountain Chant. On loan to the Maxwell Museum.

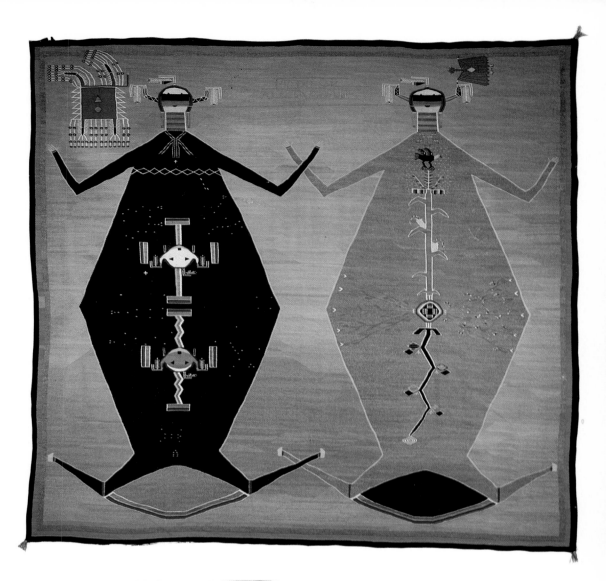

365 Mother Earth, Father Sky, possibly from Mountain Chant or Night Chant. Woven and signed by Altnabah, 1930's. Museum of Northern Arizona, Flagstaff. Photo by Anthony Richardson.

366 Rug, 1927, 162 cm x 168 cm. 10 warps, 44 wefts. Gladys Manuelito, weaver. The Sacred Twins, Female Feather Chant. Handspun wool with carded, natural and aniline colors. Gift of Lynette Newcomb Wilson, 84.61.1.

151

At Ganado, the women of the family with which anthropologist Gladys Reichard worked did occasional ceremonial rugs, but presumably they were protected and guided by Red Point (Miguelito), a respected singer and head of his family, in the same way as Klah guided his female relatives. Reichard reports that Ganado weaver Hastiin Gaani's wife had the Shooting-way sung over her before she began weaving rugs from that chant (Reichards 1936, 160). This need for protection persists to this day with traditional weavers. Desbah Tutt Nez of Red Rock, believes that her singer-husband's power and knowledge protect her from any evil associated with her rugs. In this case, the singer does not provide his wife with designs as did Klah for his family (Edith Kennedy 1981, personal communication).

Although Klah is credited with beginning the weaving of accurate copies of drypaintings, many followed his example in the 1920's and 30's. Because of Klah's fame, brought about by his skill, the preservation of so many documented pieces by him in museums, and his biography by Frances Newcomb, most early 20th century drypainting rugs are ascribed to him and his family by dealers and collectors. However, there were actually many other weavers doing the same type of rugs during that period. They are all rather large, 10' to 12' square, much larger than anything of the sort woven today, and are generally of handspun wool with grey or tan backgrounds and aniline-dyed colors. A large rug in the Art Museum at Utah State University, Logan, representing Black God from The Nightway, was woven in the 1920's by Mrs. Albert "Chick" Sandoval. Sandoval was the interpreter for anthropologist Edward Sapir, and although probably not a Nightway singer himself, was quite knowledgeable about the ceremony (James Faris personal communication, 1986). Sapir himself bought a rug in 1929 made by the wife of Manuel Denetsone of Crystal, N.M. and Sandoval made comments on what was accurate and what was not in the rug. These comments and a drawing of the rug are illustrated in *American Anthropologist* (Sapir 1935, 609-616).

365 illustrates a very unusual and important drypainting rug of the period which is actually signed by the weaver. It is a representation of the Mother Earth, Father Sky painting from the Nightway. In the center, over the line of pollen connecting the mouths of the holy couple, are the faint letters done in white wool against the brown ground "Made by Atlnabah". Atlnabah and Marie were the daughters of Miguelito and Maria Antonia of the Ganado area who taught Gladys Reichard to weave. Although Reichard said they were the finest weavers of their day, and although they were made famous through her many books on weaving, no examples are presently associated with their names, except this one. It is highly unusual for a weaver of this period to sign a rug, let alone a drypainting piece, in such a prominent place. The rug is also unusual in that it has a border of plain stripes, as does the one by Atlnabah in *Navajo Shepherd and Weaver* (plate IX). Because the border encloses the painting, she has woven a so-called "spirit trail" through the border to provide the necessary opening.

152

The technical aspects of this rug—the carding, spinning and weaving—are all superior to that of Klah pieces. It is fortunate that at least one identifiable ceremonial pattern rug from this talented weaver has survived for the appreciation of subsequent generations. Those rugs which copy the drypaintings exactly represent only a fraction of the ceremonial types produced during the 1920's, 30's and 40's. *Ye'iis* were far more numerous.

Another type of rug, pictorials, became popular. These drew individual elements from Navajo religion, contained *ye'iis* and other motifs such as a cornstalk with birds, a tobacco plant or a type of basket used in ceremonies (**367** and **370**). The hint of religious meaning seemed to satisfy the public's need for symbolism but gave little risk to the weaver. Also produced were rugs containing a row of *ye'iis* holding only vaguely-defined attributes. Frequently, these rows of generalized *ye'iis* have a rainbow guardian surrounding them, but there are not enough details to suggest any specific drypainting (**368**). This type is still popular today.

367 Rug, c. 1960, 121.5 cm x 85 cm. 8 warps, 24 wefts. Religious pictorial with four cornstalks with birds and a masked human figure. All handspun with natural and aniline colors. Gift of Dale and Marilyn Warman, 79.69.10.

Later, around 1950, another more pictorial type of rug developed which showed the *ye'ii bicheii* dance from the Nightway. In these, the actual dance is shown with masked impersonators and, more recently, with naturalistically-rendered men and women greeting the dancers (**361**). This style has been taken yet one step further with the depiction of two Navajo holding up a *ye'ii bicheii* rug complete with tassels (Kauffman and Selser 1985, Fig. 95). *Ye'ii bicheii* rugs usually show the dancers in profile while in *ye'ii* rugs the supernaturals are shown full-face as they are in the drypaintings (**369**). As mentioned above, a true *ye'ii bicheii* rug must have a figure of Talking God in the composition to qualify for the title.

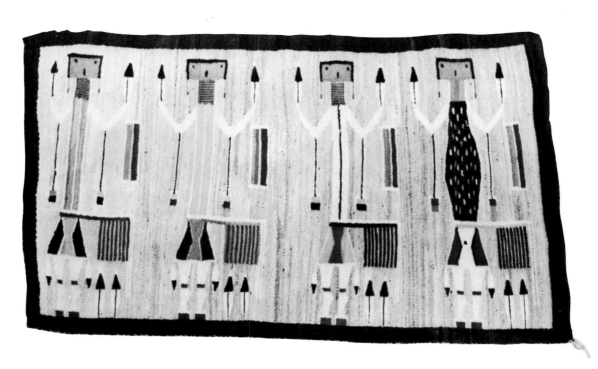

368 Rug, sandpainting, Farmington area, 1956-57, 127 cm x 76 cm. 12 warps, 50 wefts. Dorothy Funston, weaver. Won second prize at Gallup Ceremonial in 1957. Two-ply aniline dyed commercial yarn. Handspun natural white wool warp. Some carded handspun beige in wefts. Gift of Mr. and Mrs. Gilbert Maxwell, 63.34.71.

369 Rug, *Ye'ii*, Lukachukai, c. 1934, 121.5 cm x 73.5 cm. 8 warps, 32 wefts. All handspun wool with natural, vegetal and aniline colors. Gift of W.W. Hill, 65.47.9.

370 Rug, Donnehotso, 1976, 136.5 cm x 107 cm. Lena Chy, weaver. All handspun wool with natural, vegetal and aniline colors. Gift of Edwin D. Kennedy through the Maxwell Museum Association, 85.49.5.

372 Rug, 1920-40, 107.5 cm x 207 cm. 7 warps, 24 wefts. One *Ye'ii* has no facial features and another has only one eye. Handspun with natural, carded and aniline colors. Gift of Mr. and Mrs. Rufus Carter, 81.40.1.

371 Rug, Ganado, 1920-40, 178 cm x 96.5 cm. 7 warps, 24 wefts. *Ye'ii* and animals. All handspun wool with natural, carded and aniline colors and a cotton string warp. Transfer from the Harwood Foundation, Taos, 80.51.51.

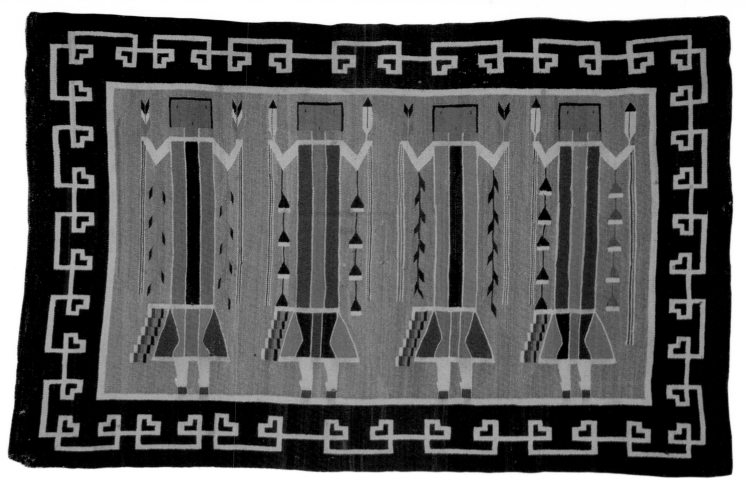

373 Rug, 1920-40, 166 cm x 112 cm. 9 warps, 40 wefts. *Ye'ii*. All handspun wool with natural and aniline dyes. Gift of Edwin L. Kennedy through the Maxwell Museum Association, 80.5.13.

374 Rug, *Ye'ii*, Farmington Area, 1960's, 140 cm x 9.5 cm. 12 warps, 44 wefts. Four-ply aniline dyed commercial yarn. Cotton string warp. Gift of Mr. and Mrs. Edwin L. Kennedy, 69.67.32.

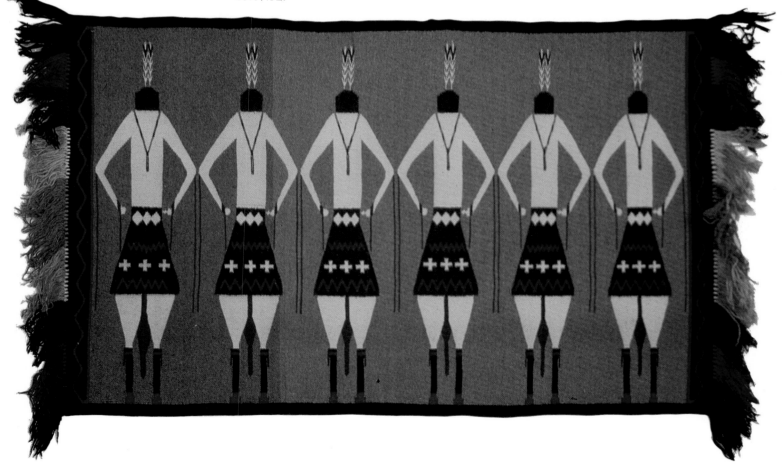

375 Rug, *Ye'ii*, Shiprock-Farmington Area, 1920-40, 71 cm x 62 cm. 10 warps, 40 wefts (handspun) and 10 warps, 48 wefts (commercial). Four-ply aniline dyed commercial yarn. Handspun wool with natural and aniline colors. Cotton string warp. Gift of Miss Elizabeth Elder, 68.16.3.

376 Rug, adaptation of *Ye'ii Bicheii* dance from Nightway, Shiprock, 1960's, 91.2 cm x 144 cm. 11 warps, 40 wefts. Four-ply commercial aniline dyed yarn. Handspun white warp. Gift of Mr. and Mrs. Edwin L. Kennedy, 69.67.28.

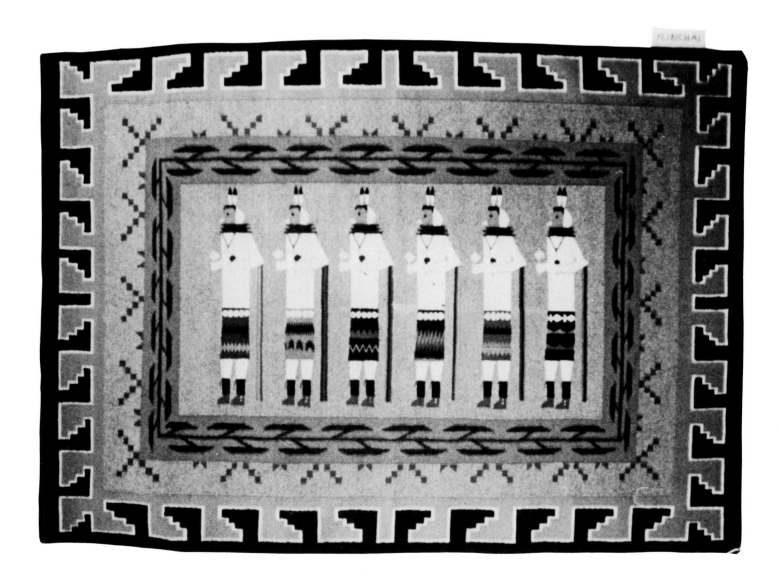

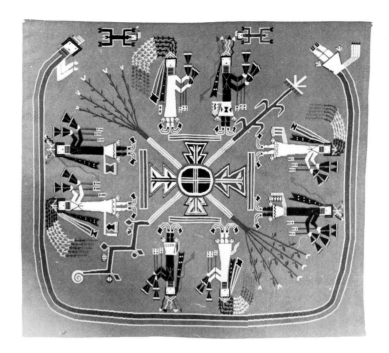

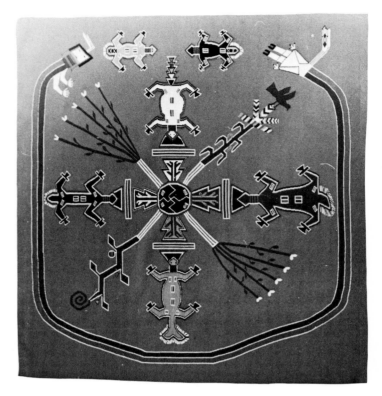

377 Rug, sandpainting, Red Rock, 1960's, 164 cm x 160 cm. 15 warps, 52 wefts. The Water Chant. Anna Mae Lamson, weaver. Two-ply aniline dyed commercial yarn. Handspun natural white warp. Gift of Mr. and Mrs. Edwin L. Kennedy, 70.75.2.

378 Rug, sandpainting, Red Rock, 1960's, 141 cm x 150.5 cm. The Water Chant. Alberta Thomas, weaver. Two-ply aniline dyed commercial yarn. Handspun natural white warp. Gift of Mr. and Mrs. Edwin L. Kennedy, 70.75.3.

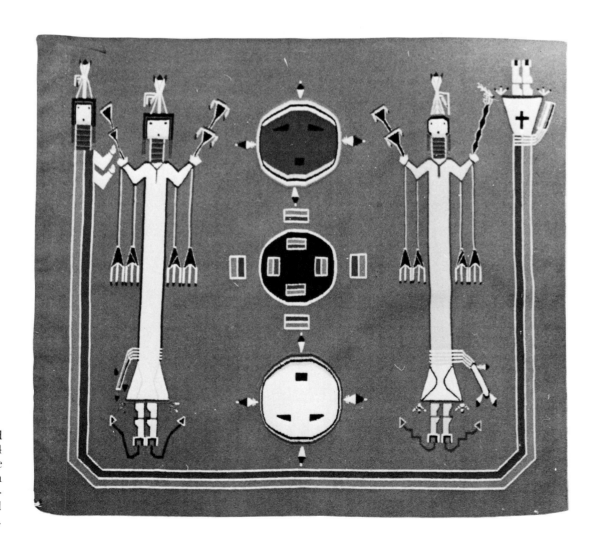

379 Rug, sandpainting, Red Rock, 1960's, 133 cm x 124 cm. 14 warps, 56 wefts. The Water Chant. Alberta Thomas, weaver. All two-ply aniline dyed commercial yarn. Gift of Mr. and Mrs. Edwin L. Kennedy, 70.75.4.

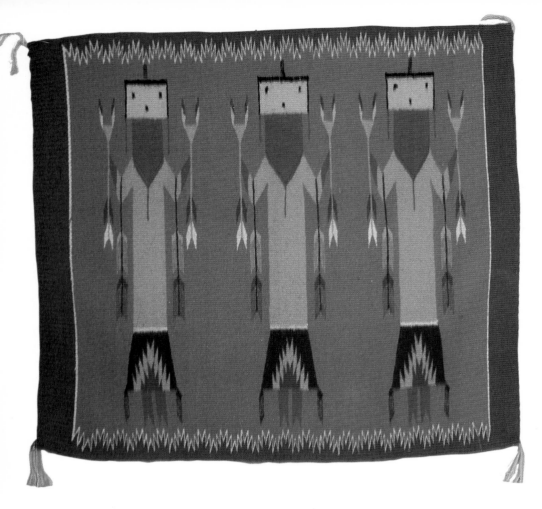

380 Rug, 1960-70, 73 cm x 68 cm. 8 warps, 62 wefts. Stella Jim, weaver. All four-ply commercial aniline dyed yarn. Gift of Edwin L. Kennedy through the Maxwell Museum Association, 80.5.8.

381 Rug, 1960-70, 162.5 cm x 135 cm. 12 warps, 50 wefts. Mrs. Tom Lee, weaver. Ye'ii. All two-ply aniline dyed commercial yarn. Gift of Edwin L. Kennedy through the Maxwell Museum Association, 79.45.68.

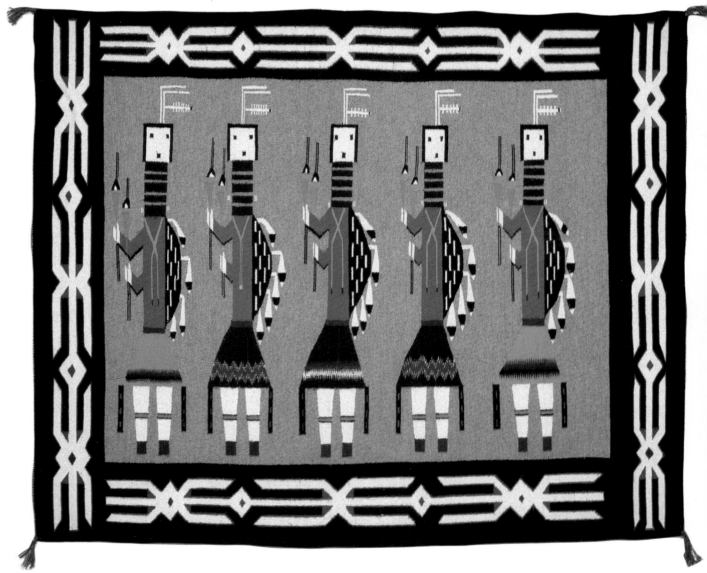

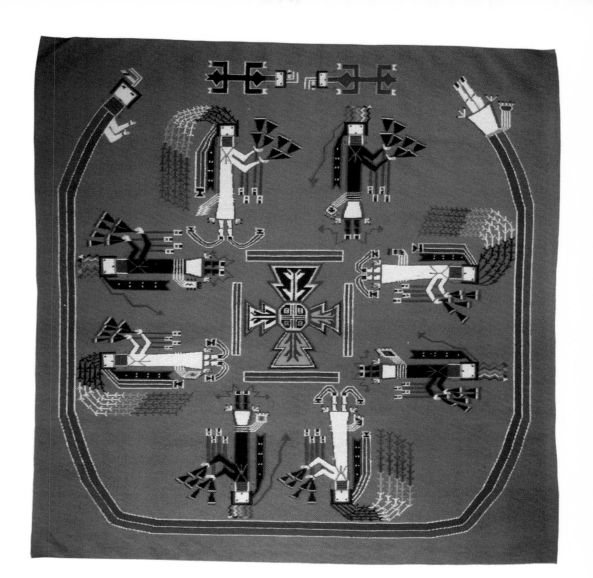

382 Rug, sandpainting, Red Rock, 1960's, 157.5 cm x 156 cm. 14 warps, 54 wefts. The Water Chant. This rug and **377, 378,** and **379** make a complete set of copies of the sandpaintings of the Water Chant as published in Wheelwright 1946; 195-201. Alberta Thomas, weaver. Two-ply aniline dyed commercial yarn. Gift of Mr. and Mrs. Edwin L. Kennedy, 70.75.1.

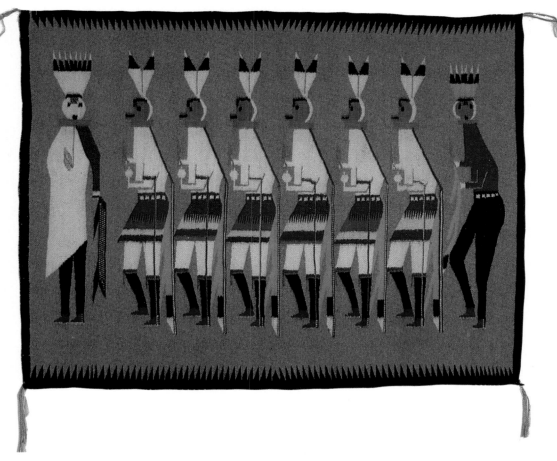

383 Rug, 1958 or 59, 123 cm x 94 cm. 10 warps, 40 wefts. Ye'ii Bicheii. Won third prize at the Arizona State Fair, 1959. All four-ply aniline dyed commercial yarn. Gift of Edwin L. Kennedy through the Maxwell Museum Association, 80.5.7.

159

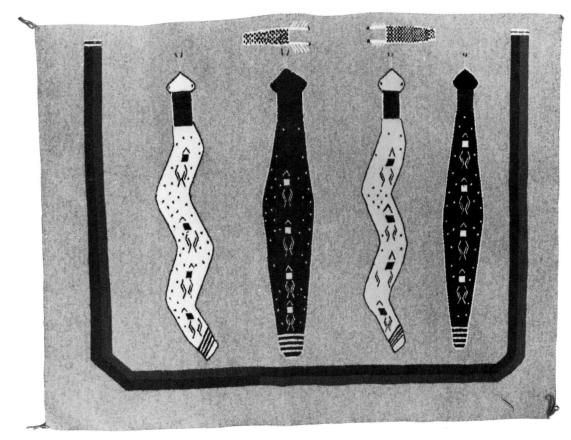

384 Rug, sandpainting, Red Rock, 1960's, 128 cm x 103 cm. 13 warps, 52 wefts. Beautyway: Big Snakes. Desbah Tutt Nez, weaver. This rug is part of a complete set of copies of published illustrations of the Beautyway Sandpaintings and were commissioned by Mr. Kennedy. See Wyman 1957:Plate I—XVI. Two-ply aniline dyed commercial yarn. Handspun natural white warp. Gift of Mr. and Mrs. Edwin L. Kennedy, 69.67.1.

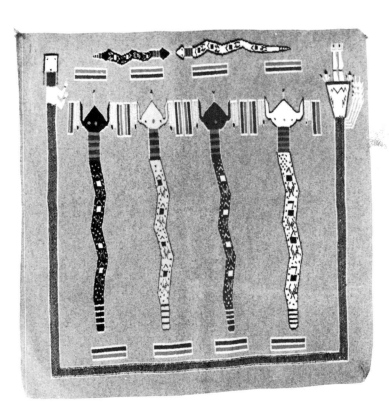

385 Rug, sandpainting, Red Rock, 1960's, 104 cm x 109 cm. 10 warps, 40 wefts. Beautyway: Crooked Big Snakes. Desbah Tutt Nez, weaver. Two-ply aniline dyed commercial yarn. Natural white handspun warp. Gift of Mr. and Mrs. Edwin L. Kennedy, 69.67.2.

386 Rug, sandpainting, Red Rock, 1960's, 104 cm x 107 cm. 14 warps, 52 wefts. Beautyway: Snakes on Their House. Desbah Tutt Nez, weaver. Two-ply aniline dyed commercial yarn. Handspun natural white warp. Gift of Mr. and Mrs. Edwin L. Kennedy, 69.67.3.

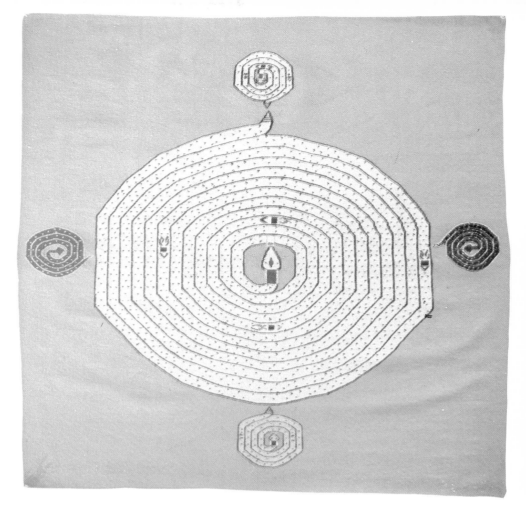

387 Rug, sandpainting, Red Rock, 1960's, 135.5 cm x 131 cm. 14 warps, 52 wefts. Beautyway: Big snake with No End. Desbah Tutt Nez, weaver. Two-ply aniline dyed commercial yarn. Handspun natural white warp. Gift of Mr. and Mrs. Edwin L. Kennedy, 69.67.6.

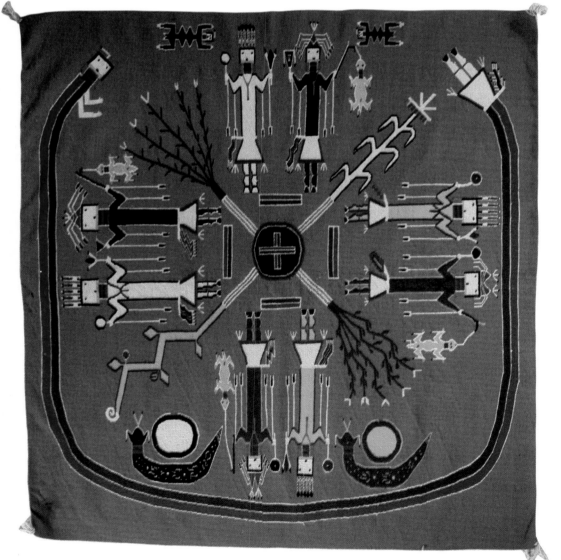

388 Rug, sandpainting, Red Rock, 1960's, 139 cm x 148.5 cm. 13 warps, 60 wefts. Beautyway: People of the Myth. Anna Mae Lamson, weaver. Two-ply aniline dyed commercial yarn. Handspun natural white warp. Gift of Mr. and Mrs. Edwin L. Kennedy, 69.67.9.

161

Changes in Ceremonial Weaving Style

Ceremonial weavings are, therefore, a type of textile that probably originated to provide ethnographers and other interested visitors with a record of a drypainting a bit finer and more decorative than the usual drawing. No ceremonial rug is known prior to 1883 when the first ethnographers began working with the Navajo. The commercialization of the form through *ye'ii* and other figures derived from chantways began around 1910. During the late 19th and early 20th centuries, great change took place in Navajo weaving in general, as the original functions of the wearing blanket, bedding and saddle blanket were disappearing. Traders then, in their effort to keep weaving alive since it was important financially to the Navajo, suggested new patterns and forms that appealed to Anglo customers. Traders J.B. Moore at Crystal, N.M. and Lorenzo Hubbell of Ganado, Arizona encouraged weavers to produce patterns that they believed would be popular. It was likely a trader who suggested that a *ye'ii* figure be placed in a rug. The controversy and fear associated with that decision seem to prove, that the first weaver was pressured by a trader or collector rather than originating the idea herself, although the layout, design details and color combinations were hers. *Ye'ii* and other ceremonial patterns were immediately popular with customers, in part because many Anglo collectors and tourists liked native American arts with "symbolism" and hidden meaning. Religious objects are considered therefore to be far more "ethnic" or "truly Indian". Collectors can relate or identify with figurative art that "tells a story" more easily than to geometric patterns. Even in geometric pieces many will search for deep significance in every triangle or zigzag.

Weavings with religious motifs are not used by the Navajo themselves as, for example, Muslims use prayer rugs for their devotions. However, this was not true in the past. When old literature on religion was examined, it was found that Matthews (1887) mentions sand being brought in and removed in blankets, but he does not mention the kind of blanket used. Stevenson in 1891 shows a sweat lodge entrance covered with black and white striped blankets (probably Navajo made) and coverings of the doorways as gifts from the patient to the singer. Although he explains that at other times in the ceremony blankets are spread out and prayer sticks and cigarettes laid on them, Stevenson does not specify "Navajo blanket". Only in one instance does Stevenson say a "Navajo blanket" is placed on the ground outside the entrance of the hogan on the south side for the patient to sit on. None of the early publications illustrate or mention a particular type of pattern vital to any ceremony. At the Kinaalda (girls' puberty ceremony) the home may have stacks of textiles for visitors to sit on, but these would be of no particular pattern.

Weavers will frequently change some detail of a drypainting rug in order to avoid harm from so much power being rendered in permanent form. This can be as subtle as reversing the colors of the rainbow guardian or the number of feathers in a headdress, or as obvious as the vaguely rendered *ye'ii* mentioned above (Sapir 1935, 609-18). Since about 1950, there has been a marked increase in the number of drypainting rugs produced, due to the encouragement of traders. Most of these rugs contain some small change or even a major inaccuracy. Only a few women, like Desbah Tutt Nez and her daughters from Red Rock, will weave absolutely exact copies. Desbah, as noted earlier, has the protection of her husband, but her daughters Alberta Thomas and Anna Mae Lamson have had numerous sings. This family of weavers derives its designs directly from books supplied by the traders Troy and Edith Kennedy (1981, personal communication). The most readily available publications are those on the Beautyway and Nightway, so these are the rugs most commonly produced today. There are also frequently-performed sings so that weavers without access to books would have some familiarity with the symbols. As more books on Navajo ceremonialism have become available, both new studies and reprints of old ones, the variety of drypainting rugs has also increased. Reichard (1936, 156-57) reported that men "draw or paint the composition on paper or cardboard; the women copy as faithfully as they can". This practice does not seem to occur today, having been replaced by copying from the numerous postcards, books, periodicals and museum catalogs now available. Because today's better roads provide fast transportation throughout the Reservation, weavers are increasingly sophisticated and can buy any book on weaving or ceremonialism that is on the market. Traders such as the Kennedys also have rare and out-of-print books which are loaned to the best weavers who make exact copies.

The growing desirability of ceremonial weavings is reflected in the high prices paid for them. James said that the first *ye'ii* rug sold for "several hundred dollars" (1914, 140). Although the size of this first rug is not recorded, subsequent pieces by the same weaver were about five feet by seven feet in size. In J.B. Moore's illustrated mail-order catalogs, customers could order geometric rugs in the dimensions and colors they wanted. When Moore was charging $1 per square foot and using this as an average figure for the period, geometric rugs of the size of these first *ye'ii* would sell for $35 to $50. Clearly, quite a premium was being paid for the unusual subject matter of ceremonials. Lynette Newcomb Wilson remembers her parents selling Klah's rugs for around $5,000 during the depression of the 1930's (1981, personal communication). The great financial reward for weaving ceremonial pattern rugs is a powerful incentive for taking the spiritual risks, and provides more than enough money to pay for any sings that become required as a result of the risk.

Currently, the ceremonial design rugs of greatest value are those of large size, with fine weave (that is with a high warp and weft count per inch), and accurate reproductions of unusual sandpaintings. Although the earliest-known ceremonial rug was woven from Germantown yarn, subsequent ones until about the 1950's are almost invariably handspun native wool. From the 1950s on, yarns were once again predominant. Reichard's chief complaint about the drypainting rugs of her day was that the colors could not even begin to approximate the actual colors of the sand used. (1936, 154). This situation has changed with the greater availability of commercial "desert colored" yarns which are purposely stocked at posts in the appropriate colors for drypainting. Some students of weaving consider the use of commercial yarns (spun and dyed in a factory) to be a debasement of the textile art; however, ceremonial design rugs require a great variety of subtle colors and the weavers would have to spend months to prepare their own yarns. By purchasing commercial yarns, the women can spend all their time on the weaving process itself, which is extremely difficult. Lines and figures executed in sand with an easy movement of a dry-painter's arm and fingers are, for the weaver, a challenging technical problem. Circular patterns are perhaps the most difficult to weave. While the rug pattern in **387** with its five snakes appears simple, the fact that they are coiled makes this a more complex problem for the weaver than most viewers would imagine. On the Navajo loom, pattern is created by the crossing of the horizontal wefts over the vertical warps which normally results in motifs with right angles. Circular patterns require careful planning and counting of the warps in order to make the curves gradual and yet not interfere with the structural strength of the rug. The weaver has not completely solved the problem in rendering a circular design in the rug in **387**, as the "circular" snakes are really formed by many small angles. Since ceremonial weaving is the only Navajo type that depends on completely accurate translations of an original design, the talent and energies of the weaver need to be devoted to solving intricate technical problems. The weavers are quite proud of this ability, although it is not always apparent to the casual viewer who may see the rug only as a beautiful image or interesting anthropological artifact and forgetting the special skill that set the rug apart from either a drypainting or a drawing of a drypainting.

390 Rug, sandpainting, Red Rock, 1960's, 111 cm x 108.5 cm. 12 warps, 56 wefts. Beautyway: Sandpainting at Dropped-out Mountain. Anna Mae Lamson, weaver. Two-ply aniline dyed commercial yarn. Handspun natural white warp. Gift of Mr. and Mrs. Edwin L. Kennedy, 69.67.4.

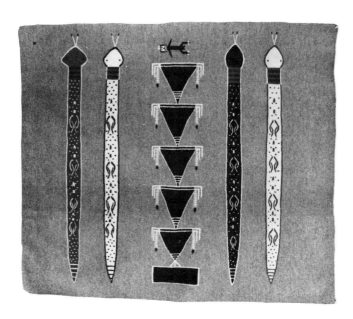

389 Rug, sandpainting, Red Rock, 1960's, 112.5 cm x 109.5 cm. 12 warps, 48 wefts. Beautyway: Snakes and Clouds. Anna Mae Lamson, weaver. Two-ply aniline dyed commercial yarn. Handspun natural white and beige warp. Gift of Mr. and Mrs. Edwin L. Kennedy, 69.67.5.

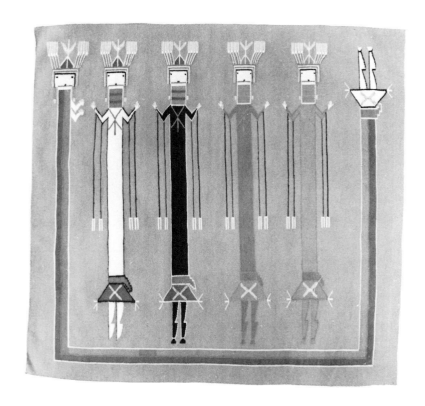

391 Rug, sandpainting, Red Rock, 1960's, 115 cm x 112 cm. 14 warps, 40 wefts. Beautyway: Snake Pollen People. Lorraine Tallman, weaver. Two-ply aniline dyed commercial yarn. Handspun natural white warp. Gift of Mr. and Mrs. Edwin L. Kennedy, 69.67.7.

163

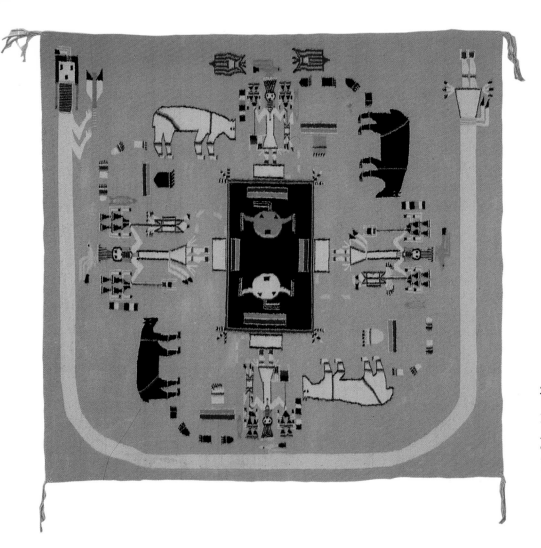

392 Rug, sandpainting, Red Rock, 1960's, 120 cm x 121 cm. 12 warps, 52 wefts. Beautyway: At Moved-out Mountain. Mrs. James Etcitty, weaver. Two-ply aniline dyed commercial yarn. Cotton string warp. Gift of Mr. and Mrs. Edwin L. Kennedy, 69.67.12.

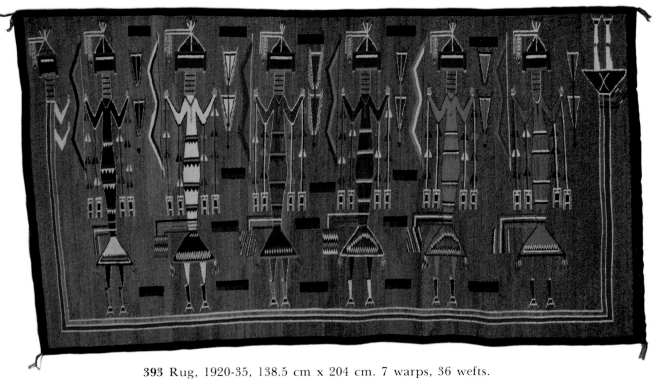

393 Rug, 1920-35, 138.5 cm x 204 cm. 7 warps, 36 wefts. Collected by Mr. Fickinger in the 1930's. Large amounts of orange characteristic of rugs made in the 1920's. Handspun wool with natural, carded, aniline colors. Gift of Paul Fickinger, 81.37.1.

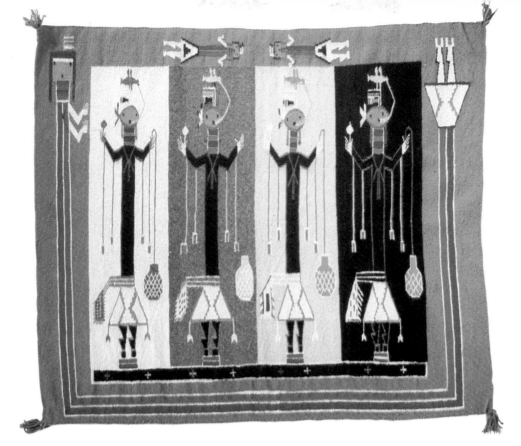

394 Rug, sandpainting, 1960's, 122.5 cm x 113 cm. 11 warps, 36 wefts. Nightway: Water Sprinklers. Clara Nez, weaver. Four-ply aniline dyed commercial yarn. Handspun natural white wool warp. Gift of Mr. and Mrs. Edwin L. Kennedy, 70.75.9.

395 Rug, Red Rock, 1960-70, 93.5 cm x 67.5 cm. 15 warps, 56 wefts. Grace Joe, weaver. Inexact rendering of the Water Sprinklers, Mountain Chant. All two-ply commercial yarn with natural and aniline colors. Gift of Edwin L. Kennedy through the Maxwell Museum Association, 80.5.12.

165

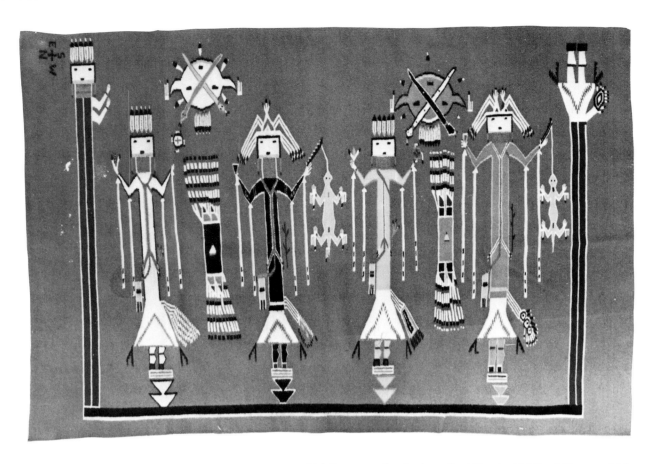

396 Rug, sandpainting, Red Rock, 1960's, 151 cm x 106 cm. 11 warps, 60 wefts. Beautyway: The Mountain Gods. Ruby Denea, weaver. Two-ply aniline dyed commercial yarn. Handspun natural white warp. Gift of Mr. and Mrs. Edwin L. Kennedy, 69.67.8.

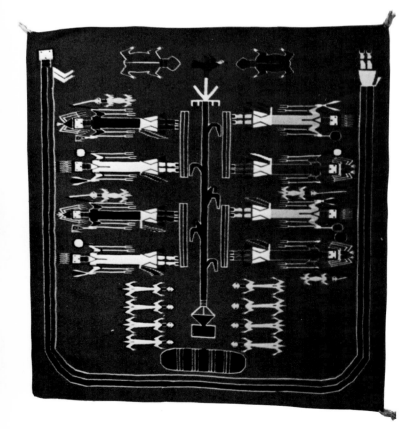

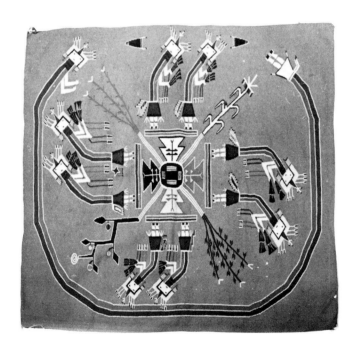

397 Rug, sandpainting, Red Rock, 1960's, 164.5 cm x 156 cm. 11 warps, 44 wefts. Beautyway: People with Weasel Skins. Desbah Tutt Nez, weaver. Two-ply aniline dyed commercial yarn. Handspun natural white warp. Gift of Mr. and Mrs. Edwin L. Kennedy, 69.67.10.

398 Rug, sandpainting, Red Rock, 1960's, 166 cm x 151.5 cm. 14 warps, 52 wefts. Beautyway: Rainbow People. Desbah Tutt Nez, weaver. Two-ply aniline dyed commercial yarn. Handspun natural white warp. Gift of Mr. and Mrs. Edwin L. Kennedy, 69.67.11.

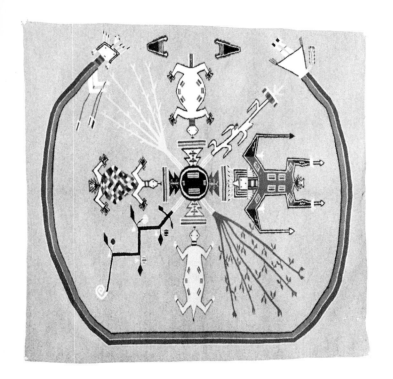

399 Rug, sandpainting, Red Rock, 1961, 146 cm x 144 cm. 14 warps, 60 wefts. Beautyway: Water Creatures. Anna Mae Lamson, weaver. Won first prize at Gallup Ceremonial in 1962. Two-ply aniline dyed commercial yarn. Handspun natural white warp. Gift of Mr. and Mrs. Edwin L. Kennedy, 69.67.13.

400 Rug, sandpainting, Red Rock, 1960's, 116 cm x 114.5 cm. 14 warps, 56 wefts. Beautyway: Sun and Moon. Desbah Tutt Nez, weaver. Two-ply aniline dyed commercial yarn. Handspun natural white warp. Gift of Mr. and Mrs. Edwin L. Kennedy, 69.67.16.

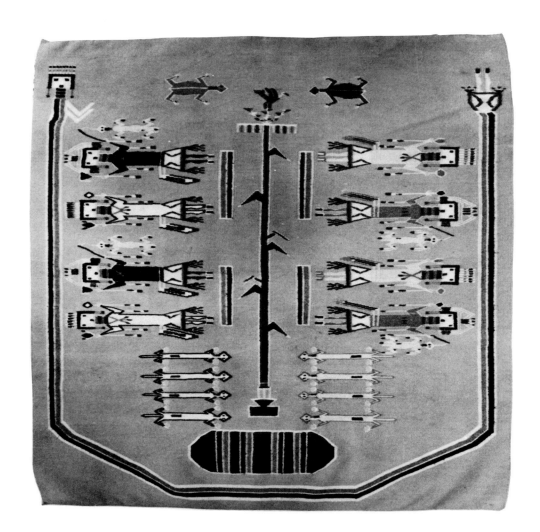

401 Rug, sandpainting, 1960's, 148 cm x 146 cm. 9 warps, 44 wefts. Beautyway: People with Weasel Skins. Mrs. James Etcitty, weaver. Four-ply aniline dyed commercial yarn. Handspun natural white warp. Gift of Mr. and Mrs. Edwin L. Kennedy, 69.67.29.

402 Rug, Blessingway, 1960-70, 146.5 cm x 91.5 cm. 10 warps, 36 wefts. Betty Tyler, weaver. All two-ply aniline dyed commercial yarn. Gift of Edwin L. Kennedy through the Maxwell Museum Association, 79.45.64.

403 Rug, Red Rock, láte 1960's. 12 warps, 40 wefts. Anna Mae Lamson, weaver. Hail Chant, People of the Storm. All commercial two-ply yarn with aniline colors. Gift of Edwin L. Kennedy through the Maxwell Museum Association, 79.45.66.

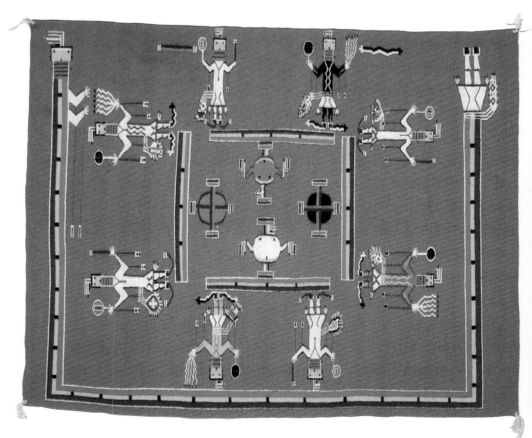

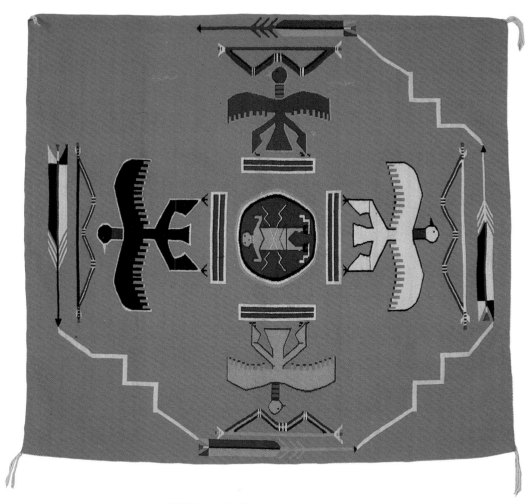

404 Rug, Red Rock, 1966, 160.5 cm x 150 cm. 15 warps, 60 wefts. Vera Begay, weaver. All two-ply commercial wool with aniline colors. Gift of Edwin D. Kennedy through the Maxwell Museum Association, 85.49.1.

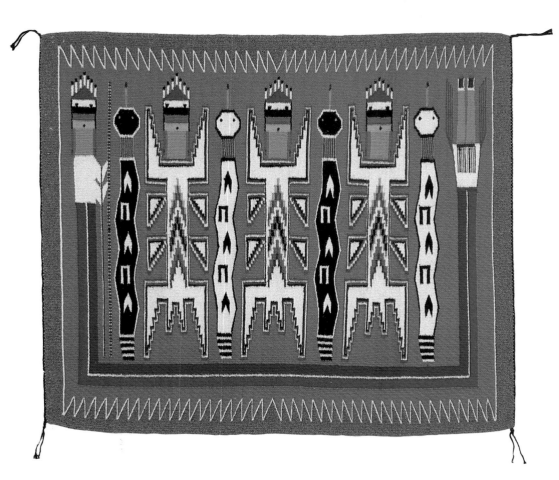

405 Rug, 1960-70, 103.3 cm x 89.3 cm. 8 warps, 44 wefts. Eva March, weaver. All four-ply aniline dyed commercial yarns. Gift of Edwin L. Kennedy through the Maxwell Museum Association, 80.5.9.

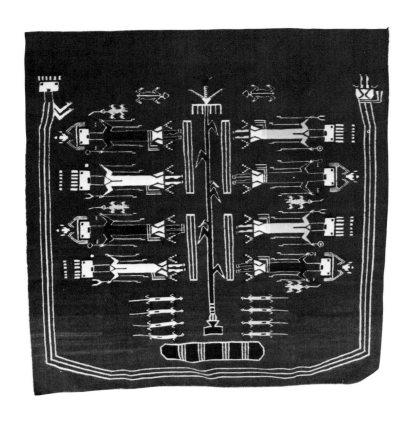

406 Rug, sandpainting, Red Rock, 1960's, 145 cm x 150 cm. 20 warps, 46 wefts. Beautyway: People with Weasel Skins. Mrs. James Etcitty, weaver. Handspun natural and carded wool. Two-ply aniline dyed commercial yarn. Gift of Mr. and Mrs. Edwin L. Kennedy, 69.67.30.

407 Rug, sandpainting, Two Grey Hills (Tohatchi), c. 1961, 188 cm x 137.5 cm. 10 warps, 52 wefts. Possible adaptation of Mountain Gods. Patsy Millie, weaver. All handspun wool with natural, carded and aniline colors. Gift of Mr. and Mrs. Gilbert Maxwell, 63.34.131.

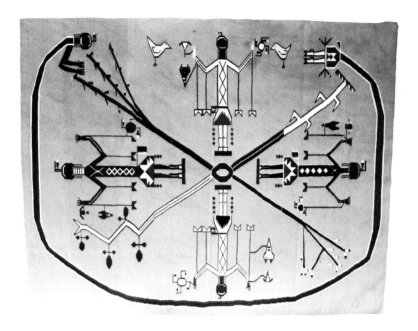

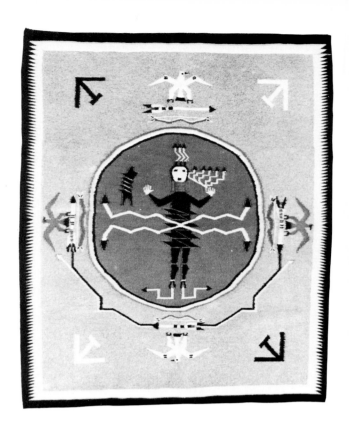

408 Rug, sandpainting, perhaps from Windway, 1960's, 186 cm x 152.5 cm. 14 warps, 52 wefts. Vera Begay, weaver. Three-ply aniline dyed commercial yarn. Handspun natural white wool warp. Gift of Mr. and Mrs. Edwin L. Kennedy, 70.75.6.

409 Rug, sandpainting, Shiprock, c. 1961, 126.5 cm x 100.5 cm. 11 warps, 32 wefts. Mrs. Tom Peshlakai, weaver. Shooting Way, Female Branch: Sun with figure of Nayenezgani. Copy of a painting by Hosteen Nez. Three-ply aniline dyed commercial yarn. Two-ply natural white commercial yarn warp. Gift of Mr. and Mrs. Gilbert Maxwell, 63.34.129.

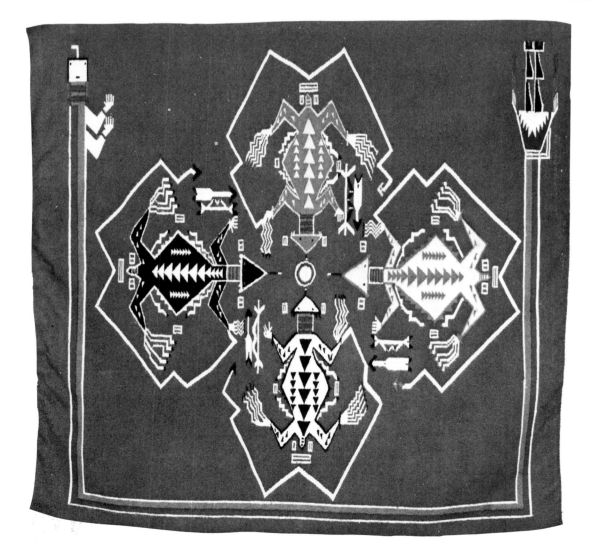

410 Rug, Red Rock, c. 1970, 123 cm x 124.5 cm. 15 warps, 64 wefts. Vera Begay, weaver. Drypainting, Horned Toad People, from the Red Ant Chant. Won second prize from the 1971 New Mexico State Fair. Two-ply aniline dyed yarns. Gift of Edwin L. Kennedy through the Maxwell Museum Association, 80.5.10.

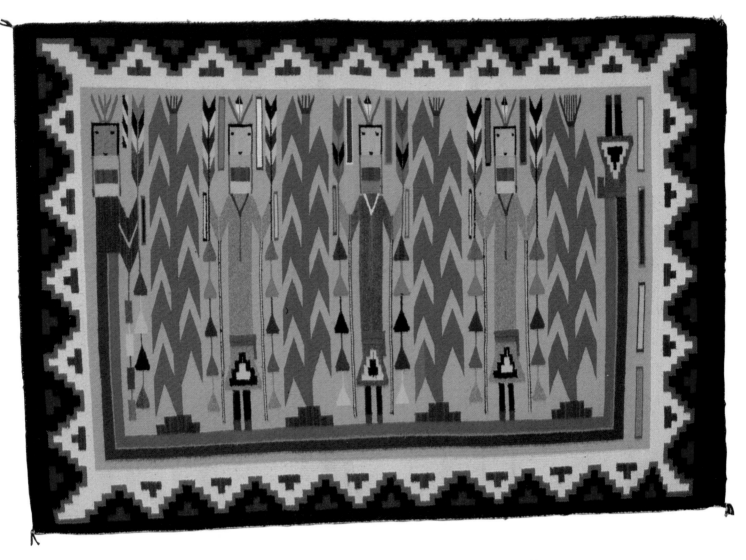

411 Rug, 1960-70, 163 cm x 119 cm. 8 warps, 40 wefts. Ye'ii.
Four-ply aniline dyed commercial yarn and white handspun.
Gift of Edwin L. Kennedy through the Maxwell Museum
Association, 79.45.67.

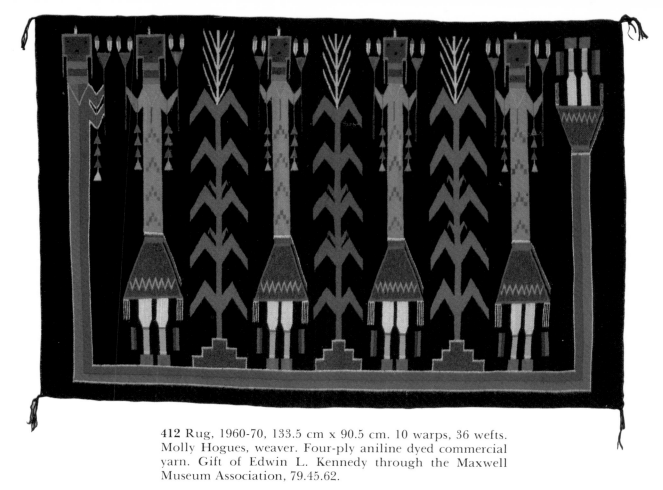

412 Rug, 1960-70, 133.5 cm x 90.5 cm. 10 warps, 36 wefts. Molly Hogues, weaver. Four-ply aniline dyed commercial yarn. Gift of Edwin L. Kennedy through the Maxwell Museum Association, 79.45.62.

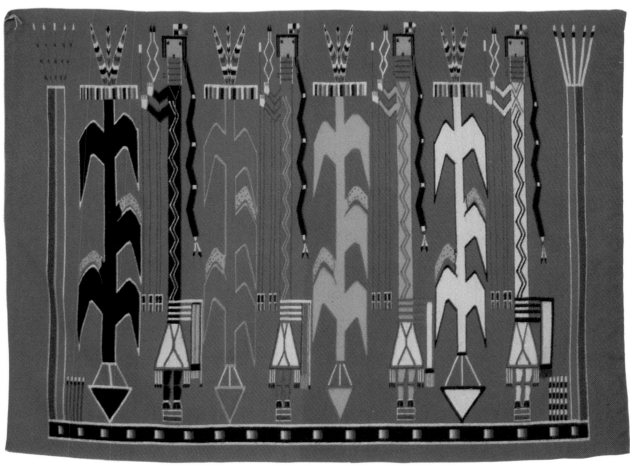

413 Rug, Red Rock, 1960-70, 161.5 cm x 121 cm. 14 warps, 60 wefts. Betty Yazzie, weaver. All commercial two-ply yarn with natural and aniline colors. Gift of Edwin L. Kennedy through the Maxwell Museum Association, 79.45.63.

173

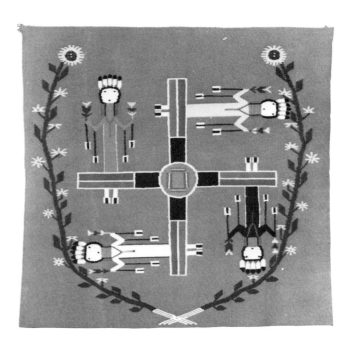

414 Rug, sandpainting, 1960's, 151 cm x 143 cm. 13 warps, 50 wefts. Mary Lewis, weaver. Rainbow People. Could be from any of six different chants: Mountain, Beauty, Plume, Wind, Male Shooting, or Night. Two-ply aniline dyed commercial yarn. Cotton string warp. Gift of Mr. and Mrs. Edwin L. Kennedy, 70.75.8.

415 Rug, sandpainting, 1960's, 111 cm x 114 cm. 10 warps, 44 wefts. May Rose Tyler, weaver. Big God Way: Sun Flower People. Four-ply aniline dyed commercial yarn. Two-ply natural white warp. Gift of Mr. and Mrs. Edwin L. Kennedy, 69.67.19.

416 Rug, sandpainting, Red Rock, 1960's, 139 cm x 141 cm. 12 warps, 56 wefts. Desbah Tutt Nez, weaver. Two-ply aniline dyed commercial yarn. Handspun natural white wool warp. Gift of Mr. and Mrs. Edwin L. Kennedy, 70.75.5.

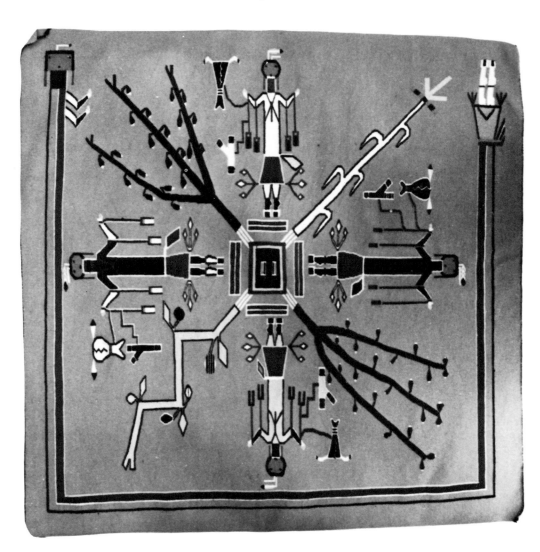

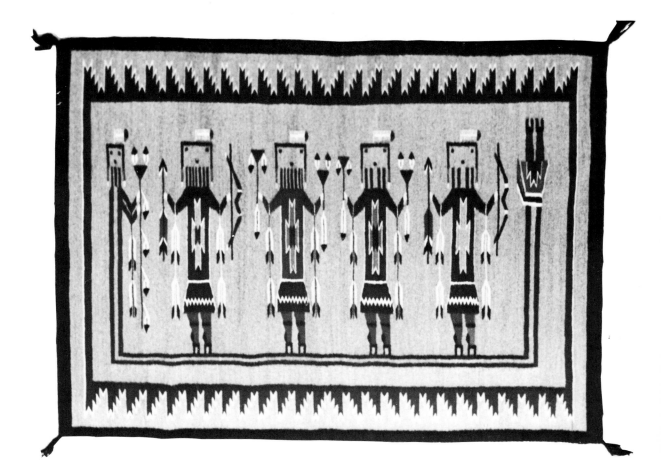

417 Rug, sandpainting, Shiprock, 1966-67, 117.5 cm x 87.5 cm. 9 warps, 52 wefts. Lucy Chase, weaver. Won first prize and Special United Indian Traders Award at the Gallup Ceremonial in 1967. All handspun wool with natural, carded, vegetal and aniline colors. Gift of Mr. and Mrs. Gilbert Maxwell, 75.324.1.

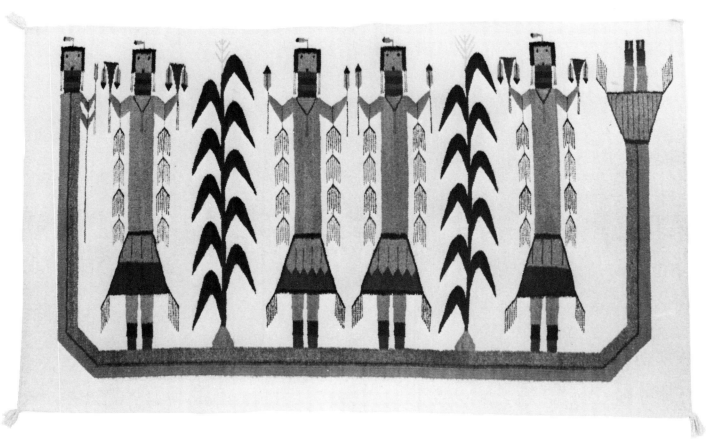

418 Rug, sandpainting, c. 1957, 149 cm x 91.5 cm. 9 warps, 30 wefts. Perhaps adaptation of Mountain Gods, see Maxwell 1963:34, fig. 20. Formerly in Don Watson Collection. All handspun wool with natural and aniline colors. Gift of Mr. and Mrs. Gilbert Maxwell, 63.34.148.

The Weavers

Among the finest weavers of ceremonial pattern rugs today are the family of Desbah Tutt Nez (**419**). Desbah's mother, Naskai Bitsie was a famous weaver, but she died before she could teach Desbah who learned from her stepmother, Boutsin Bitsie. Desbah made her first rug in 1928 at the age of 18. It was a white background *ye'ii*, something like Big Thunder (**355**), and her first sandpainting rug was the Whirling Logs.

Desbah's two daughters learned from their mother; Anna Mae Lamson (**420**) at age 8, and Alberta Thomas (**421**) at age 10. They are all excellent weavers now, but Desbah does few pieces any more. Both daughters, now middle aged, say they stole yarn from Desbah when they were young and wove on little boards. They did the spinning for their mother. Now the women use commercial yarn supplied to them by the Kennedys. It is a fine, two-ply yarn imported from Canada (Condon Yarn Co.) in colors specifically ordered by the trader at Red Rock, Edith Kennedy. One day, Alberta was found sitting, respinning the commercial yarn until it was very fine in diameter. When asked why she did not hand-spin her own wool, she smiled and said she was too lazy. Obviously, this was a quiet joke, since any artist who will respin already fine yarn and weave such elaborate patterns is far from lazy.

419 Desbah Tutt Nez. 1982. Photo by Marian Rodee.

420 Anna Mae Lamson, 1982. Photo by Marian Rodee.

421 Alberta Thomas, 1982. Photo by Marian Rodee.

Alberta's daughters do not weave. When asked if they do, the answer was no, "she's a nurse's aide", an illustration of the present situation where a woman who is able to secure a good job does not weave. Alberta did, however, look after her granddaughters Treina and Joanne Junes one summer. She taught them to weave on the traditional little board loom and to make the equally-traditional striped first rug. (**422**). The little girls did not keep on with their weaving as they only stayed with their grandmother that one summer. Alberta keeps a loom for the older girl, Treina to work on when she visits. The loom is larger than the learning board and the design is a more complex Chinle/Crystal type.

423 Early ceremonial pattern rug from Red Rock, early 1950's. The Whirling Logs, Night Chant with Talking God and Calling God also from this chant. Photo by Anthony Richardson. Private Collection.

422 Joanne and Treina Junes, 1982. Photo by Marian Rodee.

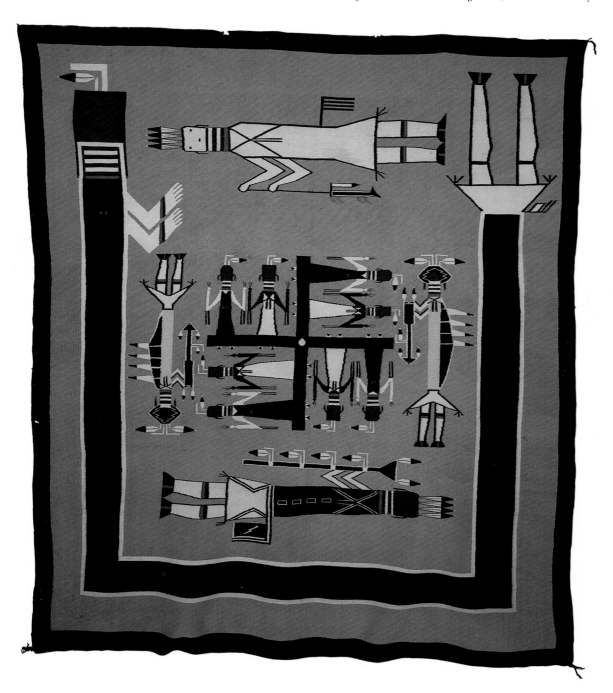

177

424 Rug, 1960-70, 174 cm x 105 cm. 9 warps, 38 wefts. Louise Dale Frazier, weaver. Generalized drypainting. Handspun wool in natural, carded and aniline colors and four-ply commercial yarn in aniline colors. Gift of Edwin L. Kennedy through the Maxwell Museum Association, 80.5.11.

425 Rug, c. 1930, 162.5 cm x 108 cm. 8 warps, 30 wefts. Yarn is very poorly spun giving the textile a bumpy appearance. All handspun wool with natural and aniline colors. Gift of Muril E. Hagen through the Maxwell Museum Association, 83.39.8.

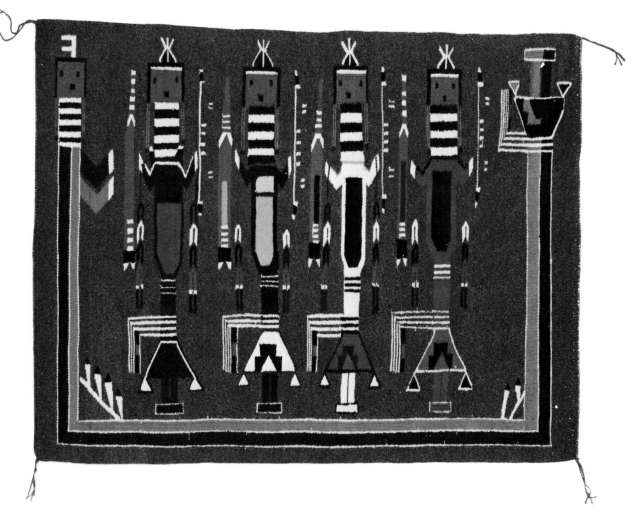

426 Rug, 1960's, 113 cm x 93 cm. 8 warps, 44 wefts. The Mountain Gods, All two-ply commercial yarn with aniline colors. Gift of Edwin L. Kennedy, 79.45.69.

Alberta works on two looms at once, one on the eastern side of the house and one on the west, to catch the sunlight all day. When visited, she had the beginning of a large, complex sandpainting (six feet by four feet) on the west-facing loom. It was to be very elaborate and fine. The tension on the loom was extraordinarily tight and held taut by inserting a metal bar which Alberta's husband helped her adjust. Because the weaving was difficult and copying the design from the book, loaned by the Kennedys, was tedious, the weaving was expected to take five to six months to complete. Alberta had started a smaller rug in the east-facing loom. She described it as an old, 1945-style, white *ye'ii* rug. She obviously enjoyed creating this piece by working out the design in her head. She marked the warps by laying-in the position of the major figures with strands of yarn.

The trader Troy Kennedy is a descendant of one of the pioneer families of the Farmington area. Troy's father, Roy, freighted merchandise from Durango to Fruitland and bought the post of Lukachukai in 1928. Another son, Earl, took this post over, but it has since burned down. The post building at Red Rock probably dates to the 1890's and was built by Carlos Stalworthy and later sold to Jewel McGee. It was from McGee that Troy and his wife Edith bought a partnership in 1948. Later, in 1966, they bought the entire post. The older, back part of the post with its *viga* and *latia* ceiling and

dirt floors was photographed in the 1930s by Laura Gilpin (Gilpin 1968, 84-85). The post was remodeled in 1965 or 66, and the old part was covered up and is visible now only in one of the back storerooms.

When the Kennedys arrived in 1948, the local weavers were making white background *ye'iis* as Desbah Tutt Nez refered to above. The Kennedys felt the Navajo religion was disappearing and that the paintings should be preserved through weaving. They had observed that there were increasingly fewer medicine men in the area. These traders have worked steadily from the late 1940's to the present in encouraging local women to make exact copies and to do more technically perfect work. 423 shows one of the early examples from the late 1940's which was probably woven by Paul Brady's wife or Geneva Smith, wife of Jessie Smith (Troy Kennedy, personal communication 1985). It is a simplified version of the Whirling Logs from Nightway but with the unusual additions of two large Talking Gods and two Humpback Gods—important figures in the Nightway, but never shown in this drypainting. The entire composition is out of proportion.

Drypainting rugs, since their beginning in the 1880's, have constituted only a tiny portion of the total production of Navajo weaving. To the present, this style of weaving is attempted by only a few excellent weavers and only with appropriate religious protection.

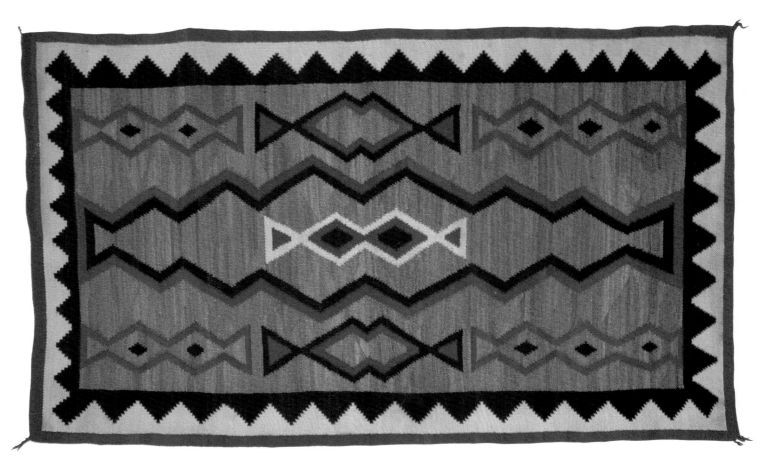

427 Rug, Ganado, 1900-20, 282 cm x 129 cm. 5 warps, 16 wefts. All handspun wool with natural and aniline colors. Gift of Lois Minium, 82.44.1.

428 Rug, Ganado, 1920-40, 283 cm x 145.5 cm. 8 warps, 24 wefts. All handspun wool with natural, carded and aniline colors. Gift of Hazel Beebe, 81.46.77.

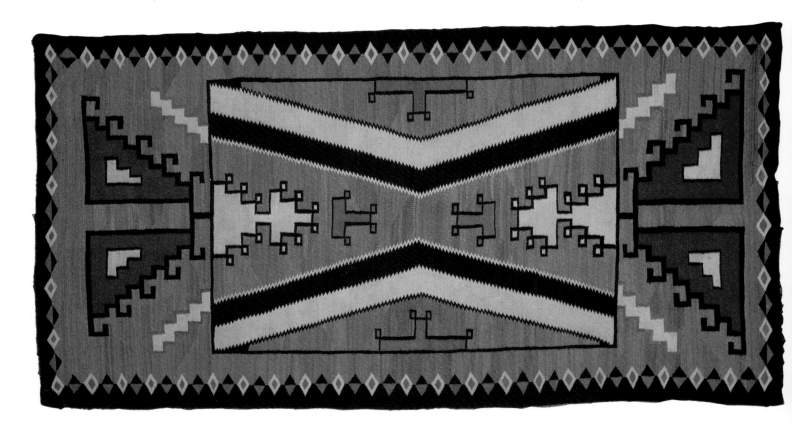

429 Rug, possibly Ganado, 1920-40, 258 cm x 239 cm. 7 warps, 22 wefts. Handspun wool with natural, handspun and aniline colors. Gift of Ronnie L. Galloway, 77.33.2.

430 Rug, Ganado, 226.5 cm x 123.5 cm. 7 warps, 20 wefts. All handspun wool with natural carded and aniline colors. Gift of Muril Hagen, the Rex and Margaret A. Prunty Memorial Collection, 83.39.10.

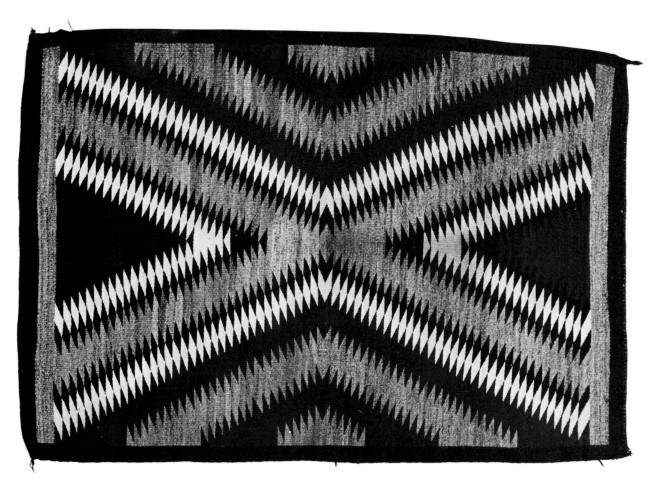

431 Rug, probably Ganado, 1920-40, 150 cm x 138 cm. 7 warps, 28 wefts. All handspun wool with natural, carded and aniline colors. Gift of Mr. and Mrs. Rufus Carter, 77.3.26.

432 Rug, possibly Ganado, 1920-40, 126 cm x 94 cm. 6 warps, 28 wefts. All handspun wool with natural, carded and aniline colors. Gift of Mr. and Mrs. Julian Shapero, 78.36.4.

433 Rug, Ganado style, 1920-40, 141 cm x 119.5 cm. 9 warps, 28 wefts. All hand-spun wool with natural and carded colors and cotton string warp. Gift of Mr. and Mrs. J.A. Joe, 76.86.1.

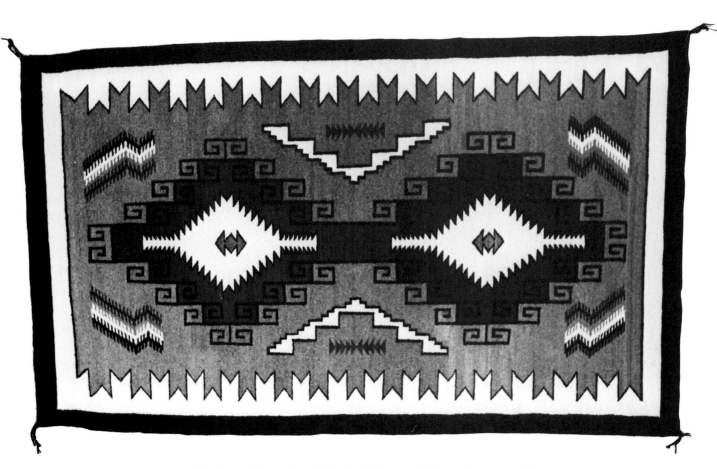

434 Rug, Klagetoh, 1920-40, 198 cm x 126 cm. 7 warps, 30 wefts. Esther Billie, weaver. All handspun wool with natural, carded and aniline colors. Gift of Mr. Read Mullan, 64.84.2.

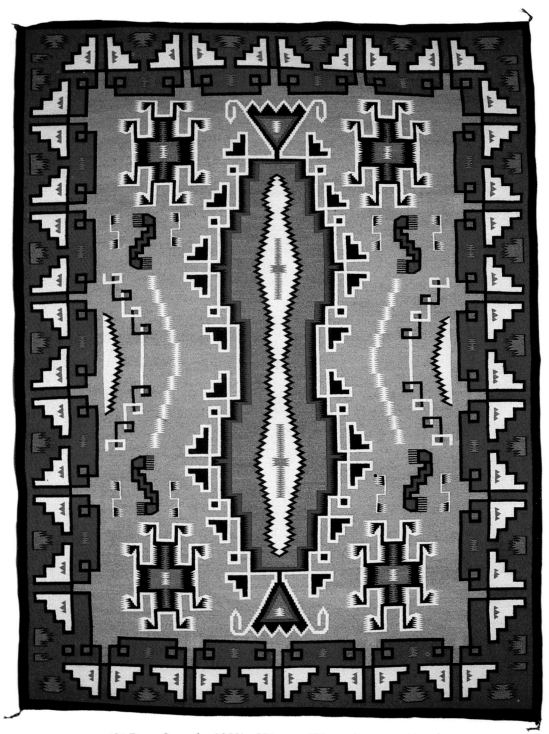

435 Rug, Ganado, 1960's, 381 cm x 275 cm. 7 warps, 44 wefts. Mary Begay, weaver. All handspun wool with natural, carded and aniline colors. Gift of Mr. and Mrs. Edwin L. Kennedy, 69.67.22.

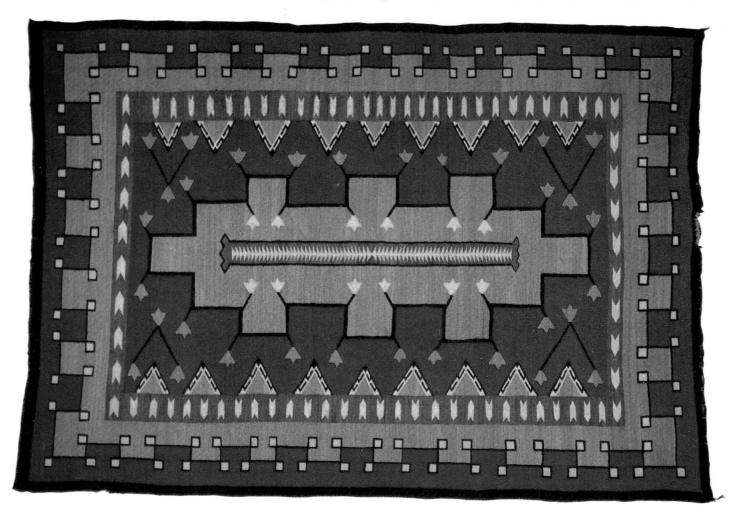

436 Rug, Ganado, 1920-40, 259 cm x 194 cm. 8 warps, 26 wefts. All handspun wool with natural, carded and aniline colors. Gift of Mrs. N.W. Shiarella, 76.40.1.

437 Rug, Ganado, 1960-70, 230 cm x 178.5 cm. 8 warps, 30 wefts. Redhouse Girl, weaver. Handspun wool with natural and aniline colors, gray is a four-ply commercial yarn. Gift of Edwin L. Kennedy through the Maxwell Museum Associaton, 80.5.2.

438 Rug, Ganado, 1951, 141 cm x 75 cm. 10 warps, 32 wefts. See Maxwell 1963:38, fig. 28. All handspun wool with natural, carded and aniline colors. Gift of Mr. and Mrs. Gilbert Maxwell, 73.9.55.

439 Rug, Ganado, c. 1930, 157 cm x 90 cm. 7 warps, 18 wefts. This rug was placed in the doorway of the New Mexico exhibit at the Century of Progress Exhibit in Chicago, 1933. All handspun wool with natural, carded and aniline colors. Gift of Mr. Tobe Turpin, 63.47.1.

440 Rug, Ganado, c. 1950, 153.5 cm x 107 cm. 10 warps, 26 wefts. All handspun wool with natural, carded and aniline colors. Gift of Mr. and Mrs. Gilbert Maxwell, 63.34.106.

441 Rug, Ganado, 1960's, 197 cm x 180.5 cm. 10 warps, 26 wefts. Hand-spun wool with natural white and aniline black. Four-ply aniline dyed synthetic yarns. Gift of Mr. and Mrs. Edwin L. Kennedy, 69.67.23.

442 Rug, Ganado, c. 1970, 139 cm x 95 cm. 10 warps, 38 wefts. All hand-spun wool with natural, carded and aniline colors and a cotton string warp. Gift of Dale and Marilyn Warman, 79.69.8.

Tees Nos Pos and Red Mesa

Tees Nos Pos in the Four Corners area is the center of a very complex weaving style. The trading post there was built in 1905 by Hambleton Bridger Noel who found that rugs woven by the local Navajo women were of high quality—perhaps due to the influence of a Mrs. Wilson, presumably a missionary in the area around 1890.

Tees Nos Pos rugs frequently have a wide border containing a series of large T's. The central portion is usually filled with a complex design similar to the terraced rectangle that occurs on many modern Ganado rugs. Feathers and arrows are commonly incorporated into the pattern as are many other small elements. Because a wide variety of colors are used, commercial yarns and aniline-dyed handspun wool are the typical yarns used in this area.

Red Mesa is near Tees Nos Pos. Rugs made there are done in what is called the outline style in which every design element (usually a zigzag or a series of them) is outlined in a contrasting color. This is one of the few survivals of the old eyedazzler patterns of the last century, but few rugs are produced in this style now.

Opposite page, top:
444 Rug, Red Mesa, 1900-10, 247 cm x 145 cm. 6 warps, 24 wefts. Bought by V. Olsen of Farmington in 1910. See Maxwell 1963:36, fig. 23. This rug documents a beginning date for the development of the outline style. All handspun wool with natural, carded and aniline colors. Gift of Mr. and Mrs. Gilbert Maxwell, 63.34.143.

Opposite page, bottom:
445 Rug, 1975, 239 cm x 180 cm. 12 warps, 40 wefts. Louise Benally, weaver. Won third prize in 1975 Gallup Intertribal Ceremonial. All commercial two- and four-ply yarns with aniline colors. Gift of Edwin D. Kennedy through the Maxwell Museum Association, 85.49.4.

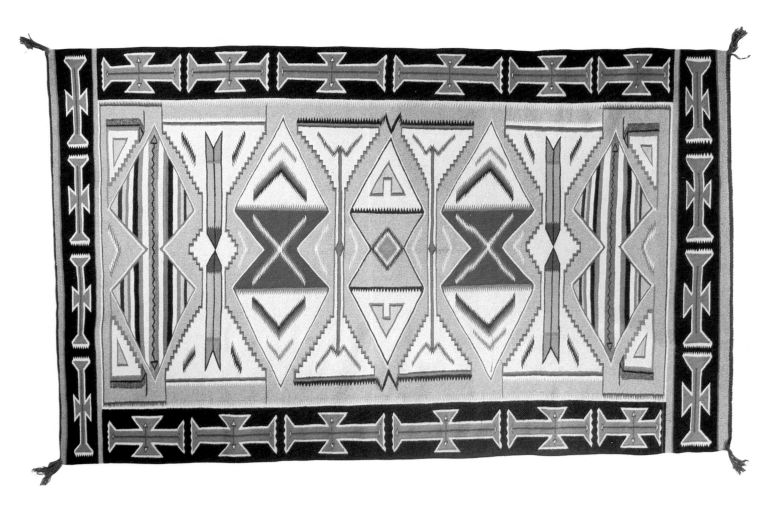

443 Rug, Tees Nos Pos, 1960's, 273 cm x 173 cm. 10 warps, 44 wefts. Sally Begay, weaver. Handspun wool with natural, carded and aniline colors. Four-ply aniline dyed commercial yarn. Gift of Mr. and Mrs. Edwin L. Kennedy, 69.67.27.

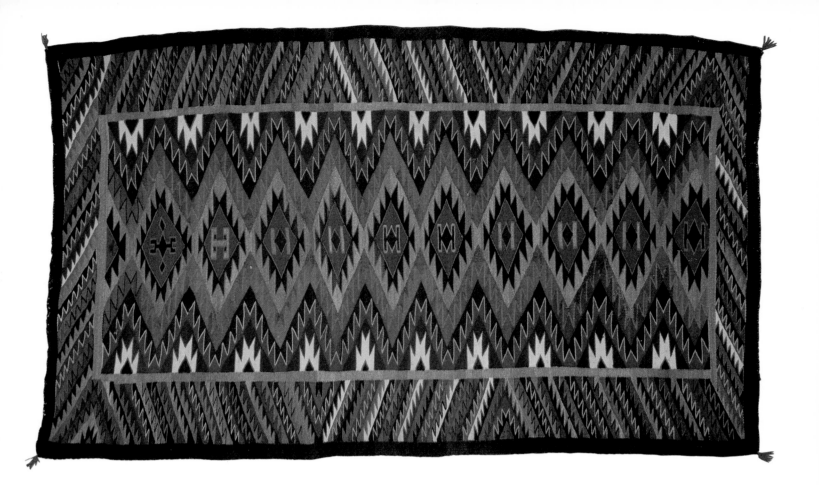

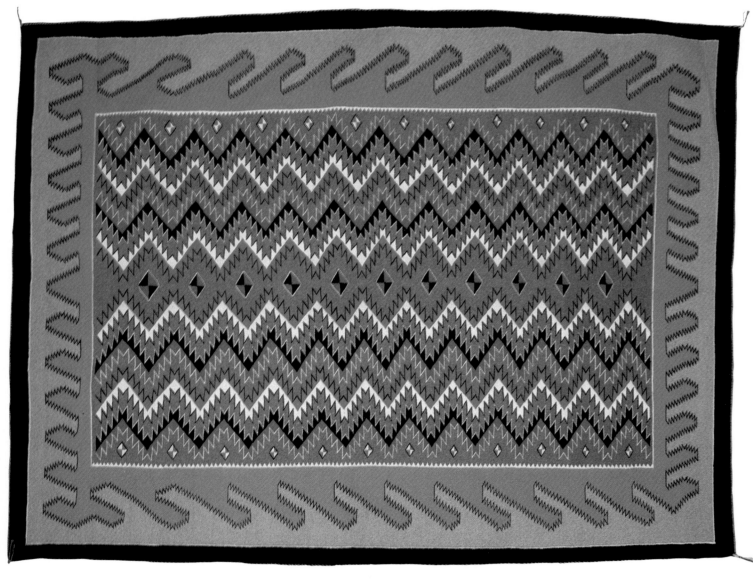

446 Rug, Tees Nos Pos, c. 1950, 184 cm x 102.5 cm. 9 warps, 26 wefts. See Maxwell 1963:24, fig. 10. Handspun wool with natural, carded and aniline colors. Four-ply commercial aniline dyed orange and blue yarn. Gift of Mr. and Mrs. Gilbert Maxwell, 63.34.108.

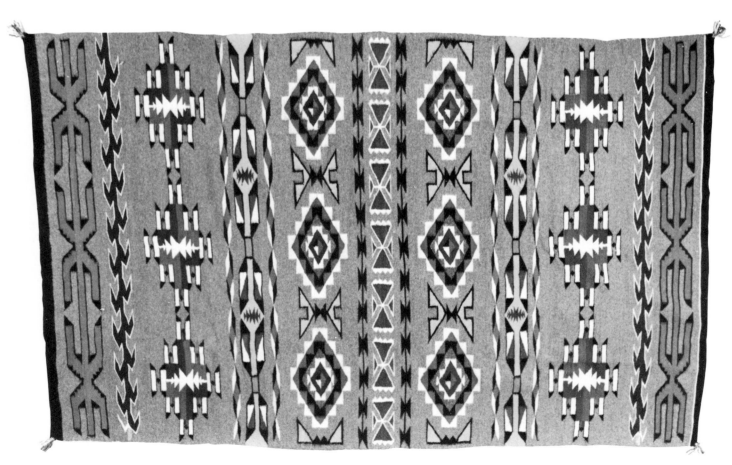

447 Rug, Tees Nos Pos, c. 1961-62, 291.5 cm x 194.5 cm. 10 warps, 26 wefts. Mrs. Charles Huskay, weaver. Won second prize at Gallup Ceremonial in 1962. All handspun wool with natural, carded and aniline colors. Gift of Mr. Read Mullan, 64.84.1.

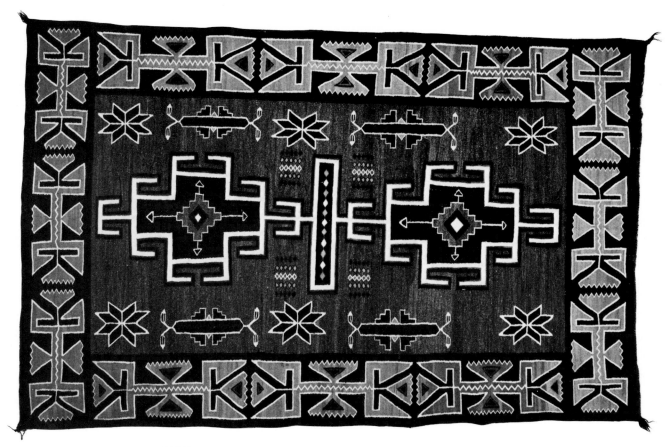

448 Rug, Tees Nos Pos, 1920-40, 276.5 cm x 183 cm. 11 warps, 26 wefts. All handspun wool with natural, carded and aniline colors. Gift of Doris Owen, 76.50.1.

449 Rug, Tees Nos Pos, 1960's, 300 cm x 95 cm. 12 warps, 44 wefts (handspun) and 10 warps, 52 wefts (commercial). Handspun wool with natural, carded and aniline colors. Four-ply aniline dyed commercial yarn. Gift of Mr. and Mrs. Edwin L. Kennedy,l 69.67.26.

450 Rug, Tees Nos Pos, 1960-70, 281.5 cm x 165 cm. 13 warps, 36 wefts. Old Lady Huskay, weaver. All four-ply aniline dyed commercial yarn. Gift of Edwin L. Kennedy through the Maxwell Museum Association, 79.45.71.

451 Rug, Tees Nos Pos, c. 1970, 199.5 cm x 110 cm. 11 warps, 44 wefts. Maude Dale, weaver. All four-ply aniline dyed commercial yarn. Gift of Edwin L. Kennedy through the Maxwell Museum Association, 80.5.5.

452 Rug, Tees Nos Pos, 1960-70, 175.5 cm x 99 cm. 13 warps, 34 wefts. Minnie Begay, weaver. All commercial two-ply yarns with natural and aniline colors. Gift of Edwin L. Kennedy through the Maxwell Museum Association, 79.45.70.

453 Rug, Red Mesa, 1920-40, 147 cm x 108 cm. 5 warps, 22 wefts. All handspun wool with natural, carded and aniline colors. Gift of Mrs. Lawrence Milne, 63.33.1.

454 Rug, Red Mesa, 1920-30, 232 cm x 143 cm. 10 warps, 30 wefts. All handspun wool with natural and aniline colors. Gift of Mrs. Dan Falvey, 74.30.2.

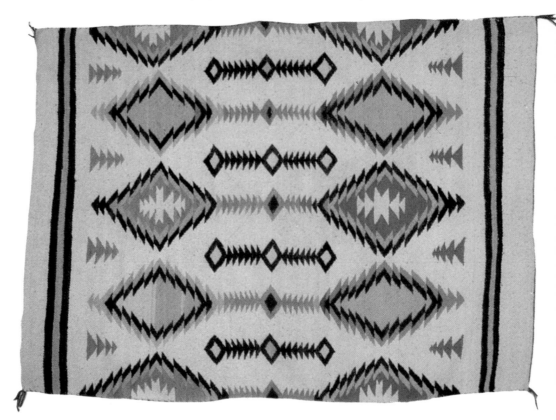

455 Rug, Chinle Revival, 1930's, 221 cm x 184 cm. 8 warps, 28 wefts. All handspun wool with natural and aniline colors. Gift of William Phelps, 76.47.1.

456 Rug, Chinle, 1930's, 46 cm x 44 cm. 8 warps, 20 wefts. Chinle Revival style bought at the Thunderbird Lodge, Chinle in 1936. All handspun wool with natural and vegetal colors. Gift of Edmund Shaw, 79.44.6.

457 Rug, Fort Wingate School, 1944, 157.5 cm. 8 warps, 44 wefts. Mr. Maxwell notes that these experimental dyes were expensive and this rug was one of only seventy-five made with chrome dyes. All handspun wool with carded and chrome-dyed colors. Gift of Mr. and Mrs. Gilbert Maxwell, 63.34.86.

458 (left) Pillow, 1985, 43 cm x 40 cm. 6 warps, 24 wefts. Alice Alonzo, weaver. All handspun wool with natural, carded and vegetal colors. Gift of Howard and Marian Rodee, 85.35.3. (center) Pillow, 1985, 40 cm x 38 cm. 6 warps, 36 wefts. Annie Pino, weaver. All handspun wool with vegetal colors. Tan; walnut, natural gray, black; pinyon pitch, brown; wild sweet potato. Gift of Howard and Marian Rodee, 85.35.2. (right) Pillow, 1985, 42.5 cm x 33 cm. 8 warps, 40 wefts. Annie Nez Martine, weaver. All handspun wool with natural white and vegetal colors. Green; sage, tan; juniper bark, light gold; Navajo tea. Gift of Howard and Marian Rodee, 85.35.1.

459 Rug, Chinle Revival, 1930's, 136.5 cm x 75.5 cm. 8 warps, 36 wefts. All handspun wool with natural, vegetal and aniline colors. Gift of Muril E. Hagen, the Rex and Margaret A. Prunty Memorial Collection, 83.39.7.

460 Rug, Chinle, 1930's, 193 cm x 112.5 cm. 6 warps, 20 wefts. Made near the mouth of Canyon de Chelly (Chinle). The documentation on the date and provenience of this rug indicate that not all weavers in this area adopted the new vegetal style. All handspun wool with natural, carded and aniline colors. Gift of Mr. Edward C. Groesbeck, 69.4.3.

461 Rug, 1930's, 143.5 cm x 99 cm. 6 warps, 18 wefts. All handspun wool with natural, carded and aniline colors. Gift of Mrs. Lawrence Milne, 63.33.2.

462 Rug, Chinle, c. 1935, 242 cm x 166 cm. 9 warps, 28 wefts. All handspun wool with natural, aniline and Dupont dyes. Gift of Mr. and Mrs. Gilbert Maxwell, 63.34.175.

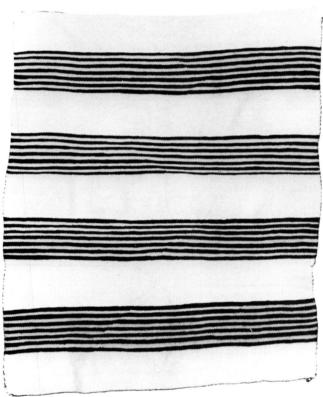

463 Rug, Chinle, 1930-34, 119 cm x 95 cm. 10 warps, 24 wefts. Bought by Dr. Hill at Chinle in 1934. All handspun wool with natural and vegetal colors. Gift of Dr. W.W. Hill, 65.47.3.

464 Rug, Chinle, 1934, 135 cm x 84 cm. 7 warps, 22 wefts. All handspun wool with natural and vegetal colors. Gift of Dr. W.W. Hill, 67.47.4.

465 Rug, Chinle, c. 1934, 127.5 cm x 66 cm. 10 warps, 26 wefts. All handspun wool with natural, carded and vegetal colors. Gift of W.W. Hill, 65.47.7.

466 Rug, Crystal, 1954, 127 cm x 86 cm. 8 warps, 26 wefts. All handspun wool with natural, carded and vegetal colors. Gift of Mr. and Mrs. Gilbert Maxwell, 73.9.57.

467 Rug, Wide Ruins, 1960's, 132 cm x 85 cm. 8 warps, 40 wefts. Annie Apache, weaver. All handspun wool with natural and vegetal colors. Gift of Mr. and Mrs. Edwin L. Kennedy, 69.67.36.

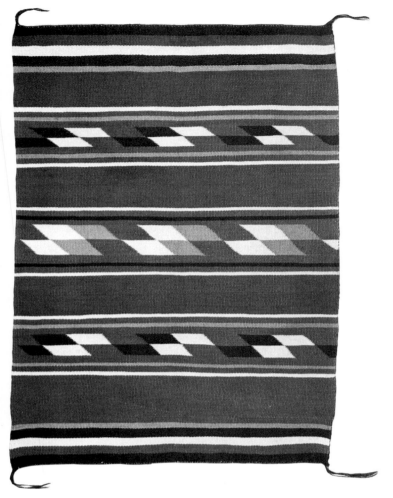

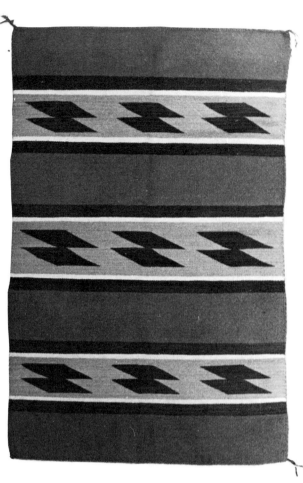

468 Rug, possibly Wide Ruins, 1960-70, 110 cm x 78.8 cm. 8 warps, 36 wefts. All handspun wool with natural and vegetal colors. Gift of Dr. David Gale, 82.60.3.

469 Rug, Wide Ruins, 1960's, 127 cm x 76 cm. 9 warps, 28 wefts. Emma K. Joe, weaver. All handspun wool with natural and vegetal colors. Gift of Mr. and Mrs. Edwin L. Kennedy, 69.67.35.

470 Rug, possibly Wide Ruins or Chinle, 1960's, 92 cm x 55 cm. 8 warps, 48 wefts. Four-ply aniline dyed commercial yarn. Cotton string warp. Gift of Mr. and Mrs. Edwin L. Kennedy, 69.67.44.

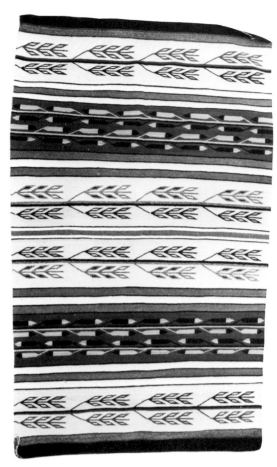

471 Rug, Nazlini, 1953, 217 cm x 125 cm. 10 warps, 26 wefts. Mary Van Winkle, weaver. All handspun wool with natural, carded and aniline colors. Gift of Mr. and Mrs. Gilbert Maxwell, 63.34.146.

472 Rug, 1960's, 285 cm x 185 cm. 8 warps, 36 wefts. All handspun wool with natural, carded and vegetal colors. Gift of Mr. and Mrs. Edwin L. Kennedy, 69.67.25.

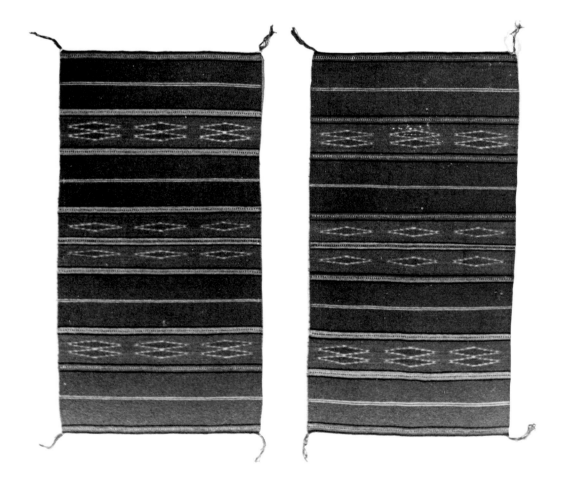

473a Rug, Pine Springs, 1960-61, 109 cm x 56.5 cm. 10 warps, 44 wefts. Ellen Smith, weaver. Won special award at Gallup Ceremonial in 1961. All handspun wool with natural and vegetal colors. Gift of Mr. and Mrs. Gilbert Maxwell, 63.34.127a.

473b Rug, Pine Springs, 1960-61, 108.5 cm x 55 cm. 10 warps, 44 wefts. Angie Smith (age 14), weaver, granddaughter of Ellen Smith who wove 63.34.127a. Won second prize in the juvenile division at the Gallup Ceremonial in 1961. All handspun wool with natural and vegetal colors. Gift of Mr. and Mrs. Gilbert Maxwell, 63.34.127b.

Four Corners

Most of the Maxwell Museum's weavings from this area are illustrated in the Sandpainting Design and Twill sections. The two specimens here, both pillow backs or throws, are of a generalized style notable for the use of bright colors similar to those of the sandpainting textiles from this area.

474 Pillow top, Four Corners Area, 1960's, 55 cm x 46 cm. 8 warps, 28 wefts. All handspun wool with natural, carded and aniline colors. Gift of Mr. and Mrs. Edwin L. Kennedy, 69.67.41.

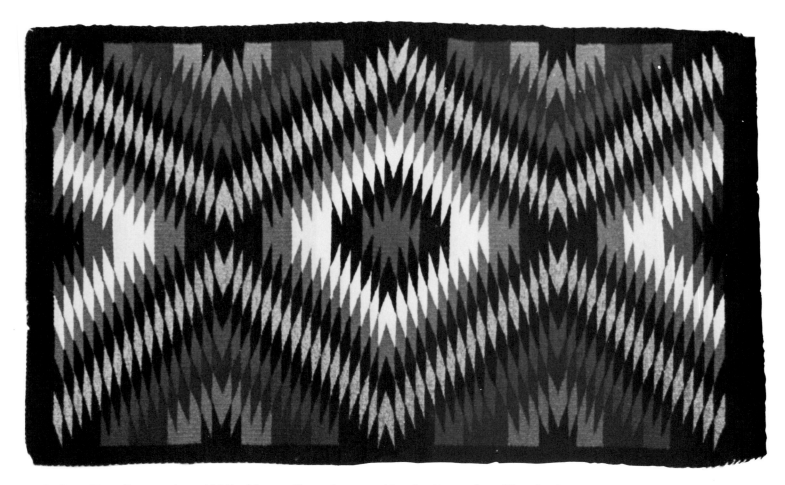

475 Rug, Four Corners Area, 1960's, 99 cm x 63 cm. 8 warps, 40 wefts. Four-ply aniline dyed commercial yarn. Cotton string warp. Gift of Mr. and Mrs. Edwin L. Kennedy, 69.67.46.

Unknown Provenience

Many twentieth-century Navajo textiles are of a pattern that cannot readily be attributed to any particular weaving area. They may have originated near one of the previously mentioned trading posts such as Ganado or Two Grey Hills but lack the characteristics of these styles. Most may be from locales where traders did not encourage manufacture of an identifiable local products.

476 Rug, 1923-24, 155 cm x 101 cm. 7 warps, 26 wefts. Purchased at Zuni Pueblo in 1923-24. All handspun wool with natural and carded colors. Gift of Peter Gonzales, The Clara Gonzales Collection, 77.35.1.

477 Rug, 1920-40, 181 cm x 98.5 cm. 6 warps, 18 wefts. All handspun wool in natural and aniline colors. Gift of Mr. and Mrs. Rufus Carter, 77.3.27.

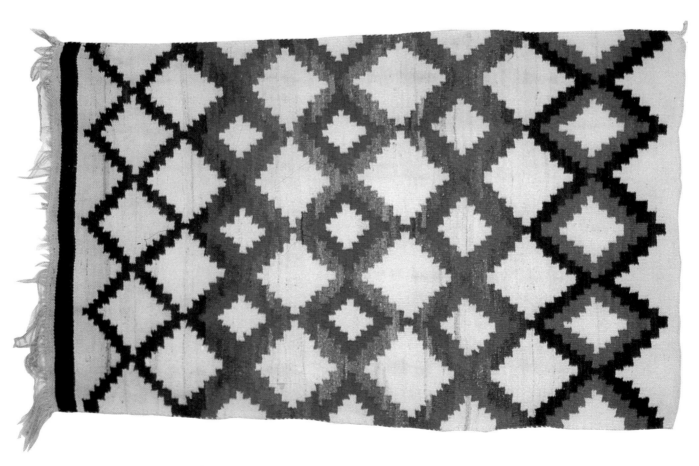

478 Rug, early 1930's, 157.5 cm x 103 cm. 7 warps, 24 wefts. Purchased at Casa Linda Motel, Gallup, New Mexico in 1937. All handspun wool with natural, carded and aniline colors. Unusual fringe on one edge cord Gift of Edmund Shaw, 79.44.8.

479 Rug, 1920-40, 167 cm x 118 cm. 7 warps, 24 wefts. All handspun wool with natural and aniline colors. Gift of Mrs. Prudence E. Oakes, 66.113.4.

480 Saddle blanket, 1920-40, 59 cm x 64 cm. 8 warps, 40 wefts. All handspun wool with natural, carded and aniline colors. Donor unknown, 74.28.3.

481 Rug, c. 1930, 123.5 cm x 80 cm. 8 warps, 36 wefts. Bought at Mesa Verde, Colorado. All handspun wool with natural, vegetal and carded colors. Gift of Dr. W.W. Hill, 65.47.5.

482 Rug, c. 1930, 92.5 cm x 44.5 cm. 8 warps, 26 wefts. Bought at Mesa Verde, Colorado. All handspun wool with natural and carded colors. Gift of Dr. W.W. Hill, 65.47.6.

483 Rug, possibly Chinle, 1920-40, 200 cm x 118 cm. 6 warps, 16 weft. All handspun wool with natural and carded colors. Donor unknown, 74.28.4.

484 Rug, 1920-40, 190 cm x 144 cm. 5 warps, 24 wefts. All handspun wool with natural, carded and aniline colors. Gift of Mrs. Prudence E. Oakes, 66.113.4.

485 Rug, 1920-40, 104 cm x 66 cm. 12 warps, 28 wefts. All handspun wool with natural, carded and aniline colors. Gift of Hazel Beebe, 81.46.79.

486 Rug, 304 cm x 160.5 cm. 6 warps, 28 wefts. All handspun wool with natural, carded and aniline dyes. Gift of Muril E. Hagen, the Rex and Margaret A. Prunty Memorial Collection, 83.39.9.

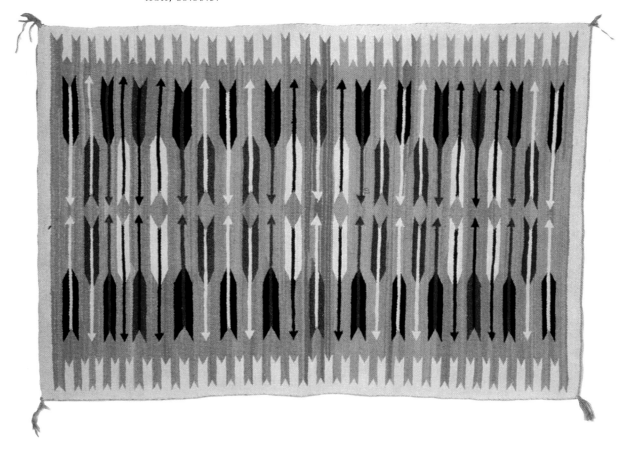

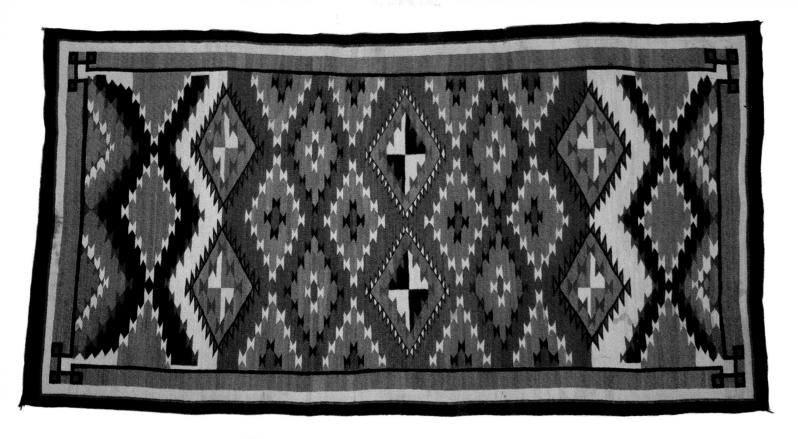

487 Rug, probably from Klagetoh, 1940-60, 110.5 cm x 56.5 cm. 7 warps, 22 wefts. All handspun wool with natural and aniline colors. Gift of Mr. and Mrs. J.A. Joe, 76.71.1.

488 Rug, 1930's, 162 cm x 91 cm. 6 warps, 26 wefts. All handspun wool with natural and aniline colors. Gift of Mr. and Mrs. Gilbert Maxwell, 72.49.58.

489 Rug, 1920-40, 128 cm x 75 cm. 7 warps, 20 wefts. All handspun wool with natural, carded and aniline colors. Gift of Mrs. Lawrence Milne, 63.33.3.

490 Rug, 1920-40, 196 cm x 129.5 cm. 7 warps, 28 wefts. All handspun wool with natural, carded and aniline colors. Gift of Mr. and Mrs. Bruce Ulbright through the Maxwell Museum Association, 83.38.11.

491 Rug, 1920-40, 174 cm x 119 cm. 6 warps, 34 wefts. All handspun wool in natural and carded colors. Gift of Mrs. O.D. Johnson, 76.59.4.

492 Rug, early 1930's, 114.3 cm x 65.7 cm. 8 warps, 24 wefts. Purchased at Crownpoint in 1937. All handspun wool with natural and aniline colors. Gift of Edmund Shaw, 79.44.7.

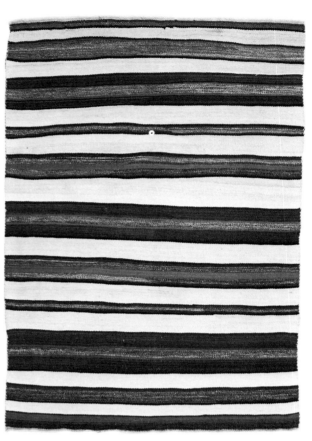

493 Rug, 1920-40, 196 cm x 110 cm. 5 warps, 22 wefts. All handspun wool with natural and aniline colors. Some brown is four-ply aniline dyed commercial yarn. Gift of Mr. and Mrs. Rufus Carter, 77.3.29.

494 Rug or blanket, 1920-40, 188 cm x 130 cm. 5 warps, 24 wefts. A Navajo interpretation of a Spanish American blanket style. All handspun wool with natural, carded and aniline colors. Gift of Mrs. O.D. Johnson, 76.59.2.

495 Rug, 1920-40, 117 cm x 109 cm. 6 warps, 22 wefts. All handspun wool with natural, carded and aniline colors. Gift of Mr. and Mrs. Julian Shapero, 78.36.3.

496 Rug, early 1930's, 143 cm x 91.2 cm. 6 warps, 24 wefts. Purchased in Cubero, New Mexico (near Laguna Pueblo) in 1937. All handspun wool, natural, carded and aniline colors. Gift of Edmund Shaw, 79.44.9.

497 Rug, possibly Tees Nos Pos, 1940-60, 140 cm x 103 cm. 9 warps, 22 wefts. All handspun wool with natural, carded and aniline colors. Gift of Joseph W. Phelps, 78.37.1.

498 Rug, 1880-1900, 179.6 cm x 128.7 cm. 14 warps, 26 wefts. It is very unusual to have a large rug done in the twill technique. The pattern is also very rare for a twill textile. All handspun wool with natural and aniline colors and a cotton string warp. Gift of Mrs. H.A. Batten, 79.45.5.

210

499 Blanket, 1880-90, 141.5 cm x 87 cm. Purchased from Carlsbad Caverns Supply Co. in 1946. Registered with Laboratory of Anthropology, Santa Fe, no. 626. Twill weave. All handspun wool with natural, vegetal (indigo) and aniline colors. Gift of Mr. and Mrs. Gilbert Maxwell, 63.34.183.

500 Saddle blanket, 1880-1900, 102 cm x 75.5 cm. purchased in 1946 from Carlsbad Caverns Supply Co. Registered with the Laboratory of Anthropology, Santa Fe, no. 645. Diagonal twill weave. All handspun wool with natural and aniline colors. Gift of Mr. and Mrs. Gilbert Maxwell, 63.34.181.

501 Saddle blanket, 1895-1910, 126 cm x 77 cm. Plain twill weave. All handspun wool with natural, carded, vegetal (indigo and yellow) and aniline colors. Gift of Mrs. Lawrence Milne, 63.33.5.

502 Saddle blanket, 1900-20, 131 cm x 85.5 cm. Twill weave. All handspun wool with natural, carded and aniline colors. Gift of Mrs. Lewis Kohlhaas, 74.37.2.

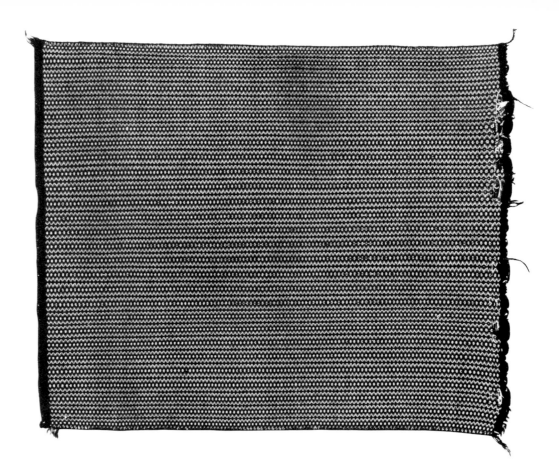

503 Saddle blanket, 1890-1910, 78 cm x 65.5 cm. 11 warps, 34 wefts. Twill, all commercial four-ply wool yarns with natural and aniline colors and a cotton string warp. Gift of Edwin L. Kennedy through the Maxwell Museum Association, 79.45.74.

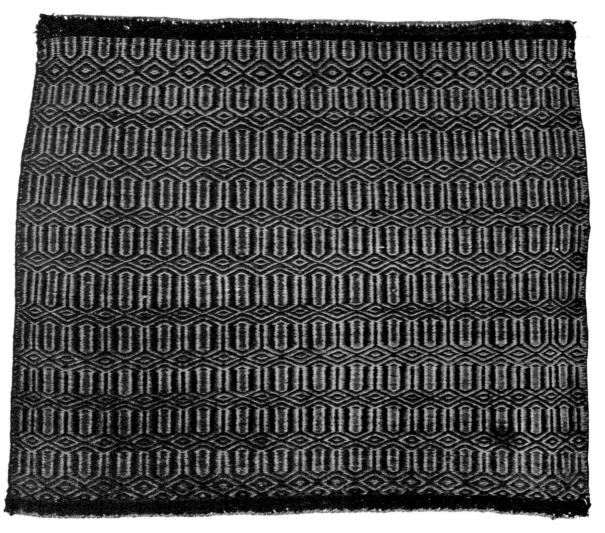

504 Saddle blanket, 1920-40, 76 cm x 79 cm. 4 warps, 14 wefts. Twill, all handspun wool with natural and aniline colors. Gift of Mrs. O.D. Johnson, 76.79.3.

Specialty Weaves

Two-faced textiles have a fairly complex pattern on one side and simple stripes on the reverse. The technique is accomplished by using four heddles attached to the warps. Two of the heddles are used to throw wefts to the front and two to the back (514, 515, 517, 518). Twills are also made by manipulating four heddles, using regularly alternating colors (black, white, gray, black, white, gray) to produce an all-over diamond pattern (331-333 and 498-510).

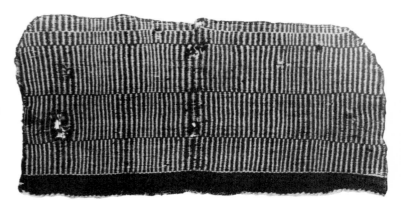

505 Saddle blanket fragment, 1880-1900, 42 cm x 85 cm. Plain twill weave. All handspun wool with natural and aniline colors. Gift of Mrs. Richard Wetherill, 55.20.43.

Twills

506 Rug, c. 1970, 139 cm x 96 cm. 4 warps, 20 wefts. Twill. All handspun with aniline and natural colors. Gift of Dale and Marilyn Warman, 79.69.9.

507 Saddle blanket, 1920-40, 131 cm x 90.8 cm. 7 warps, 28 wefts. All handspun wool with natural colors. Gift of Dr. David Gale, 82.60.4.

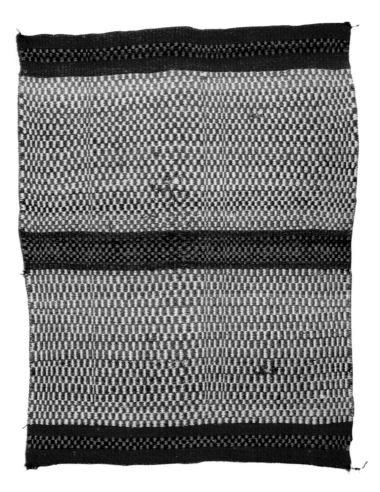

508 Saddle blanket, 1890-1900, 129 cm x 98.5 cm. 4 warps, 20 wefts. Handspun wool with natural and aniline colors. Gift of Hazel Beebe, 81.46.80.

509 Saddle blanket, 1890-1910, 141 cm x 90 cm. 12 warps, 20 wefts. Handspun wool in natural colors. Some four-ply aniline blue and green yarn. Cotton string warp. Gift of Edwin L. Kennedy through the Maxwell Museum Association, 79.45.76.

510 Saddle blanket, 1920-40, 122 cm x 73 cm. 6 warps, 16 wefts. All handspun wool with natural, carded and aniline colors. Gift of Mark Hooper, 80.5.1.

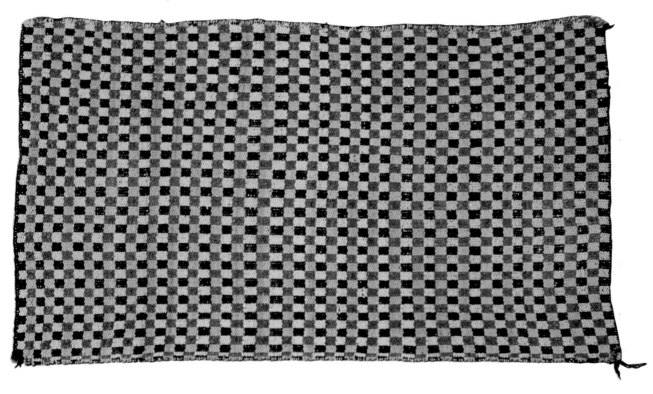

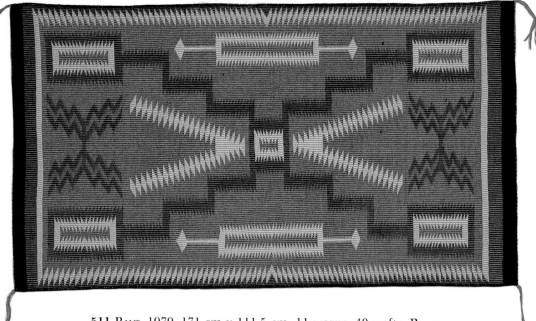

The raised-outline technique originated in the Coal Mine Mesa area. At first, the rugs were done by alternating two colors in the wefts—one color going from right to left and, instead of being carried back from left to right, the second color was used. This creates a shaded background. The style was further elaborated by producing raised outlines where two colors join simply by passing the wefts at the juncture over two warps instead of the usual one (511-513).

511 Rug, 1979, 171 cm x 111.5 cm. 11 warps, 40 wefts. Rose Keith, weaver. All commercial three-ply yarn in natural and aniline colors. Gift of Edwin D. Kennedy through the Maxwell Museum Association, 85.49.9.

512 Rug, possibly from Klagetoh, 1960-70, 147.5 cm x 78.5 cm. 8 warps, 20 wefts. Merlie Tsosie, weaver. All handspun wool with natural and aniline colors. Gift of Edwin L. Kennedy through the Maxwell Museum Association, 79.45.61.

513 Rug, 1960-70, 162.5 cm x 125.5 cm. 8 warps, 22 wefts. Lillie Littleleaf, weaver. Raised outline storm pattern. All handspun wool with natural and aniline colors. Gift of Edwin L. Kennedy through the Maxwell Museum Association, 79.45.65.

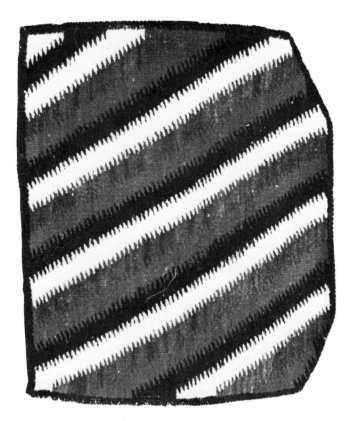

514 Saddle blanket, 1950-60, 70 cm x 88 cm. 5 warps, 18 wefts. Double weave and shaped. All handspun wool with natural and aniline colors. Gift of Mr. Tom Bahti, 61.1.10.

515 Rug, c. 1946, 147 cm x 105 cm. 6 warps, 28 wefts. Double weave. See Maxwell 1963:41, fig. 33. Handspun wool with natural, carded and aniline colors. Cotton string warp. Gift of Mr. and Mrs. Gilbert Maxwell, 63.34.152.

506 Rug, 1930-35, 77.5 cm x 58.5 cm. 7 warps, 26 wefts. Double weave with pictorial motif of cornstalks. All handspun wool with natural and aniline colors. Gift of L.G. Bell, 79.66.1.

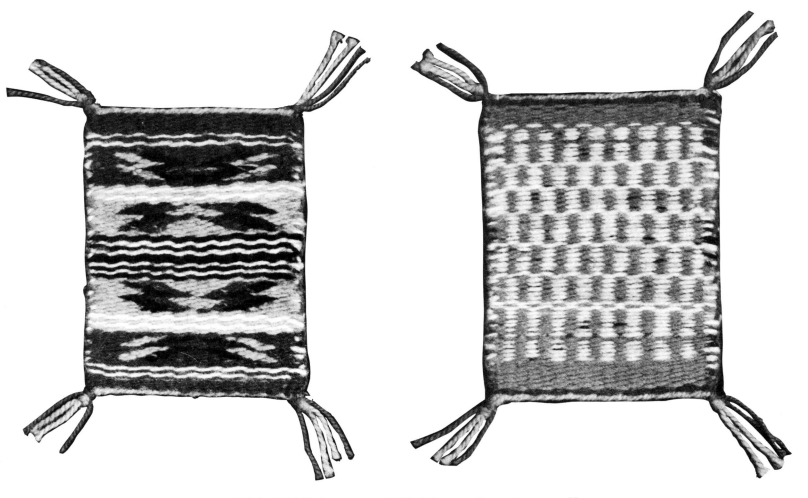

517 & 518 Miniature rug, 1978, 7.5 cm x 6 cm. 8 warps, 60 wefts. Louise Bia, weaver. Two-faced, handspun wool with natural and vegetal colors. Gift of Edwin Kennedy, Jr. through the Maxwell Museum Association, 85.49.8.

Shaggy tufted textiles are produced as saddle covers. Usually done in white, tufts of goat hair are wrapped around warps and held in by weft threads (**519**).

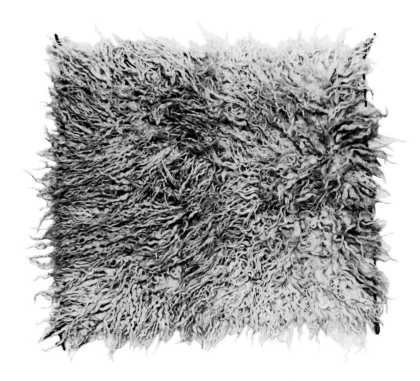

519 Rug, 1930's, 72.5 cm x 66 cm. 6 warps, 18 wefts. Tapestry weave with tufts of goat hair woven in about one inch apart. This type of textile is frequently placed in front of a loom and used by the weaver as a mat or cushion. Handspun wool in natural and aniline colors. Goat hair. Gift of Mr. Tom Bahti, 63.13.2.

217

Although pictorial elements were used in blankets as early as the 1860s, the earliest extant pictorial rugs date from the 1890s. Weavers often used representations as design patterns, altering the forms of natural objects or reversing the letters of a word to make them better suited to the composition of the rug.

520 Rug, 1910-40, 159 cm x 104.5 cm. 8 warps, 32 wefts. All handspun wool with natural, carded and aniline colors. Gift of Mr. George A. Johnston, 63.40.3.

521 Blanket, Lukachukai, 1948, 147 cm x 145.5 cm. 6 warps, 13 wefts. Mary Woodman, weaver. A copy of a Pendleton Mills machine-woven woman's shawl with a knotted maroon wool fringe on all four sides. There are no lazy lines in the piece to imitate the machine-made cloth. Handspun wool with natural and aniline colors. Four-ply natural white commercial yarn. Gift of Mr. and Mrs. Gilbert Maxwell, 63.34.115.

522 Kilt, c. 1950, 70 cm x 93 cm. 10 warps, 52 wefts. Made by a Navajo weaver as a copy of or substitute for a Pueblo embroidered kilt. Four-ply aniline dyed commercial yarn. Cotton string warp. Gift of Mr. and Mrs. Gilbert Maxwell, 67.126.3.

218

523 Rug, 1930's, 286 cm x 152 cm. 6 warps, 18 wefts. This pictorial rug apparently is part of the romanticising of Native Americans showing the stereotype of the Plains Indian with feather war bonnet which has come to represent all Indians. Notice the way in which the feet are shown, one pointing outwards and one in profile. All handspun wool natural, carded and aniline colors. Gift of Mr. and Mrs. Al Sullivan Jr., 76.48.1.

524 Rug, 1920-40, 125.5 cm x 92 cm. 10 warps, 24 wefts. All handspun wool with natural, carded and aniline colors. Purchased by Greater UNM Fund, 74.65.1.

526 Rug, 1950-60, 61 cm x 54.5 cm. 7 warps, 28 wefts. All handspun, aniline and vegetal colors. Gift of Mr. and Mrs. Bruce T. Ellis, 70.39.41.

525 Rug, 1930-35, 100 cm x 77.5 cm. 7 warps, 32 wefts. Religious pictorial using the drypainting symbol of the Sun, Moon or Wind. All handspun wool with natural and aniline colors. Gift of Mr. and Mrs. Rufus Carter, 77.3.28.

527 Rug, 1960's, 137 cm x 99 cm. 10 warps, 36 wefts. Atsuma Blackhorse, weaver. Copy of a Pablita Velarde painting. Four-ply natural and aniline dyed commercial yarn. Cotton string warp. Gift of Mr. and Mrs. Edwin L. Kennedy, 69.67.18.

220

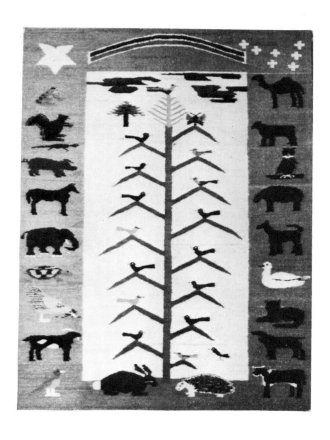

528 Rug, pictorial, Lukachukai, 1962, 170 cm x 124.5 cm. 7 warps, 30 wefts. Margaret Bochinclozy, weaver. See Maxwell 1963:40, fig. 32. All handspun wool natural, carded and aniline colors. Gift of Mr. and Mrs. Gilbert Maxwell, 63.34.172.

529 Rug, 1960-70, 121 cm x 110 cm. 8 warps, 28 wefts. Religious pictorial, a Thunderbird with zigzag arrows representing lightning radiating from his wings. Handspun with natural, carded and vegetal colors. Some gray two-ply yarn. Gift of Edwin L. Kennedy through the Maxwell Museum Association, 80.5.3.

221

Two Grey Hills: A Tradition of Perfection

The Traders

When George Bloomfield bought the trading post at Toadlena, New Mexico in 1911, he found like J.B. Moore at Crystal on the other side of the Chuska Mountains, the weaving quality very poor. In an effort to improve the textiles in his area, Bloomfield spent a great deal of time examining the rugs brought to his post, and took a personal interest in explaining to each weaver the defects in their work and how they might be corrected. With Ed Davies of the neighboring post of Two Grey Hills, (530) Bloomfield was instrumental in eliminating from local rugs their heavy, loose weave and the multiplicity of bright aniline colors.

Novices to the field of Navajo weaving are often under the mistaken impression that the term "Two Grey Hills" refers to the color and pattern of the rugs bearing that name. In fact, the "two gray hills" are actual landmarks near the trading post, but are not depicted in any of the rugs from this area (530).

The Two Grey Hills style is well known for it's simple, harmonious color combination—well carded grays, beiges and rich medium browns as well as black and white. When Bloomfield arrived, the story goes, the weavers in the area disliked red (McNitt 1962, 260). The warm beige which is today associated with Two Grey Hills weaving was found all over the reservation in the period between 1920 and 1940. The black alone is a commercial dye bought in packages at the post.

The style at Two Grey Hills owes much of its inspiration to the rugs of Crystal. J.B. Moore at Crystal issued mail-order catalogs in 1903 and 1911 so one can see that the range of patterns he was offering to his customers are similar to the later Two Grey Hills style. By around 1920, the basic elements of Two Grey Hills style rugs was firmly established. Reportedly Bloomfield and Davies also showed their weavers potsherds from the general area as an inspiration for their rugs (Southwest Saint 1983, 6). These sherds would have been Anasazi black on white types as are found at Chaco Canyon. Especially noticeable in both rugs and pottery is a multiple-outlined Z shape (see the border of **561**.)

530 The post at Two Grey Hills, 1982. Photo by Marian Rodee.

531 Rug, Two Grey Hills, perhaps Tohatchi, 1920-40, 198 cm x 154 cm. 9 warps, 40 wefts. All handspun with natural, carded and aniline colors. Gift of Harriet Carroll, 85.38.1.

532 Rug by Linda Lapahie.

533 Rug, Two Grey Hills, 1974, 91.5 cm x 63 cm. 15 warps, 100 wefts. Woven by Virginia Cohoe. All handspun wool with natural colors. Gift of Edwin L. Kennedy through the Maxwell Museum Association, 85.49.3.

223

From The Weaver's Point of View

Since most studies of the history of Navajo weaving are from the trader's and historian's viewpoint, I decided to ask the weavers their viewpoint. My conversations with the weavers in the vicinity of Two Grey Hills were concerned with when and from whom they learned to weave. There have been studies of family style within Pueblo pottery, but none for Navajo weaving. A study conducted at Hopi among potters showed that there was not so much a family style as a style held in common by men and women who learn the art from one another and work together (Stanislawski and Stanislawski, 1975). Since in traditional native American societies young artists are usually taught by older relatives this amounts to the same thing. Questions about when and from whom women learned to weave were easy for them to answer, although questions about family patterns were not.

Women weavers interviewed at the Two Grey Hills area have been in agreement that there were distinctive designs that only weavers in their family used, but they were rarely able to clearly point out or describe the designs. Their vagueness may have been caused by the complex and difficult nature of the questions they were asked to answer. Few artists in any society are able to discuss their sources and analyze compositional elements of their work and this problem was intensified with the weavers because many talked through an interpreter. Geertz recognized this problem when he wrote:

> It is the failure to realize this on the part of many students of non-Western art, and particulary of so-called "primitive art", that leads to the oft-heard comment that the peoples of such cultures don't talk, or not very much, about art—they just sculpt, sing, weave, or whatever, silent in their expertise. What is meant is that they don't talk about it the way the observer talks about it—or would like them to—in terms of its formal properties, its symbolic content, its affective values, or its stylistic features, except laconically, cryptically, and as though they had precious little hope of being understood.

But, of course, they do talk about it, as they talk about everything else striking, or suggestive, or moving, that passes through their lives—about what role it plays in this or that activity, what it may be exchanged for, what it is called, how it began, and so forth and so on. But this tends to be seen not as talk about art, but about something else—everyday life, myths, trade (Geertz 1983, 97).

The weavers tell stories of family pride and striving for technical excellence.

Aesthetics

While some writers have tried to relate current Navajo "aesthetics" primarily to a native world view, the results have been more romantic than realistic largely because Navajo weaving has been so heavily influenced by the taste of outsiders for so long. As has been presented in the foregoing chapters, in the past one hundred years, Navajo weaving has reflected a series of Anglo suggestions and economically enforced changes in materials and designs. In an attempt to save weaving and stimulate the economy on which it is based, traders all over the Reservation made suggestions to weavers to make a more saleable product. Consequently, the weaving of today looks very little like that of the mid-19th century. Even taking into consideration that much Navajo weaving of the 18th and 19th centuries was produced for people outside their own ethnic group—Spanish settlers, Anglo soldiers, Ute neighbors and even more distant Sioux and Crow Indians—"native style" is a question of degree. The very change and adaptability of the weaving style is part of the Navajo way, for they are always changing, albeit slowly, when they find new solutions that work better than the old. Because the processes of change have taken place slowly during the past century, many of today's Navajo are scarcely aware that their current rug designs are not completely traditional and of ancient origins.

Instead of probing the murky and elusive realm of Navajo weaving aesthetics, it might be more profitable to examine the views of the individual weavers and the problems of family style.

When a young woman learns to weave from an older female relative—generally her mother, grandmother or aunt—she begins by observing the elder for many hours. When she finally starts her own weaving, it is natural that she uses her teacher's patterns, for the teacher can show her how to plan the motifs and make the correct joins. As the young weaver progresses, she gradually will add more of her own design ideas. Unless all the rugs of a family can be preserved, either by owning them all or through photography, it is impossible to document a family's style. This kind of documentation is missing in Navajo weaving.

The Weavers

Lynette Nez (**534**) first learned weaving from her mother at about age 16 or 17 (c. 1950s). After her mother died, she continued to learn from her aunt Fannie Hoskay (**535**). Lynette's grandmother, Mrs. Policeboy (**536**), was also a good weaver and may be the same as the "Policegirl" mentioned as working with the trader Bloomfield in the early development of weaving in the region (McNitt 1962, 260). Lynette's own daughter, Dorothy, is learning to weave from her mother, but she is starting with thicker wool (more coarsely spun yarn). When we compare the photographs of weavings made by Mrs. Policeboy, Fannie Hoskay, and Lynette Nez, the time-spread is so great (from the 1930's until the present) that there is little similarity in the rugs, although for a time each reflected the style of her respective instructor (**534-536**). Thus, when questioned about it, women respond "yes, there is a family style", for they all learned the patterns and weaving techniques from within the family, although each eventually evolves according to her particular talents. With Lynette Nez, the only definable family style may be a tendency to use light colors.

As each weaver adds her own elements, the regional styles evolve slowly over time. For example, Two Grey Hills weaving of the 1920's through 50's is quite different from that of the 1960's to the present. The early traders there urged weavers to use patterns derived from local potsherds and the Crystal rug style influenced the Two Grey Hills style. The former standard size of 4' by 6' for rugs was influenced from Crystal. Both old and new rugs from Two Grey Hills are identifiable by certain common characteristics: including natural wool colors of black, white, grays and browns, a plain black outer border, multiple inner borders, a central medallion or double medallion with many hook motifs, and small filler elements. In examining these rugs, one notices a simplification of the patterns over the last generation. While contemporary rugs are elaborate, they do not have the many small fillers of the older examples. Also today the 4' x 6' rugs which were commonly produced fifty years ago are rarely seen today let alone the really large pieces of the past. Economics have caused most rugs now to be smaller; pieces measuring 1' x 2' are common. Earlier generations of traders supported weavers and their families with credit at their posts until a rug was completed. Now, due to government regulations, the trader's business is only conducted in cash. Therefore weavers make smaller pieces which they can finish in a few weeks and get paid for. At Two Grey Hills, the weavers have a reputation for producing complex, perfect pieces, often of miniature size and with the highest thread count per inch on the Reservation. Coarse rugs from this area are almost unknown. The exquisite, tiny, fine pieces have been highly publicized during the last forty years as "the most expensive Indian rugs".

More care goes into the preparation of materials at Two Grey Hills than at any other area except the vegetal-dye areas. Sorting and carding raw wool called "wool top" is important because one of the characteristics of this style is the use of natural sheep colors. Weavers here have preserved in their herds sheep in a wider range of colors than found elsewhere on the reservation. A weaver sorts through the wool and matches the colors carefully, for wool from one sheep will vary in color and quality from that of others of the "same" color in the flock. Likewise, the body area from which the wool is taken makes a difference in wool quality. Wool from the back of sheep is faded and sun damaged, while that from the shoulders and flanks is the best. Wool from the underbelly is short, coarse and generally very dirty. The job of carding two wool colors together to make a third is surprisingly difficult. Only a small amount of wool can be carded at one time, and it takes a practiced eye to card enough black and white, ounce by ounce, to produce enough gray for an entire rug. Absolute evenness of color throughout the rug is one sign of good quality. White wool, which is almost never a true white, is soaked with powdered gypsum to make it bright. Black can be natural (a black lamb is darkest during its first year and gets lighter over time) or, more commonly, can be "top dyed" over a dark

534 Lynette Nez.

535 Fannie Hoskay.

536 Mrs. Policeboy.

wool. Commercial dye can be bought in packages at the trading posts and is the only synthetic material used in these rugs.

The tendency to perfection in recent decades has resulted in pieces which are considered precious objects of art rather than functional rugs. A rug's fineness is measured by the number of warps and wefts per inch. Counts of over 80 wefts per inch are generally called "tapestries". The term "tapestry" refers not to its weaving technique, since even the coarsest rug or saddle blanket is done in the tapestry technique, but to the function of being hung on the wall—like old European tapestries. The smallest and finest, "tapestries" with 125 weft threads to the inch, are sometimes framed under glass. There are only a few weavers of tapestries in the Two Grey Hills area, although the proportion of these weavers to the total weaving population is probably greater there than elsewhere. All the women mentioned in this essay are tapestry weavers.

Daisy Lapahie and her daughter Linda have a style that is more similar, as seen in pictures taken the same year. The similarity is a tendency for simplicity within the generally large and complex Two Grey Hills style. The designs are spread out in Linda's rug with a lot of background color, but in Daisy's rug the ground shows primarily around the edges of the central medallion. They each have done less terracing (the breaking up of an outline with small blocks or steps) than most other weavers.

537 Daisy Lapahie at trading post.

538 Linda Lapahie at trading post.

Daisy Lapahie (537) is a weaver whose mother died and who then learned from another maternal relative, in this case her grandmother, who whipped her to make her learn. Daisy forced three of her daughters to learn weaving so they would always have extra money. One, Linda, wanted some income while she attended Navajo Community college and Daisy said "Learn to weave". She did and became a highly skilled weaver like her mother and soon earned enough to buy her own Mazda. (532 and 538) Daisy said she had ten children and her husband did not make much money and what she made on her weaving made a big difference to the family. Now that her children are grown up she can afford more luxuries with her weaving money, like a second house in Shiprock, electricity and cars.

Clara Sherman and her son James (539 and 567) share a similar style. Their earlier rugs are bold and simple, but in the last few years, probably influenced by Rose Lee's success, they have changed to a more elaborate style with a double central medallion and more terracing than in their older pieces (541). James uses more terracing (542 and 543) than his mother and both emphasize white backgrounds more than other Two Grey Hills weavers. Also, their borders are wider in proportion to the centers.

Clara Sherman, a tribal employee, had two girls but neither wanted to learn to weave. (539). However, she taught her stepson, James. James has daughters but he did not teach them. He is very shy about his weaving and did not want to talk or be photographed. Clara's husband had gone with their sheep up into the Chuska Mountains for the summer. She and the family will go up to visit them from time to time. The Navajo Nation has passed rules to protect the land from overgrazing. Sheep, no matter how small the size of the herd, must be pastured in the mountains in the summer. Taking down a loom and moving it can cause the edge to become uneven when the tension is released and then applied again. Summer rainstorms can also affect the evenness of edges, with the extra humidity causing the wool to expand and then contract.

Clara learned to weave from her older sister, Frannie Charles, first by carding her wool and then undoing part of her rug and putting it back in. When another sister, Yazzie Blackhorse, went to the mountains with her flock leaving a rug on her loom less than half completed, Clara worked out the remainder of the pattern from her own mind and then reversed it for the other half. Clara's mother encouraged her to do this work since otherwise the rug would get dirty or damaged. Her sister was surprised and let her keep the money for it, about $35. Clara was thirteen then and did not do a rug of her own until she was fifteen. When Clara put her warp up on the loom it was taller than the hogan. The family all laughed at her mistake, but she went ahead and wove the rug although it was larger than she had planned, especially for a first effort.

After her mother died, Clara inherited 26 sheep and now she has 300, of which 56 are the desirable brown variety which she sells to Navajos in other areas of the Reservation.

539 Clara Sherman at trading post. 1982.

540 Clara Sherman in Albuquerque at loom, 1986.

541 Rug by Clara Sherman, 1986.

543 Rug by James Sherman, 1986.

542 Rug by James Sherman, 1986.

228

Rose Lee has commented that she draws her designs out on graph paper, and this gives her rugs a complicated terracing appearance (3). The rug she designed for her mother, Ruth Teller, is smaller and has fewer terraced elements because she took into account her mother's eye troubles. (Terracing is more difficult and time-consuming to weave than a plain line.) Rose prefers a double central medallion, often with a cross motif in the center.

Rose Lee (544) came into the post with her mother Ruth Teller (545) who was one of the finest weavers in the region but no longer produces much. Rose learned from her mother before she even went to school, but only started to perfect her art in 1972.

The photograph of the two women shows a small rug, not very far along, which was commissioned. Rose hopes to have it done in time to enter it in the Gallup Ceremonial and the money it brings she plans to give to her husband and son. Rose wants to do things that will enable her to get more money for her rugs, such as being pictured in a book or winning prize ribbons. She won a grand prize ribbon at the New Mexico State Fair, but it had been placed on another rug. She tried to get the judge to rectify the mistake—she did not want the prize money—just the ribbon to add to her collection. Rose is very creative and says she sees patterns everywhere she goes—on napkins in restaurants and on billboards. She goes home and plots them on graph paper, or rather one fourth of the rug which is then reversed and doubled. Ruth Teller likes Rose's patterns better than her own so she sketches new ideas for her mother (547). This was the only instance where a woman told me she worked a pattern out on paper. Because she *is* inventive, other women in the area are liable to steal her designs and she brought her loom into the post all wrapped up.

Although Rose likes talking about her work there are many secrets connected with weaving she will not reveal. She uses metal highway markers as shed rods as they are small and smooth and well adapted to her work which is very fine. In the past she had problems keeping the edges of her rugs straight, but no longer. I said some Anglo weavers used wires along the edges of their rugs and Rose seemed interested, but her mother thought the wires would cut the wool when pulled out.

When I remarked that some people said Navajo weaving was a dying art, Rose laughed and said to give her a little girl and it would not die. She had two boys and tried to adopt a little girl but failed. Subsequently, Rose gave birth to a girl and in another eight or ten years there should be another generation at work.

Rose is well rewarded for her work and was living in a mobile home she had received in payment for a rug. Yet she was also the only weaver who expressed a real fondness for the process of weaving saying that the loom is like a friend and she only feels comfortable with something on the loom. Each rug is a little different and, she hopes, better than the one before (3).

544 Rose Lee.

545 Ruth Teller.

546 Rug by Eva Gould.

547 Larger rug by Rose Lee, smaller one by Ruth Teller.

It is fortunate and rare to find a family with photographs of themselves and their work spanning over 25 years. The earliest photograph (549) from about 1952 shows Katherine Nathaniel as a young woman with a very large rug of the typical early 20th century Two Grey Hills pattern. It is large and complex with many filler elements. Motifs from this rug were used over and over again in the style that Katherine developed from the 1960s to the present. The triangular elements with bars or dashes used as fillers in the corners of the old rug are frequently seen in the corners of new, smaller rugs. Most of Katherine's pieces of the last ten years have become standardized with a plain double stripe border, background colors predominately gray or beige, and one large central medallion with rounded corners rather than the more typical angular ones. Yet each rug, though similar to unpracticed eyes, has major differences and no two are ever the same. Motifs are elaborated or simplified, filler elements added or subtracted. The artists in this region are working with a very limited palette, yet the appearance can be altered by re-combining colors in different areas.

Katherine Nathaniel learned weaving around age 9, but her mother Eva Gould, would not teach her, therefore she learned on her own. She also received some help from her father's sister, Clara Gould Sherman. Katherine did not like her mother's rugs so she made up her own patterns. Actually Eva Gould's rugs are very coarse both in technique and pattern (546) and, according to the trader, they were never any better. I specifically asked about this since most traders will continue to buy rugs, even though they are not of top quality, from older weavers who were once excellent in remembrance of their past greatness and because

548 Katherine Nathaniel at trading post December 1973.

549 Katherine Nathaniel early 1950's.

they are also dealing with the daughters who are currently top weavers. Katherine's skill and energy in becoming one of the finest weavers in the Two Grey Hills region is outstanding. Katherine taught her daughter Alfreda and they each had a rug on the loom when I visited. The family had been documenting Alfreda's weaving progress from a girl of eight or nine to her present age (about 20) which they keep in a family album (**548-555, 557**).

Katherine was complaining about her eyes. The room where she and Alfreda were weaving had no electricity and the women were working by Coleman lanterns. The light is a little dim for such detailed work, but Katherine thought the bright white light with which she used to work had done its damage. (Eye problems are a common complaint with mature weavers and many women must give up weaving or at least really fine work in their sixties.) Katherine also had a photo of her "wool top" (just sheared and sorted wool ready for bagging) and of her favorite sheep which shows the range of natural brown wools for which the rugs of Two Grey Hills are famous.

550 Katherine Nathaniel at home, late 1970's.

552 Katherine Nathaniel at home, 1980.

551 Katherine Nathaniel at trading post, April 1978.

553 Katherine Nathaniel's rug, 1982.

When Alfreda, Katherine's daughter, began weaving at age 8 or 10 (554, 555, 557) it was natural that she used some of her mother's patterns. It is difficult to tell much from the earliest photo of Alfreda at the loom with a rug one-third finished (554). However, the small piece Alfreda holds in 555 has a central motif like the one in her mother's early rug, and the border in 555 is identical to that of the old one. Alfreda was clearly trying out new designs along with combinations of earlier ones. Recently, Katherine's son Mark, who is in his mid-20's, started to weave and 556 is one of his first rugs. The style shows none of his mother's influence; the pattern seems crowded at the ends and bare at the center. However, the technique of both Mark and Alfreda is excellent. Children of good tapestry weavers seldom produce mediocre pieces. Not only do they have excellent teachers, but they know that really fine quality weaving is well rewarded financially while mediocre weaving will not easily find a market anywhere.

554 Alfreda Nathaniel at loom, 1974.

555 Alfreda Nathaniel, 1978.

556 Mark Nathaniel's rug, 1986.

557 Alfreda Nathaniel, March 1980.

233

558 Cora Curley.

When visited, Cora Curley (**558**) and her daughter Edith Yazzie (**559**) were at home, both working at their looms which are next to each other in the house. It is easy to see how women following the traditional Navajo residence pattern or "outfit" share the same weaving style. Traditionally an older woman, the head of the family, lives together with her husband and children. As they marry the sons leave and the daughters stay with their husbands joining the household. As the daughters begin having children in their turn, they occupy houses near their mother. The women learn techniques from one another, young girls learning from older women in the outfit. Cora and Edith's rugs were only partly done but they showed me photos of recently completed pieces. I remarked that they were just like one in the Maxwell Museum (**570**) and Cora was offended. Each rug is different in color and pattern she declared. The differences are subtle ones, however, with minor changes in the placement of small design elements and of course the color range is from shades of gray to brown.

560 Rug, Two Grey Hills, 1927-28, 213.5 cm x 139 cm. 9 warps, 26 wefts. Won first prize at the Shiprock Fair in 1928. All handspun wool with natural, carded and aniline colors. Gift of Mr. and Mrs. Frederick Johnson, 76.5.1.

559 Edith Yazzie.

234

561 Rug, Two Grey Hills, 1945, 190 cm x 153.5 cm. 12 warps, 64 wefts. See Maxwell 1963:26, fig. 12. Bessie Many Goats, weaver. All handspun wool with natural, carded and aniline colors. Gift of Mr. and Mrs. Gilbert Maxwell, 73.8.1.

562 Rug, Two Grey Hills, 1960-65, 157 cm x 84.5 cm. 12 warps, 38 wefts. All handspun wool with natural, carded and aniline (black) colors. Purchase 70.24.1.

563 Rug, Two Grey Hills, 1925-26, 183 cm x 120 cm. 8 warps, 36 wefts. Purchased in 1927 from George Bloomfield of Toadlena, New Mexico. Rug won first prize at the Gallup Ceremonial in 1926. All handspun wool with natural, carded and aniline (black and red) colors. Gift of Mr. Julian Shapero, 76.6.1.

564 Rug, Two Grey Hills, 1920-40, 214 cm x 127 cm. 9 warps, 14 wefts. Very unusual turquoise dye along with the natural wool colors. All handspun wool with natural and aniline colors. Gift of Dr. David Gale, 82.60.1.

565 Rug, Two Grey Hills, 1920-40, 230 cm x 151 cm. 11 warps, 40 wefts. All handspun wool with natural and carded colors. Gift of Fred M. Garret, 76.49.1.

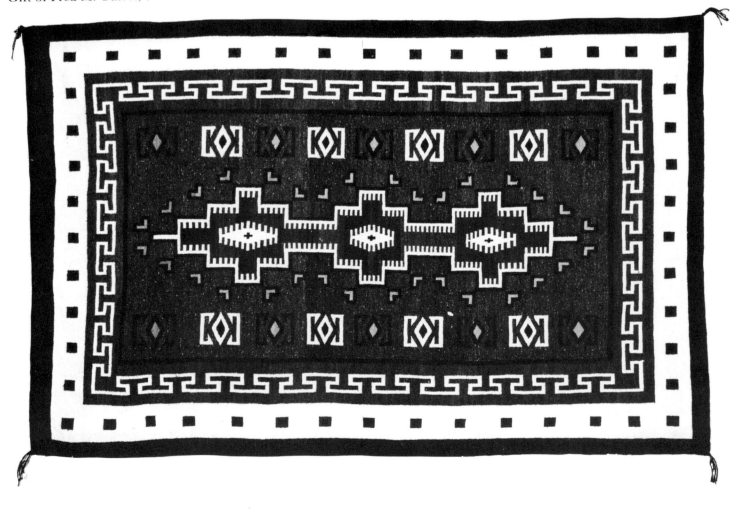

566 Rug, Two Grey Hills (Toadlena), 1961-62, 129 cm x 89.5 cm. 15 warps, 96 wefts. Rose Mike, weaver. Won first prize at Gallup Ceremonial in 1962. All handspun with natural, carded and aniline (black) colors. Gift of Mr. and Mrs. Gilbert Maxwell, 63.34.72.

567 Rug, Two Grey Hills, 1960's, 115 cm x 76 cm. 13 warps, 38 wefts. James Sherman, weaver. All handspun wool with natural, carded and aniline (black) colors. Gift of Mr. and Mrs. Edwin L. Kennedy, 69.67.38.

Photography was not done by the Navajo in the earlier part of the 20th century but photos were taken by the many visiting professional photographers who traveled through the West and by the Anglos who settled on or near the Reservation. When the Polaroid camera was introduced, by the 1960's, the hobby of family photography came to this segment of the American population. The Navajo especially liked the Polaroid, for although the film is expensive, they did not have to send a finished roll of film a long distance to be developed. The results are instant and easy.

The evolution of the weaving style in the Two Grey Hills area has been the result of interaction among various groups—the trader with the customer, the trader with the weaver, and generations of weavers with one another. Older women pass on their traditions, younger women take the family traditions and add something of their own and slowly over the years this complex interaction produces visual changes.

568 Polaroid of Martha Duboise and her rug and the post tag. Photo by Bill Malone, reproduced by Anthony Richardson.

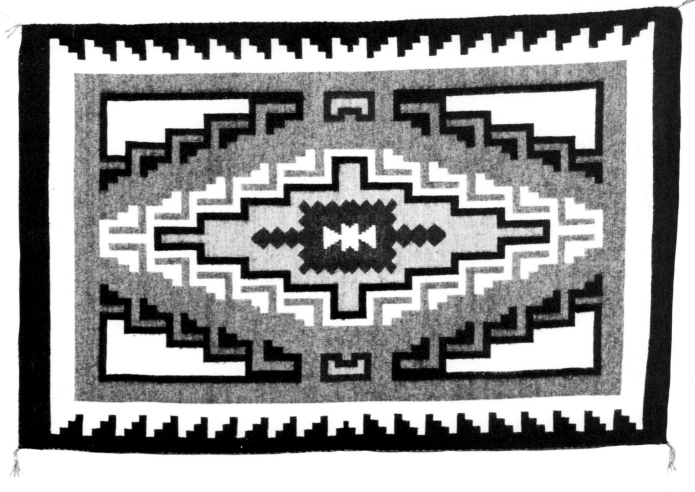

569 Rug, Two Grey Hills, 1960-70, 123.5 cm x 88 cm. 15 warps, 60 wefts. Woven by Bessie Deal. All handspun wool with natural and aniline colors. Gift of Edwin D. Kennedy through the Maxwell Museum Association, 85.49.2.

570 Rug, Two Grey Hills, 1960's, 185.5 cm x 119.5 cm. 14 warps, 70 wefts. Cora Curley, weaver. All handspun wool with natural, carded and aniline (black) colors. Gift of Mr. and Mrs. Edwin L. Kennedy, 69.67.17.

571 Miniature rug, Two Grey Hills style, 1977, 14.5 cm x 11 cm. 16 warps, 70 wefts. Alberta Thomas of Red Rock, weaver. All handspun wool with natural colors. Gift of Edwin Kennedy Jr., through the Maxwell Museum Association, 85.49.6.

CURRENT WEAVING CONDITIONS

The major rug styles of the 20th century, Ganado, Two Grey Hills and Vegetal Revival, were all developed by traders working together with the weavers in their areas to develop a new trade item to support the Navajo economy and Navajo weaving tradition. Until 1900, the old trade network was used by most weavers to dispose of their textiles (Bailey and Bailey 1986, 60). In the early 20th century, the posts became the major outlets for rugs, and now the situation has changed again for a number of reasons.

Since the mid-twentieth century, weavers as a group have tended to be the least-educated of Navajo women. With better education available since the end of World War II, and with more job opportunities on the reservation as a result of the energy boom of the 1960's, more women have gone out of the house to work. Only among the older and middle-aged women who have little education and a limited knowledge of English is weaving still an important activity. When I asked a well-known weaver why her own daughter did not weave she replied "Oh she's a nurse's aide". In other words, weaving is thought of as a last resort when money is needed. Several weavers who received large amounts of money from a legal settlement stopped weaving until the money was spent. Hand weaving is a very time consuming activity and not really economically profitable in a developed society. Many non-Indian handweavers have noted the same problem, that is, they cannot really charge a price for their creations that is commensurate with the time spent. Consequently, during periods of economic recession, the number of rugs woven increases; and in periods of high employment and royalties from the energy industry, the quantity of rugs woven decreases.

The impracticality is a result of the Navajo's resistance to change the type of loom they use. Weaving is still done on a primitive vertical loom with each textile warped separately and mounted from the crossbars of the frame. Although more finished wood is commonly used today instead of the rough tree branches of the past, the form of the loom is unchanged. Attempts at time-saving are done with materials and dyes, not technique.

The present economic basis for Navajo weaving indicates that the way in which women learn to weave is also changing. Very few girls any longer learn to weave from their mother or aunt at the age seven to ten. Now, at the age of sixteen to twenty-eight they learn to weave when, as young adults, they develop tastes for expensive items like cars, or wish to supplement their husbands' incomes. Still, in more remote and less developed areas of the Reservation, girls learn at a younger age; but in more prosperous regions teenagers and women in their twenties learn when they begin to have children and want extra money without leaving home. The women who take up weaving later are usually the daughters of the best weavers and have the example of the financial success of their mothers as models. Although mediocre weavers are poorly paid for their work, those who take the time and energy to become excellent weavers are well rewarded. A finely-woven handspun rug of elaborate design can sell for as much as $20,000, although the weaver herself may only receive one-third of the final selling price. One weaver even traded a rug for a house trailer. Perhaps a weaver can do two or three such textiles in a year, and, like two-income families everywhere this extra money often determines whether a family lives well or just gets by. It is also the custom in those traditional extended families to share the wealth with all the members. Such families often live together in a compound of loosely grouped houses and livestock corrals and clan relatives, no matter where they reside, can make a claim on a prosperous weaver.

Three generations of the Yazzie family illustrate many of these economic trends. The women spend most of the year in the valley around the post of Red Rock, Arizona which is not far from the agency town of Shiprock, New Mexico. They get their yarns from the post which is run by Troy and Edith Kennedy. In the summer, the women take their flocks to sheep camps in the Lukachukai Mountains above Red Rock. They have very few sheep, but the tribal government has made a legal requirement of the former custom of pasturing of flocks in the lowlands in the winter and in the mountains during the summer. Grace Joe, who is probably in her late seventies, spends most of her summers at the camp (572). Her daughter, Betty Joe Yazzie, goes back and forth daily to her home in the valley (573). Grace speaks only Navajo and her daughter is bilingual with a heavy accent and acts as interpreter for her mother. Both women learned weaving as children. The third generation is represented by Bessie Yazzie who speaks English easily with only a slight accent (574). She began weaving in 1982 at the age of twenty-seven. She has small children and, needing a source of extra income, followed the examples of her mother and grandmother by becoming an excellent weaver. She is the only one of six daughters who does not have regular employment. Her first small rug sold for $100, the second (the same size) $300 and the third, when complete, will fetch close to $1,000.

The Yazzie women also illustrate another trend in weaving: the breakdown of regional styles. Originally, the post was the center of a circle attracting people in the immediate vicinity to do business. The traders then had a very real influence on their customers and often were the only representatives of the Anglo-American world with which these Navajo dealt. However, more schools roads, electricity and that demon, television,

572 Grace Joe at the loom at her summer sheep camp in the Lukachukai Mountains, 1982. Photo by Marian Rodee.

573 Betty Joe Yazzie at her loom in her camp in the Lukachukai Mountains, 1982. Photo by Marian Rodee.

574 Bessie Yazzie in the post at Red Rock. 1982. Photo by Marian Rodee.

575 Betty Joe Yazzie's "red rug". 1982. Photo by Marian Rodee.

meant greater sophistication on the part of weavers. They could travel easily to other posts and buy books illustrating weavings. Soon, women were weaving styles from other areas quite commonly, so that nowadays unless one knows that a weaver lives in a certain area, a textile is best described as Ganado or Two Grey Hills "styles". Grace Joe works in the ceremonial pattern tradition of Red Rock (395), but the piece on her loom in the photo is a classic Two Grey Hills style. Betty Joe Yazzie has a Two Grey Hills rug on her loom at her sheep camp, but had a "red rug" or Ganado on a loom at her winter home in the valley (575). Generally, weavers who work in a style from another region execute simpler patterns, perhaps because they do not have an older relative to teach them the technical intricacies of the style.

Some dealers maintain that Navajo weaving is a dying art. With increasing economic prosperity, few average weavers will produce ordinary rugs, but there will continue to be incentives for the really excellent artists to sell fine pieces, now often made as wall hangings, that will greatly augment their families' income. There is also a spiritual importance to Navajo weaving. Most women felt, at least on a sub-conscious level, that weaving is an important part of being an Navajo woman. Most women have tried weaving at least once, sometimes within the family, other times at a formal class sponsored by the tribe or by watching a demonstration weaver at one of the tourist centers. They usually try it only once because it is too difficult or their regular job is easier. Traditional religion and custom empahsize the role of woman as weaver, and with more pressure for them to join the American melting pot, weaving is increasingly a respected symbol of Navajo womanhood but a less practiced art.

Current trends in rug weaving

The tendency has been toward increasingly finer weaving with perfectly straight edges and balanced patterns that are seldom more than a weft pick or two off balance. That is, many Navajo rugs have a large central motif with identical designs in each of the four corners. When such a rug is folded in half in either direction the pattern remains the same. In a fine quality rug, color must be evenly matched throughout the rug. This requires dyeing or carding the wool carefully and all at one time to insure a perfect color match.

In the Pueblos, there has been an increasing tendency among potters to sign their pottery during the 20th century. This phenomenon was reportedly begun by the now famous potter Maria Martinez and her husband in 1919 at the suggestion of Kenneth Chapman, an early student of Pueblo pottery. Gradually, other potters signed their work and changed an anonymous craft made for their own household use, as souvenirs, or curios into "Works of Art" created for aesthetic reasons. The recent emphasis on famous artists has produced a blend of tradition and individual creativity. In weaving, however, the Navajo have been reluctant to sign their pieces. (It is much easier to write one's name with a polishing stone on the bottom of an unfired pot). The tags commonly attached to rugs today give not only the price, but also the weaver's name and area of the Reservation. These tags have been the only way of identifying the weavers. In the last ten years, Polaroid pictures have been attached to the tag showing the weaver with the rug at the moment she has sold it (560). A few weavers, such as the Johns family of Monument Valley, are weaving their initials into their rugs. Others have embroidered their initials in after the rug was completed. Bill Malone, the trader at the Hubbell Trading Post at Ganado, Arizona, has requested the salaried weavers, working there at the National Park Service Visitors Center, to weave their initials, date and the post initials into their rugs. Although the names and styles of a handful of master weavers are known to a small number of dealers and collectors, the weavers will not receive the greater monetary rewards given to "artists" over "craftsmen" in our society until weavers receive the same prominence as Pueblo potters.

576 Herman Coffey and assistants at the Crownpoint Auction, 1985. Photo by Anthony Richardson.

NEW APPROACHES TO MARKETING NAVAJO
WEAVING: CROWNPOINT AND RAMAH

Crown Point

Initiated in 1968, the auction at Crownpoint, N.M. is the oldest and most successful Navajo—run auction of native weaving. (Crownpoint is the capital of the Eastern Navajo Agency and on the road to Chaco Canyon National Monument about 150 miles northwest of Albuquerque.) Lavonne Palmer, a local trader with too many rugs in stock that year, suggested an auction and Kent Fitzgerald, Superintendent of the Eastern Navajo Agency, supported the project. Weavers were informed of the upcoming auction through the local chapter house and, with the rugs donated by Mrs. Palmer and those brought in by local women, between forty and fifty pieces were sold that first night, largely to people in the Crownpoint community. Initially, the weavers paid annual dues and were issued cards, but now the process has become simpler. Any Navajo weaver may bring her rugs to the auction where the rugs are tagged. Half the tag stays with the weaver and the other half is pinned to the rug. On the night of the auction, the weaver presents her tag and receives either money (checks) or the unsold rug. All accounts are settled the night of the auction. The buyers pay by check or cash at one table and the weavers receive their checks or rugs at another. No traders or dealers may use the auction to dispose of their surplus inventory. To cover expenses, ten percent of the selling price goes to the Association. Ena Chavez, who now organizes the auction, and Herman Coffey, the auctioneer, are both paid for their time and the volunteers who assist them are given small amounts to cover their gasoline and baby sitting expenses. The auctions are held at 7 p.m. every sixth Friday in the Crownpoint High School gym. The evening has become a social occasion, with a chili dinner served in the cafeteria and craftsmen selling other items at scattered tables. Today between two and three hundred weavers bring rugs ahead of time for each auction. The audience averages about 250 people including around 150 bidders for the 280 to 350 available pieces. The auctions have been successful for all and are now held throughout the year drawing weavers from all over the Reservation (**576**). The hottest bidding centers around the rugs under $300 and especially those under $100. Many big, expensive rugs are withdrawn for want of a single bidder; anyone in the market for a larger piece can often find one here at about a fourth of the retail price.

Ena Chavez tries to maintain the quality of the textiles by excluding rugs with cotton warps and, of course, Mexican copies. She makes suggestions to the weavers for future inprovements and what the minimum or starting price should be. If a weaver does not take her advice, Ena will still accept the rug, albeit reluctantly. One of her regular suggestions is that the weavers spin and dye their own yarns to save money. The skeins of prepared yarns, sold by the tribe as Shiprock Wool, sell for about $2.50 each. Shiprock Wool starts as raw Navajo wool which is sent to a factory where it is cleaned, spun and dyed in popular "Navajo" colors. The spinning machines are programmed to put small irregularities or "bumps" into the yarn so that when the yarn is woven it is very difficult to distinguish the finished weaving from a handspun piece. Yet, the commercial yarn rugs still have a certain perfect regularity of color and surface and a slightly limp feeling which is not characteristic of handspun rugs. The time saved by using prepared yarns offsets the higher cost. The Museum of Northern Arizona commissioned a rug in 1980 (Gallagher 1981, 22-27) and of the five hundred and sixty hours spent in making the rug, four hundred and two were required for yarn preparation. So much time is saved with little change in the visual effect that about eighty per cent of all rugs today are made with some sort of commercial yarn.

The variety of patterns, sizes and quality of rugs are a matter of chance at any of the auctions. Weavers with famous names generally do not enter their rug since they are assured of good prices for their weaving from traders and gallery owners with whom they deal. The quality of weavings at the Crownpoint auctions is generally quite good, however. Keith Guard, a dealer in Navajo textiles in Las Cruces, periodically visits the auction to replenish his inventory. Guard had entered some of the rugs purchased at Crownpoint into the Gallup Ceremonial and has won a number of blue ribbons (Guard 1985, personal communication). He comments:

> At the auction, we can buy what we call "honest rugs"; not always prize winners or collector's items, but rugs made in the old way, rugs in which the weaver raised the sheep, sheared, cleaned, carded, and spun the wool before weaving the rug. This class of rugs is fast disappearing from the commercial market.

Other dealers within the region also buy much of their stock at the auction, citing that weavers get more money for their rugs through the auction than through the old trading post system. Other buyers are area people, employees of the government agencies serving the Navajo, residents of Gallup and Grants, the two nearest Anglo commuities, and people from Albuquerque and Santa Fe. Tourists, carrying yellowing articles about the auction clipped from their hometown newspapers, frequently plan their trips in order to attend. Its proximity to the Albuquerque—Santa Fe metropolitan area contributes to the auction's success. Bringing the rugs to a larger population center such as Los Angeles or New York City would only add to the expenses and complexity of the auction process. Besides there is a mystique for Anglo buyers who travel to "Indian country" to buy almost directly from the weavers with the standards of quality and genuineness guaranteed by an auction on federal lands.

The Crownpoint auction is successful from both the weavers' and the buyers' point of view, and yet this form of merchandizing has not replaced the traditional wholesale/trader market. Mrs. Chavez has reported other auctions from time to time on the Reservation, and the tribal government has contacted her about starting one on a regular basis elsewhere.

Ramah

In November 1984, the weavers at the Ramah Navajo Reservation in Pine Hill, N.M. formed a cooperative association to find ways of improving the quality of their weaving and to obtain better prices for it. They wanted to find a market niche—something that was uniquely "Ramah". Led by Ramah Navajo School Board Community Planner Yin May Lee and Berniece Cojo of the Ramah community, they invited outside specialists to visit. Maria Varela—one of the founders of the Spanish American wool corporation Tierra Wools in Tierra Amarilla, N.M.—spent a day at Pine Hill. She told the weavers of her experiences in setting up the Tierra Wools corporation and advised them to develop an organization, insure the quality of the products and stabilize production. This last goal would be a difficult one to achieve within a traditional Navajo community where each woman's first responsibilities are as wife and mother. The quantity of weavings she can produce depend on her family responsibilities and seasonal activities.

Another part of this program included the weavers visiting the Maxwell Museum of Anthropology at the University of New Mexico in Albuquerque where they were shown examples of textiles in the extensive collection, both old and new. The weavers examined the collection carefully, even using a magnifying lamp to see details. The weavers looked for old examples from Ramah on which to base a revival style, but found no documented pieces in the collections of this or any other New Mexico museums.

A most influential outsider has been Lyle McNeal of Utah State University in Logan, who maintains a herd of *churro* sheep. McNeal started a project to preserve a breed that was almost extinct, and has become involved in trying to re-establish the *churro* in the economy of the Southeast. The *churro* breed was originally brought to the Southwest by Spanish settlers. Its long, greaseless wool is well-suited to handspinning and weaving. The *churro* is a lean animal, less meaty than the breeds currently raised by the Navajo. Sheep serve many purposes for a Navajo family. Wool is sold for cash, and used by family weavers, and older animals are slaughtered for food, especially on ceremonial occasions.

Some Ramah weavers faced the sheep problem and have decided on a compromise. They have bred a few of their meaty ewes to a *churro* ram bought from the herd in Logan. The lambs were born in the spring of 1986.

Each weaver plans to have five or six *churro* sheep whose wool will be used for weaving only.

The Ramah weavers attended the conference "Wool on a Small Scale" at Utah State University in June, 1985, where they examined the *churro* herd there and experimented with various spinning wheels and a wool carding machine. One of the conference participants donated a wheel to the Association and some weavers have been practicing with it. Most weavers are hesitant to depart from anything that is not traditionally Navajo in the preparation of their materials. Some of the weavers also attended a sheep-shearing school in Logan, an intensive one week course. Lyle McNeal also gave a similar shearing workshop at Ramah.

Among the Navajo weavers, everything is discussed and decided upon in a group. With the assistance of planners, the weavers have been exposed to the ideas of outsiders who come to talk, and they have travelled on and off the Reservation for ideas. Recently a group from Ramah visited the studio of two contemporary Anglo tapestry weavers in Albuquerque. Resources within the Ramah community are also utilized. Katie Henio, a master weaver and dyer, gave a day-long demonstration of dyeing with local plants and took some of the women on a plant-collecting trip (**577-583**). Throughout it all, the women have discussed each new proposal and decided what was best for them. They have agreed, to use handspun *churro* wool as much as possible in their textiles, and to dye with local plants.

The weaving they have chosen to make first is a pillow cover (**458**), and each will be labeled with the cooperative association's tag giving the weaver's name and the dyes she used. The first group of pillow covers that were made were lined up in front of the members and their quality and designs were discussed. It was at that point they decided that only handspun, vegetal-dyed pieces were acceptable, and anything made of commerical dyes or yarns was rejected. The designs were required to be even, the edges of the pieces straight, and the wefts packed down to cover the warps.

The idea of starting the enterprise with pillow covers was a good one. They are small, relatively simple to make and conform with the modern American taste for large, over-stuffed sofas strew with interesting pillows. Most importantly, pillows are inexpensive, even compared with the smallest rugs. At first, the weavers' association had no funds to purchase its members' work (**584**) but now they have a revolving loan fund begun with foundation money. A middleman in the Albuquerque area is now purchasing the woven squares and paying a seamstress to make them into pillows which adds to the cost of the finished pieces.

The weavers of Ramah want to receive more money for their work and some recognition both for themselves and their community. The association leaders took several pieces of weaving to the Crownpoint auction, but the estimate of what they would bring was less than they could get through their old marketing system. This system is a bit different from other areas on the main Reservation. Some weavers are members of fundamentalist Protestant churches and they sell their rugs to members in other areas of the Southwest and on the revival meeting circuits. Many rugs are sold in

Gallup and Albuquerque and to local government employees. (This system has replaced the marketing vaccum left when the Bond family closed their trading post business about ten years ago.) The Ramah weavers are facing the same problem that craftsmen everywhere face—how to market their creations and receive a price commensurate with the effort expended. Adding to the problem is the desire of the weavers to maintain a traditional Navajo lifestyle in an area remote from major marketing centers.

577 Rose Henio sorting dye plants at the community center at Pine Hill, New Mexico. (Ramah Navajo Reservation). Photo by Anthony Richardson.

578 Katie Henio boiling fermented prickly pear cactus fruit to produce a red dye bath. Community Center at Pine Hill, New Mexico, 1985. Photo by Anthony Richardson.

579 Annie Pino and Rose Henio carding and spinning. Community Center at Pine Hill, New Mexico, 1985. Photo by Anthony Richardson.

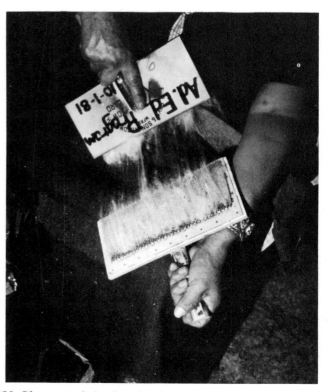

580 Closeup of the hands of Annie Pino showing how to card, comb, and straighten the wool. Community Center at Pine Hill, New Mexico, 1985. Photo by Anthony Richardson.

581 Annie Martine spinning. Pine Hill, New Mexico, 1985. Photo by Anthony Richardson.

582 Rose Henio drawing the yarn off her spindle.

583 Katie Henio winding a skein of wool after it has been spun. Pine Hill, New Mexico, 1985. Photo by Anthony Richardson.

584 Author and Yin May Lee, community planner, holding two Ramah rugs. Pine Hill, New Mexico, 1985. Photo by Anthony Richardson.

5. Care of Textiles

Rewoven repairs of Navajo textiles have been traditional since at least the turn of the twentieth century. Some pieces of Classical weaving are found with dated tags of the Fred Harvey Company fastened to the selvage cords, making it clear exactly when the restoration was done. If a piece is to be rewoven, great care should be taken with the selection of the restorer. He or she should have respect for the integrity of the textile by leaving as much of the original piece as feasible, and adding as little new work as possible. Every edge cord and piece of original yarn will be significant to students and museum curators of the future.

Cleaning is best left to professionals. Dry cleaning is safe but tends to dry out the wool eventually. Cleaners of oriental rugs are generally experienced in cleaning handmade rugs. They use a washing method with large screens. The danger in washing rugs, especially at home, is that the dyes are soluable in water. The special screening method used by professionals does not allow the dyes to go into solution.

The traditional hand-cleaning method used in the Southwest includes taking the rug onto a cement patio or driveway in the winter and brushing it with a broom and some clean snow. This surface cleaning method prevents the dyes from running or bleeding. This method is not advised, however, as it puts a bit of strain on a rug. Although the dyes used by the Navajo are fast if package directions are followed, the method used most often leads to running. On the reservation, where water is quite precious, weavers tend not to rinse the excess dye out of the wool. The wool is thus filled with extra dye just waiting to be released in a washing tub. There are companies that remove bled dyes from weaving, and this process has become popular with many collectors. However, it is not advisable for two reasons. First, it changes the color of the rug, as the chemicals remove both wanted and unwanted dyes indiscriminately. Second, it is not known what effect these chemicals will have on the structure of the wool over a long period of time. Collectors should consider the long-range significance of their actions if only to ensure that there are textiles around for the next generation to collect.

The single-most dangerous agent for textiles is sunlight. Direct exposure must be avoided. All colors will fade, including natural wools. Chemical dyes may fade more quickly, but natural dyes are also susceptible to sunlight. Sunlight will also weaken the wool fibers, causing structural damage. Cleanliness is important; dirt particles are abrasive and will also make the rug more attractive to insects. To cut down on washing or dry cleaning, rugs should be vacuumed periodically. If a rug or blanket is especially fragile or has many holes, it can be vacuumed at minimum suction through a piece of light screening to prevent further damage. Very old and/or fragile pieces should not, of course, be walked upon.

Insects are also a major problem to rugs. Frequent inpsection and cleanliness are the best defense. Many people think that sealing up textiles with a large quantity of moth crystals (paradichlorobenzene or PDB) is enough. Moth crystals, however, will not kill moths, but only discourage the adults from laying their eggs. If the textiles are already infected with moth eggs PDB will not prevent them from hatching or kill the destructive larvae. Modern rugs are sometimes woven with moth-egg-infested wool, so even new weaving should be carefully examined before it is put away in trunk or closet. This is not to discourage the use of moth balls or crystals in conjuction with cleaning and frequent inspection. Incidentally, PDB should be used in a sealed container; otherwise it will evaporate quickly, and the fumes are dangerous to breathe. The crystals should not be sprinkled directly on the textiles but enclosed in some sort of container, either one commercially made or a small homemade cotton bag.

Stored textiles should either be layed out flat or rolled on tubes which can be gleaned from carpet stores. Of course, rollers do not have to be used, since textiles can be rolled on themselves. Rugs used on the floor should be placed over a pad to protect them from being cut by sharp heels.

Rugs and blankets which are hung on walls have more stress on them than those stored rolled in a dark cabinet, so some care must be taken to hang them properly. Most important, nails should *never* be used. A strip of material, either velcro or drapery heading, can be sewn along the top of the piece, with the needle passed carefully between the warps as the weaver placed her wefts. A rug should always be hung from the warps, as they were made quite strong to last through the constant beating with the weaver's comb. Also, the weaver created her pattern in the direction on the warps are best viewed that way. A dowel rod can then be passed through the heading and attached by brackets to the wall. With the velcro method, one strip is sewn to the rugs, while the other is nailed or stapled to a board, and the board in turn is nailed to the wall. Support along the entire top of the rug is the key consideration. Hanging rugs should also be frequently vacuumed and inspected. With proper care, much of today's weaving will eventually appear in museum catalogue of the next generation.

Reading List

Amsden, Charles A.
[1934] *Navaho Weaving, Its Technic and History.* Glorieta, N.M.: Rio
1971 Grande Press.

Bailey, Garrick and Roberta Glenn Bailey
1986 *A History of the Navajos: The Reservation Years.* Santa Fe:
School of American Research Press.

Bennett, Noël and Tiana Bighouse
1970 *Working with the Wool: How to Weave a Navajo Rug.*
Flagstaff, Arizona: Northland Press.

Bennett, Noël
1974 *The Weaver's Pathway: A Clarification of the "Spirit Trail" in
Navajo Weaving.* Flagstaff: Northland Press.

Berlant, Anthony and Mary Hunt Kahlenberg
1977 *Walk in Beauty: The Navajo and Their Blankets.* Boston: New
York Graphic Society.

Bloom, Lansing B.
1927 "Early Weaving In New Mexico", *New Mexico Historical
Review.* July, 1927 (Reprint) pp. 8-238.

Brugge, David M.
1983 "Navajo Prehistory and History to 1850", *Handbook of North
America Indians.* Vol. 10 Washington: Smithsonian Institution.
pp. 489-501.

Dockstader, Frederick J.
1954 *The Kachina and the White Man.* Albuquerque: University of
New Mexico Pres. Revised and enlarged edition 1985

Dyk, Walter, ed.
1967 *Son of Old Man Hat: A Navajo Autobiography* [1938] Lincoln:
University of Nebraska Press.

Fisher, Nora, ed.
1979 *Spanish Textile Tradition of New Mexico and Colorado.*
Santa Fe: Museum of N.M. Press.

Franciscan Fathers
1910 *An Ethnologic Dictonary of the Navajo Language.* St.
Michaels, Arizona: The Franciscan Fathers.

Gallagher, Marsha
1981 "The Weaver and the Wool: The Process of Navajo Weaving".
Plateau 52 (4): pp. 22-27

Geertz. Clifford
1983 *Local Knowledge.* New York: Basic Books, Inc.

Gilpin, Laura
1965 *The Enduring Navajo.* Austin: University of Texas Press.

Gregg, Josiah
1844 *Commerce of the Prairies: Or, the Journal of a Santa Fe Trader,
During Eight Expeditions Across the Great Western Prairies,
and a Residence of Nearly Nine Years in Northern Mexico.* 2
Vols. New York: Henry G. Langley. (Reprinted: University of
Oklahoma Press, Norman, 1954.)

Gustafson, Paula
1980 *Salish Weaving.* Seattle: University of Washington Press.

Hanson, Charles E. and Veronica Sue Walters
1976 "The Early Fur Trade in Northwestern Nebraska." *Nebraska
History,* Vol. 57 Number 4. pp. 1-21.

Hanson, Charles E. Jr.
1970 "The Mexican Traders". *The Museum of the Fur Trade
Quarterly.* Vol. 6, no. 3 pp. 2-6.

Hill, W. W.
1948 "Navajo Trading and Trading Ritual: A Study of Cultural
Dynamics" in *Southwestern Journal of Anthropology.* Vol. 4.
pp. 371-396.

James, George Wharton
[1914] *Indian Blankets and Their Makes.*
1974 New York: Dover Press.

Kauffman, Alice and Christopher Selser
1985 *The Navajo Weaving Tradition: 1650 to the Present.* New
York: E.P. Dutton, Inc.

Kent, Kate Peck
1982 *Navajo Weaving, Three Centuries of Change.* Santa Fe: School
of American Research Press.
1983 *Pueblo Indian Textiles: A Living Tradition.* Santa Fe: School
of American Research Press.

Kent, Susan
1982 "Hogans, Sacred Circles and Symbols; The Navajo use of
Space". *Navajo Religion and Culture: Selected Views* Santa Fe:
Museum of New Mexico Press. pp. 128-37.

Kluckhohn, Clyde W.W. Hill and Lucy W. Kluckhohn
1971 *Navaho Material Culture.* Cambridge, Mass.: Belknap Press of
Howard University Press.

Matthews, Washington
1884 *Navajo Weavers.* pp. 371-391 in *Third Annual Report of the
Bureau of American Ethnology* for the Years 1881-1882. Wash.
Reprinted: Filter Press. Palmer Lake, Co. 1968
1887 "The Mountain Chant: A Navajo Ceremony", in *Fifth Annual
Report of the Bureau of American Ethnology.* Washington,
D.C. Govt. Printing Office. pp. 379-467.
1897 *Navajo Legends. Memoirs of the American Folklore Society* 5.
Menasha, Wis. (Reprinted: Kraus Reprint, N.Y., 1969.)
1902 *The Night Chant: A Navajo Ceremony. Memoirs of the
American Museum of Natural History* 6 N.Y.

Maxwell, Gilbert
[1963] *Navajo Rugs, Past Present and Future.*
1983 Palm Desert, Ca: Best-West Publications. Reprint, 1983 with
additions by Bill and Sande Bobb. Santa Fe: Heritage Arts

McGreevey, Susan B.
1982 *Woven Holy People: Navajo Sand Painting Textiles.* Santa Fe:
Wheelwright Museum of the American Indian.

McNitt, Frank
1962 *The Indian Traders.* Norman: University of Oklahoma Press.

Merrimack, Valley Textile Museum
1977 *Homespun to Factory Made: Woolen Textiles in America,
1776-1876.* North Andover, Mass.

Newcomb, Frances
1964 *Hosteen Klah.* Norman: University of Oklahoma Press.

Parezo, Nancy J.
1983 *Navajo Sandpaintings: From Religious Act to Commercial
Art.* Tucson: univeristy of Arizona Press.

Pinxten, Rik, Ingrid van Doven and Frank Harvey
1983 *The Anthropology of Space.* Philadelphia: University of
Pennsylvania Press.

Reichard, Gladys
1936 *Navajo Shephard and Weaver.* New York: J.J. Augustin.
1950 *Navaho Religion.* Princeton: Princeton University Press.
Reprinted 1974.

Rodee, Marian
1977 *Southwestern Weaving.* Albuquerque: University of New
Mexico Press.
1978 "Multiple Pattern Germantown Rugs". *American Indian Art.*
pp. 44-49.
1981 *Old Navajo Rugs: Their Development from 1900 to 1940.*
Albuquerque: University of New Mexico Press.

Sapir, Edward
1935 "A Navajo Sand Painting Blanket" in American Anthropologist n.s.37. pp. 609-616.

Southwestern Saint
1983 April. Vol 3 #3. pp. 6-8.

Stanislawski, Michael B. and Barbara B. Stanislawski
1975 "Hopi and Hopi-Tewa Ceramic Tradition Network". In
Spatial Organization of Culture. Jan Hodder ed. London:
Duckworth Press. pp. 61-76.

Stevenson, James
1891 "Ceremonial of Hasjelti Dailjis", in *Eighth Annual Report of
the Bureau of American Ethnology* Washington D.C.: Government Printing Office.

Stoller, Irene P.
1976 "The Revival Period in Navajo Weaving" in *Proceedings of
the Irene Emery Roundtable on Museum Textiles.* Washington: The Textile Museum pp. 453-461.

Tanner, Clara Lee
1968 *Southwest Indian Craft Arts.* Tucson: University of Arizona
Press.

Wheat, Joe Ben
1976 "Documentary Basis for Material Changes and Design Styles
in Navajo Blanket Weaving" in *Proceedings of the Irene
Emery Roundtable on Museum Textiles.* Washington: The
Textile Museum. pp. 420-440.

Wheelwright, Museum
1980 *Shared Horizons: Navajo Textiles.* Santa Fe.

Wyman, Leland C.
1983 *Southwest Indian Drypainting.* Albuquerque: University of
New Mexico Press.

Index

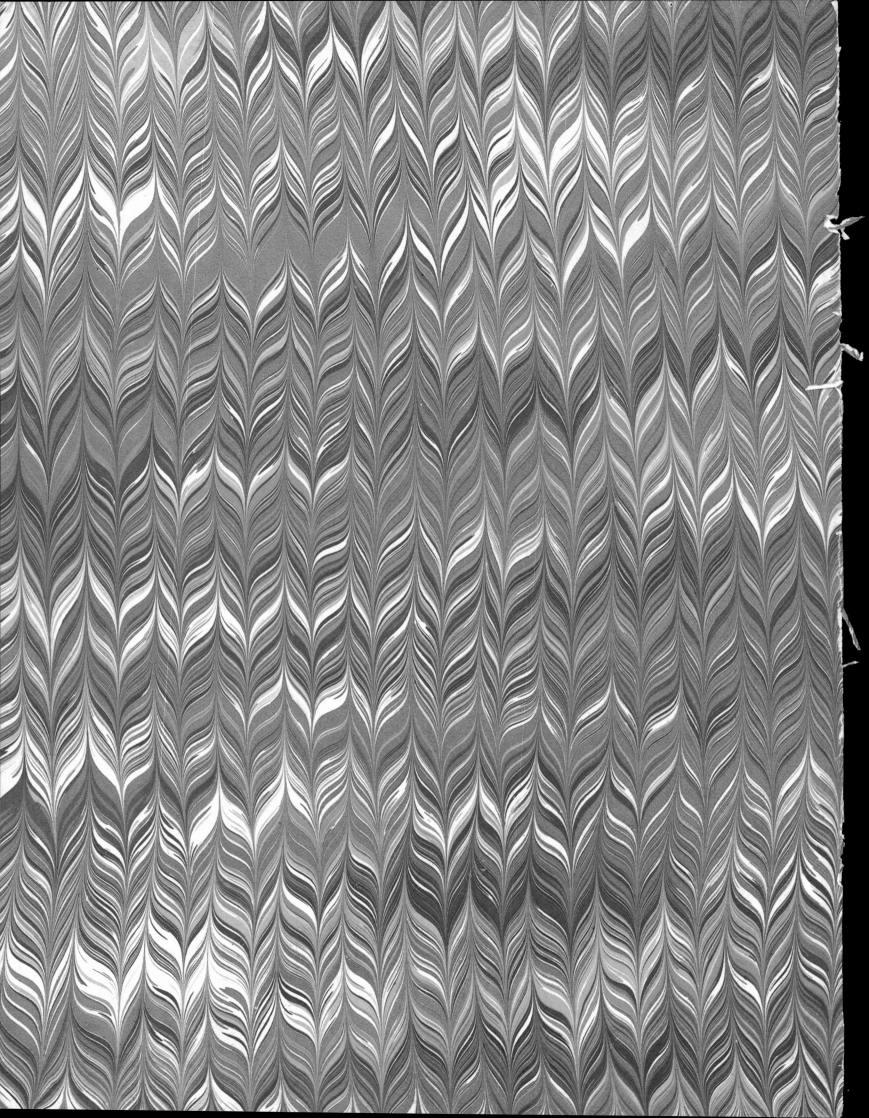